PERSONAL BECOMING

PERSONAL BECOMING

BY

ANDREW TALLON

IN HONOR OF KARL RAHNER AT 75

MARQUETTE UNIVERSITY PRESS
MILWAUKEE, WISCONSIN

Original edition published by The Thomist Press, Washington, D.C. 20017,
The Thomist, Vol. 43, No. 1, Jan. 1979. Reproduction right granted.

Revised edition
© Copyright 1982, Marquette University Press

ISBN 0-87462-522-X

TABLE OF CONTENTS

PERSONAL BECOMING

(KARL RAHNER'S CHRISTIAN ANTHROPOLOGY)

PART ONE

Personal Becoming: Karl Rahner's Philosophical Anthropology

PART TWO

Personal Becoming as Interpersonal Becoming: Karl Rahner's Theological Anthropology

This second, corrected, 1980 edition of *Personal Becoming* has a bonus for the Rahner scholar, a complete bibliography of Rahner as subject. I have gratefully used the bibliography of secondary literature, 1948-1978, by Albert Raffelt (in *Wagnis Theologie*, pp. 598-622), which contains 646 entries. (I have excluded the 36 entries—Nos. 464-500, Raffelt's numbering—mostly very brief, e.g., one page, in German newspapers, on the occasion of Rahners 70th birthday.) This completes and updates my two previously published bibliographies (1973 and 1978), used by Raffelt, to whom I am happy to return the compliment.

I would like most especially to acknowledge the care and support of Dr. Robert Engbring, Director of Marquette University Press, who guided this work to completion.

FOREWORD

By Karl Rahner

My Dear Colleague,

You have written a book-length study: *Personal Becoming*: The Concept of Person in Karl Rahner's Transcendental Anthropology. This is naturally a great honor for me and I thank you sincerely and warmly for it. You have asked me to write a brief Foreword to your study. This Foreword can certainly not be the occasion of summarizing it in a kind of review and of judging it from my own standpoint. To do so would be to exceed the possibilities and the limits of such a Foreword, which can only be the sign of my thanks for the attention you have paid my work, a work theological and to a certain extent also philosophical.

You have, however, in our correspondence, proposed three questions to me and suggested that in this Foreword I say something briefly in response to these three questions. Such answers can also perhaps be of some small service to the readers of your study and facilitate for them, in some small way, their understanding of your work. I will therefore try to answer your questions insofar as I can do so briefly.

1. You ask me whether it is also my own view that personal becoming [*das personale Werden*], becoming a person [*Personwerden*], is the central idea of my philosophico-theological anthropology. Before I try to answer this question, may I point out to the readers of this Foreword that you ask about the central idea of my *anthropology?* As a theologian, of course, I ask also about God, Christ, and the Church, thus about themes in which becoming a person can naturally not be simply *the* key concept, *the* central idea, even though I myself have always striven to show that in Christianity theology and anthropology mutually interpenetrate and condition one another more than is evident in the Church and in theology as it was

1

usually taught. Your question thus refers—and your readers must keep this clearly in mind right from the start—to my anthropology. But once this is clear, and I may then come to my reply to your question, I become unsure. I could give a straightforward answer " Yes " to the question, on the condition that it is presupposed that one always keeps clear that the concept of becoming a person, on the one hand, does not exclude but rather includes the concept of an original constituting of the person through the creative act of God, by which act the person already *is,* and, on the other hand, that the fact that person is constituted originally means right from the start precisely a becoming in which this person must first become in the history of his freedom, until he is definitively perfected in freedom in the presence of God. But if I thus answer your first question with a " Yes," then I must come back and ask myself whether such a concept of becoming a person is not self-evident for a Christian theologian (and philosopher), and whether it ought not be a central idea *for everyone,* even if perhaps expressed in other words. If that were the case then it could hardly be so " original " a concept as to be made the central idea precisely of *my* anthropology.

But perhaps your question does not intend a special particularity and originality of my anthropology (which I am not claiming) but rather inquires only about a principle of organization according to which the *membra disiecta* of an anthropology can be gathered, an anthropology which I have never written as a structured whole. If, under these conditions, one makes becoming a person the key concept, the central idea of my anthropology (which is possible, as I have said), then of course everything comes down to the exact content one gives this concept, thereby doing justice to my anthropology or, better yet, to the things themselves.

In this context it is decisive, as you emphasize in your letter, that one notice that the transcendence of man as finite spirit toward God, the absolute being in person, toward mystery in the fullest sense, is necessarily mediated through the (finite) other [*das (endliche) andere*], through matter, body, the surrounding world of things [*Umwelt*], the social world [*Mitwelt*], (the *personal* other [" *den* " *anderen*]), through history and word, " mediations " which I myself certainly neither sufficiently nor thoroughly worked out in their unity and difference.

2. With that I come to your second question. You ask whether there has been a certain development in my concept of person. I would answer: obviously and hopefully, because, I hope, I have not always repeated the same thing and certainly could not have said everything at one time, because, in my own history, hopefully, I have kept on learning something new. I admit that I myself have hardly ever reflected on this development of my thought in general and of my concept of person in particular so that I could myself indicate precisely the stages of this development. Obviously, in *Spirit in the World* this concept of person would still be very rudimentary and not very explicit. This is due, even prescinding from the fact that this book stands at the beginning of my philosophical and theological work, simply from the nature of this work as dealing with a question in the *history* of philosophy. Since a single article of Aquinas's *Summa* was to be interpreted in that work, a restriction is already thereby given, which was by no means to sketch a whole anthropology and to structure it through the concept of person and the concept of becoming a person. With Thomas it is the case (this is his limitation) that the other which allows finite spirit to return to itself is the neutral " object " [*der materiellen* " *Gegenstand* "]: he [Thomas] does not consider in *this* connection that the other in the true sense [*das eigentliche andere*] is another *person* [" *der* " *andere ist*], whom the subject encounters in knowledge, freedom, and love, in genuine interpersonal history [*in echter interpersonaler Geschichte*]. This formal framework, which is signified by the neutral " object " [*dem materiellen* " *Gegenstand* "], must, however, be viewed in its formal abstraction, and by no means merely signifies the material object in its mere neuter thingness; it must, of course, be filled out and in its content be differentiated if a genuine anthropology is to emerge. Thus, my dear Professor Tallon, you have correctly seen that for me the other,

which mediates the person to itself, ever more clearly emerges as the personal other [" *der* " *andere*], whom the person in knowledge and love encounters, and that the human environment is such only as a human and personal world in which man lives in order to come to himself, so that in love he abides with the other and thereby experiences what is meant by " God," who is the sphere and the ultimate guarantee of interhuman love.

3. This said, I can also relatively easily and briefly answer your third question in which you ask about two critical objections that one can possibly raise against my concept of personal becoming, objections against which you yourself defend me. The starting point for an anthropology is of course intersubjectivity and not an " interobjectivity " (if I may so speak). For Thomas, object is a formal concept, one that simply indicates a " vis-à-vis " [" *Gegenüber* "], with the question still left open, if perhaps overlooked, how this object is precisely to be characterized. The necessary and important distinction between thing-object and another person encountered in intersubjectivity is in Thomas certainly not yet given at the very start of his anthropology. For me, however, it is clear that the original approach wherein genuine mediation both for transcendence toward God and for the person's coming to himself is supposed to be thought, this mediation is the other person in intersubjectivity. It is clear (to come to the second objection you mention) that the horizon of our transcendence [*Transzendentalität*] is neither " nothing " nor an impersonal " it," but rather the personal God, leaving open the question how the experience of the boundlessness and openness of the transcendence of finite spirit is to be interpreted carefully and more exactly as *experience* of God. Experience of one's own transcendence (as freedom) is in finite spirit the experience of freedom as a given, and thereby we see a first hint for the necessity of thinking the whence and the whither of this transcendence as *personal*. Of course I am aware that the philosophical question of the personality of God needs a more thorough treatment than it was given in my works. My stu-

dent, David J. Roy, in his dissertation at Münster (*Personal God Discourse*: An Unfolding of the Problematic), has written an exceptionally extensive work, hermeneutical in nature, on how we can conceive of our language as language about God as person. There he does not deal immediately with the analogous assertion that God is a person, but with our speaking about God as person and with our necessity for doing so. The author uses the term of " dialogical " transcendentality. I refer to this vast work (whether it has been published or not, I do not know) not in order to develop the problem further here, but only to make clear, on the one hand, that I am conscious of the incompleteness of my own reflections on this question, but that, on the other hand, the position about which you ask is of course my own position, as Roy in his work, in addition to Bernard Lonergan, not insignificantly refers to my work. That must—unfortunately—suffice for now as an answer to your third question.

I wish for your study the attention which is its due. With best wishes, I am

Sincerely yours,

KARL RAHNER, S. J.

List of Abbreviations

GW1 .... *Geist in Welt*, first ed.
GW2 .... *Geist in Welt*, second ed.
GWS .... *Geist in Welt*, Spanish GW2
GWF .... *Geist in Welt*, French GW2
SW .... *Spirit in the World*, English GW2 (Dych)
HW1 .... *Hörer des Wortes*, first ed.
HW2 .... *Hörer des Wortes*, second ed.
HWF .... *L'homme à l'écoute du Verbe*, HW1 and HW2 (Hofbeck)
HWE .... *Hearers of the Word*, English HW2 (Richards)
LW .... *Listening to the Word*, English HW1 (Donceel)
STh, I-XII .... *Schriften zur Theologie*, Volumes I-XII
ThI, I-XIV .... *Theological Investigations*, Volumes I-XIV, English translation of STH, I-X
ThT .... *Zur Theologie des Todes*
ThD .... *Theology of Death*, English ThT
PH .... *Das Problem des Hominisation*
HE .... *Hominisation*, English PH
SG .... *Sendung und Gnade*
MG .... *Mission and Grace*, I-III, English SG
VP .... *Visions and Prophecies*
DEC .... *The Dynamic Element in the Church*
LThK .... *Lexicon für Theologie und Kirche*
SM .... *Sacramentum Mundi*
KThW .... *Kleines Theologisches Wörterbuch*
CThD .... *Concise Theological Dictionary*, English KThW

AUTHOR'S PREFACE

A FOREWORD is usually an afterword, written when the work is done, an occasion to do things the work itself couldn't do—such as thank those who helped it happen—and things it perhaps should have done, but failed to do. Both of these needs become clear after the fact, though it often helps the reader, as he eases his way into the book proper, to find the kinds of statements one remembers to put into forewords. I will divide these remarks into two sections, the first to preview this study, the second to introduce Rahner's approach to Thomas.

1. *Approaching This Study.* In 1969 I presented my dissertation at Louvain entitled *Personization:* Person as Becoming in Karl Rahner's Philosophical Anthropology. In that study I limited myself to Rahner's four purely philosophical works: GW, HW, "Introduction au concept de philosophie existentiale chez Heidegger," and "A Verdade em S. Tomás de Aquino." I described it as the first of two studies, the second of which, inappropriate for a purely philosophical dissertation, would continue the investigation into Rahner's theological works, still continuing. Since Rahner's relevant theological writings have in general been short, being mostly articles, in journals and lexicons, and contributions to the series *Quaestiones Disputatae,* and since I am not a professional theologian, the study of the concept of person as found in his *theological* anthropology has taken the form of an exposition of the development, in selected essays in STh, of that concept as already found and metaphysically grounded in his *philosophical* anthropology. The word development is not idly chosen. Rahner's *Personbegriff* underwent changes between 1937, when he was at work on GW, and (at least) 1965, the date of STh VI.*

* Editor's Note—This present work includes only two parts, completely reworked, from an earlier Louvain dissertation. The third, fourth, and fifth sec-

To search for a metaphysics of person as becoming is obviously not to view person as a static, fixed, or ready-made essence, but rather as dynamic, open, and self-enacting. Person is thus understood as personization—as person-becoming (*Personwerdung*)—i. e., as a potentiality to be en-acted. Ethics, however, is the chief locus of personal becoming, and thus we must remain open to the question of free ethical activity, since it is in such activity that man is most self-appropriative and self-creative, most metaphysically himself because most metaphysically becoming. Beyond this, our search must remain open without reservation, i. e., must not exclude the realm of the transcendent, of the " meta-physical " in the most traditional and classical sense of this term, i. e., God. In the context of a philosophical anthropology becoming a theological anthropology, openness to the transcendent or metaphysical means facing the fact that for man to identify himself, i. e., to talk about himself as he is, he must talk about God. Rahner's anthropology is open to a religious event that happens in history, an epiphany the human incarnate spirit can encounter, the face of the other who can make a difference to his personal becoming.

To study Rahner's theological writings is to become aware of a gradual evolution in his thinking on personal becoming. What was hardly mentioned in GW and barely sketched in HW was nevertheless grounded there implicitly; the *principles* were worked out, but it was left to later applications to bring out the implications, to make them explicit, and also to show some real development. Because of this developmental nature of Rahner's understanding of person, an historical approach to his writings is indicated. By taking Rahner's relevant works in their approximately original order of publication, which initially does not necessarily correspond to the order of their republication as STh or QD, we can follow that evolution. My

tions of this study pick up where the dissertation left off and trace the development of the ideas of the first two sections through Rahner's STh and other theological works. For reasons of space, some sections have been shortened, others dropped completely.

method will be to interpret each article as strongly as possible for a metaphysics of person; once having done this I will introduce material from later articles only when they make some advance over prior articles, whether it be one of doctrine, or merely one of clarity of expression or application. Since Rahner began regularly publishing everything he taught, the question of exact chronology lost importance after the early years; because of Rahner's consistency, moreover, and because his later ideas can be seen as flowing from his first principles, the question of chronology eventually becomes less a matter of crucial importance than one of personal interest.

I have restricted myself to citing only the more " scholarly " sources of Rahner's thought. Rahner often tested his ideas before an audience in one form and then expanded his talk into an article complete with bibliography, notes, and all the academic apparatus; occasionally a shorter version appeared later; usually a longer one resulted. One can, therefore, and of course with profit, read Rahner's entries in the KThW, SM, and the LThK. These formulations, being later condensations of longer works, and therefore secondary in usefulness to this study, nevertheless have the virtue of their faults; often they make the important points stand out all the more clearly for the omission of detail; often, too, later formulations are simpler because they are more mature and less tortured in style. Works of spirituality and popularization (*haute vulgarisation*) have like faults and virtues. As part of my method, notes are sometimes drawn from chronologically later essays which, though not singled out for separate discussion, still provide occasions for clarifying points less clearly made in earlier essays, for illustrating them in different or better ways, and for demonstrating Rahner's continuity and evolution of thought. Thus, unlike the early procedure, when at first no notes at all, and then reference rather than content notes sufficed, later we find so much going on, seemingly all at once, as Rahner's fertile ground virtually explodes into new applications and insights, that content notes become essential to the method of exposition.

My problem now in this "preview part" of my preface is how to offer a forward glance and still remain clear in the absence of the development of the idea the book constitutes. How am I to say, usefully and briefly, and without unnecessary repetition, what this study is going to do? My solution is to forsake a linear for a circular approach. The reason is that the reality is so simple, if not easy, both in theory and in practice, that it is in great danger of being missed completely.

The concept of person as finite spirit is the concept of a self for whom otherness is both possible and necessary for that self to *become* himself. Possible and necessary: possible because spirit, necessary because finite. "Becoming" means there is potentiality to be actualized. Actualization is always of potentiality and always requires otherness. *There is no way metaphysically to understand how a being could be conceived, could be intelligible, that had totally within itself the power fully to actualize itself and had not already done so.* Potentiality means finitude, means becoming in space and in time. Becoming means becoming oneself, not something or someone else. But this becoming is only partly through, in, with, and of oneself. Becoming means that there is "something from outside" as well as "something from inside," to use handy but guarded expressions. Man becomes a knower as active and passive, becomes a lover as active and passive, when he goes from potential knower-lover to actual knower-lover, i. e., person, through something from the "inside" and something from the "outside." The "inside" (or immanence, inwardness, interiority), or spirit, must, because unable to become spirit unassisted, relate to otherness in a relation of dependence and need (transcendence, exteriority); spirit's first otherness, in its very becoming itself, its becoming spirit, is matter, its own body, with which, in a relation so essential to itself that its very being comes only with the relation, it is constituted spirit-in-matter: *Geist in Welt.* Second otherness is the next necessary condition—and cause—of the becoming of this composite, i. e., everything and everyone else there is, from inert elements, through people loved and hated, to the immanent-transcendent God: man is *Hörer des Wortes.*

About this first incarnation something more must be said, even here, though briefly. How is materialization a spiritualization, i. e., how does spirit become itself in becoming material? *That* it happens thus must first be established, or the question of *how* will be too easily dismissed. In Kantian terms, and in the context of knowing, it is evident that empty concepts are filled when reason is materialized in sensibility (and the proverbial " no will accomplished without passion " speaks of the same incarnation of spirit now as will in space and time). Man knows and loves through otherness. *Man's being comes from otherness, and so must his becoming.* But how do we know that this becoming, which is actual in experience, in practice, is possible in thought, in theory? In other words, what is man, what is man's nature?

This question is, of course, but one way to formulate transcendental method. Transcendental method begins with experience and constructs a theory to explain how that experience is possible; but this is to ask for the nature of something, i. e., to ask what must this be if it can act thus. The mistake often made, once lip service has been paid to such statements on or of transcendental method, is not to realize that the method must be continued right into itself, i.e., into a statement of *what man's nature must be for this method to be the way into that nature.* In other words, man knows what person is by incarnating the notion in himself, by trying to make the idea happen somewhere, so that it can then be said to be real (not merely ideal), to exist (not merely be an ideal essence). Further, the idea must be materialized in society, and in society's habits (institutions); we cannot know what personal becoming means until we see whether and why we succeed or fail in refounding ourselves and society according to that idea (as Lindworksy said: each Jesuit, in becoming a Jesuit, must refound the Society of Jesus as Ignatius did). We do not first recognize the idea and then incarnate it in self and society, but rather recognize it in the very attempt to incarnate it. Sometimes we are already there before we know it, as when we are led, through good example, to adopt ethically good behavior before recognizing its value. Man becomes personal, at least in part, in trying to learn what being a person is and means. Thus transcendental method is not about man but *is* man. Ultimately this is the deepest meaning of Rahner's starting point in the question about being; really we have an awareness here that performing the question is itself an essential element in man's very becoming: questioning and its very possibility—reveals man's nature as becoming. (That transcendentality is also, at least implicitly, *dialogical,* will be noted presently.)

With Blondel, Maréchal, and Rousselot we may say that there is already and always in man a pre-conceptual and pre-voluntary dynamism written into the very nature of finite spirit as intellect and will; man's nature anticipates all persons and things, all subjects, known and loved, all truths grasped, all goods willed, in a natural (in the sense of pre-reflective, pre-deliberative) movement toward the term or horizon of finite spirit. Intellect and will, incarnated, embodied, materialized in space and time, ratify and second this already and always working movement. Rahner, following Aquinas, usually speaks only of the cognitive part of spirit's dynamism, of the intellect's natural anticipation of all the persons and things to be known: before any knowing there is an openness to all truth, and thus, in an anticipation on this " all," there is a transcendence of each " every," a transcending anticipation that Aquinas called an *excessus,* i. e., an excess of capacity to know unexhausted by any known, as intellect's openness exceeds or transcends every known. Rahner calls it *Vorgriff,* i. e., anticipation or transcendence as grasping for more than is caught in every grasp of a known person or thing. Insofar as the term of *excessus* or *Vorgriff* is God, absolute truth, the good of intellect, He is " known," or co-known, not as an object but as the necessary condition, the non-object making possible human knowledge of objects as objects.

The will, of course, though seldom treated in the same language, has a " *Vorgriff* " of its own. Like Blondel's *volonté voulante* it is a " natural," i. e., pre-*volonté voulue*, dynamism to be seconded by conscious, choosing will. Rahner does not coin a will-word, parallel to *Vorgriff*. Since *Vorgriff* (as just anticipation or transcendence or transcending anticipation) is not necessarily a knowledge-word (as distinguished from a volition-word), except insofar as one wants to make *greifen* (grasp) a term more relevant to knowing than choosing or loving, it could be considered a general word about spirit prior to any distinction into spirit's powers of intellect and will. Thus God is co-loved in every person or object chosen or loved. The unity of love of God and love of neighbor, in later essays, shows Rahner's development as well as his consistency, since the one same transcendental method, the one same idea of *Vorgriff* to horizon of spirit, at first almost solely in terms of intellect, but eventually also in terms of will, grounds his meaning of person as necessarily becoming through otherness, the ultimate otherness of God mediated by (though perhaps only unconsciously and implicitly) the proximate first and second othernesses of body and other persons. He eventually speaks of experience, a term, like Merleau-Ponty's and later Sartre's *le vécu*, which suggests a unity prior to distinctions within consciousness.

Thus personal becoming is our reason for being, and freedom is the means, because in free acts we exercise disposition over ourselves, integrate and appropriate ourselves in act, decide who and what we are becoming. But this self-actualization, this becoming myself, is possible only in self-transcendence, in the first otherness of my body and in the second otherness of the world, both of things and of persons (both human and divine). In Peter Eicher's words, " Thus man in free decision becomes person: he not only has to appropriate himself in his interiority [self] and in his own embodiment [first otherness], but also has freely to take up the relation to the thou, to the world around him, and to culture [second otherness] (*Die anthropologische Wende*, p. 362).

To conclude (though still penultimately) this part of my foreword, I must very briefly mention Christology and then add remarks on intersubjectivity and the dialogical principle. On the first point I wish only to acknowledge the force of the idea that the proper study of man is enacted man, fully actualized man, rather than potential man, since potency is known only in act; thus Christology would yield a better anthropology. The way I have just stated the matter is probably adequate to suggest why philosophically I could not proceed this way, nor did Rahner.[1]

But if I may broaden the methodological context for a moment, I can take this occasion to express a reservation; in so doing I am presenting the negative side of the discussion of intersubjectivity, thereby bridging to the other point mentioned above.

Putting aside the question of *when* to begin the study of man (i. e., whether in the unactualized man, the child, as some suggest, or in the " mature " adult, à la Sartre, with all the attendant problems of that approach), *where* exactly do we begin? With the writer, the " abstract individual," silently alone, thinking and writing, writing and thinking, or with the "concrete person," speaking and listening, in the dialogal context, the face-to-face, the I-Thou relation? The former situation is, of course, the "real" world of the philosopher-theologian, who gets no essays written (or dictated) in the latter.

In my judgment the whole debate, involving Simons, Gerken, Eicher, Heinrichs, Fischer, *et al.*, needs the perspective of Levinas as well as that of Buber and others. Granted that a philosophy that grounds all knowledge, even that of self and God, on the *conversio ad phantasmata*, can and must ultimately profess the primacy of otherness, it is one thing to lay down the foundations as Rahner did, and another to work it to yield all its possible harvest, which task Rahner left to others. In fairness to Rahner it must be said, even while critiquing him

---

[1] This is the reverse of Gaboriau's complaint, in *Le tournant théologique . . .* , that the proper study of God cannot be man.

for speaking too often of self and knowledge (bei-*sich*-sein) rather than, as later he did, of the thou and love, that Rahner never meant his statements *sensu negante* but *sensu aiente*. As he complains in STh XII (p. 425, n.), though it is true, as he has been often reproached, that he did not place personal inter-subjectivity sufficiently clearly in the foreground, the reproach, in its usual form, was nevertheless incorrect and unjustified. Between 1967, when Rahner wrote the essay—to which this note was attached, presumably in 1975 (judging by his remark on p. 607)—the two major studies of Rahner's philosophical anthropology appeared,[2] both with preface-letters by Rahner. It is easy to agree with Fischer that Rahner, by placing love at the core of intellect, opens up his otherwise apparently ego-centered metaphysics, making it—in language consciously re-

---

[2] See P. Eicher, *Die anthropologische Wende.* Karl Rahners philosophischer Weg vom Wesen des Menschen zur personalen Existenz (Freiburg [Switzerland]: Universitätsverlag, 1970) and K. Fischer, *Der Mensch als Geheimnis.* Die Anthropologie Karl Rahners (Freiburg: Herder, 1974). The implicit dialogical transcendentality that A. Gerken and Eicher agree is found in Rahner never really received explicitation at Rahner's own hand, as they must admit; see Eicher's " Kritische Betrachtung II: Auseinandersetzung um die transzendentalphilosophische Anthropologie," pp. 93-110, esp. pp. 100-101, and also his whole chapter 1 of Part IV, on Personal Existence, pp. 340-372. Fischer deals with Rahner's relation to the dialogical principle (" K. Rahners Verhältnis zum ' dialogischen Prinzip ' ") on pp. 193-205; here I must express agreement with Fischer in attributing importance to the essay by J. Heinrichs, " Sinn und Intersubjektivität. Zur Bermittlung von transzendentalphilosophischen und dialogischen Denken in einer ' transzendentaley Dialogik,' " in *Theologie und Philosophie* (1970) (45), 161-191. Suffice it to say for now—since to develop this theme further would take another study—that just as Buber finds meaning not *in* mental states but *between* persons, and as Levinas finds meaning in sense (*sens* in *sensibilité*), i. e., in pre-cognitive and pre-contractual intentionality (non-representational), which is the event of the other in the self yet remaining other, thus showing meaning and sensibility both to be reference to other, so also Heinrichs, who expresses meaning as the simultaneity of self-consciousness and consciousness of other, the event of meaning being the concrete and the self and other being abstract moments within it. Among Levinas's many works, see *Autrement qu'être ou au-delà de l'essence,* The Hague: Nijhoff (1974); see my review-article in *Man and World* (1976), (9), 451-462. I should also mention here, leaving other relevant works to be noted later, the important study by M. Theunissen, *Der Andere.* Studien zur Sozialontologie der Gegenwart (Berlin: de Gruyter, 1965). Recommended also is Eicher's " Immanenz oder Transzendenz? " in *Freiburger Zeitschrift für Philosophie und Theologie* 15 (1968), 29-62.

ferring to P. Rousselot's work on love—an ecstatic movement of spirit toward other. The essence of the finite self becomes development of self in dependence upon other: free response to another belongs to the meaning of meaning and to the meaning of man.

Rahner's use of the symbol of the heart offers another way to show his metaphysics to be both transcendental and dialogical. Although only begun (in STh II, in two essays on the heart), this theme holds the key to a phenomenology that would match the still unsurpassed metaphysics of finite spirit we find in Rahner. For were one to look for a starting point for a phenomenology that would lead to his metaphysics, it would be in the encounter of persons whose pre-intentional dispositions emerge in appeal-response dialogue, revealing intellect and will, and their embodiments, as originating from a deeper, more original unity, that of finite spirit: the lived experience of the heart, with all the ambiguity of feeling as both cognitive and affective, responding to the face of the other, precedes the distinction into knowledge and love, intellect and will, spirit and body.*

* Since the second section of this foreword is meant to lead directly into the study proper, now is the welcome moment to thank those who helped make these pages see light. I must first mention Father Daniel Shine, S. J., of Weston College and Boston College, under whose direction I began work on Rahner in 1960. I owe a great debt of gratitude also to Monsignor Albert Dondeyne, under whose direction I wrote my dissertation; although Director of the Institut Supérieur de Philosophie and extremely active in research and teaching as well as in his priestly ministry, he gave me all the time I requested and continued to correspond over the years since; to him also I owe new incentive to work on the philosophy of person and the interpersonal in Emmanuel Levinas, whose work I understand as partly complementing Rahner's. To Father Christian Wenin, then editor of the *Revue philosophique de Louvain* and now secretary of the Institute at Louvain la Neuve, very special thanks also for his humanity and personal support then and now. To Professor Paul Byrne, late and much missed Chairman of Marquette's Philosophy Department, I owe deep thanks for his constant encouragement and counsel, as colleague, chairman, and friend. To my colleagues I also say thanks for help in ideas and professional assistance; the atmosphere created in the Department by such men and women makes work great fun. To Father William Hill, O. P., editor of *The Thomist*, for accepting this study and guiding it to publication. To Marquette University, for several grants along the way, and to Kathy

2. *Approaching Rahner Approaching Aquinas.* The task of this second part of my foreword is to introduce Rahner's approach to Thomas Aquinas.

There is a contemporary way of understanding person that differs from the classical one. Rather than defining person in terms of substance and reason, the new focus is on relation and freedom.[3] Whether the latter-day focus merely makes explicit what is implicit in the traditional definition, or genuinely introduces something new, in the sense at least of something not previously thought or valued, to the present meaning of man,[4] is

Guenther, Barbara Olson, Suzanne Wilson, and Grace Jablonski for typing the manuscript, I also owe sincere thanks. More recently incurring my gratitude are Professors Jim Dagenais, Miami University of Ohio, and Howard Hong, St. Olaf's College, Director of the Kierkegaard Library. Most of all I thank my wife Mary Elizabeth Vander Vennet Tallon, for love and peace, without which there would be neither personization nor community. Last of all I thank Father Karl Rahner, S. J., whose works nourish the whole person. In discussion, in letters, and most recently in his gracious Foreword to this study, he has offered a model of wisdom and love toward personal becoming.

[3] See F. Copleston, *Contemporary Philosophy.* Studies of Logical Positivism and Existentialism (Westminster, Md.: Newman Press, 1966), 103-124: ". . . in what one may call, in a very wide sense, the idealist current in modern philosophy the tendency has been to look on consciousness, or rather self-consciousness, as the chief characteristic of personality. . . . But in the case of the modern thinkers . . . the emphasis is laid on freedom rather than on self-consciousness. Freedom becomes recognized as the chief characteristic of the human person. . . . In the eyes of certain thinkers one can become a person and one can cease to be a person . . ." (104); ". . . there has been a shift of emphasis from self-consciousness to freedom as the chief characteristic of personality" (114).

[4] J. de Finance, e. g., in his *Connaissance de l'être* (Paris: Desclée de Brouwer, 1966), 481-494, after manifesting his awareness of the contemporary focus on freedom and relation rather than on substance and reason, says (480): "As a matter of fact, especially for about the last forty years, it has been the social and ' relational ' character of the person that has been getting all the attention: the person appears as essentially oriented and open toward the other: the I is possible and has meaning only in relation to a you." He concludes that Boethius's definition correctly understood still provides the best framework for a metaphysics of person: ". . . it is still the old definition of Boethius, revised and corrected by St. Thomas, which provides the most satisfactory framework for a metaphysics of person. The other definitions are valuable only to the degree that they lean on it and make explicit one or other aspect of it" (481). " The ethical, axiological, and relational definitions of person enunciate important truths in the phenomenological and moral orders, but they cannot intend to characterize immediately what makes per-

another question. I mention the change to point out that it is really thanks to Rahner's works later than SW that he could be included among those taking the contemporary viewpoint. The concept of person as free and as the cause and effect of relation, relation understood as act, as bond, and as force-field or community, is so evident in his theological anthropology [5] that one is drawn to seek the roots and bases for that position in the works to which Rahner himself consistently directs anyone seeking the metaphysical underpinnings of his theological edifice. It seemed logical to expect a doctrine of person in SW, since this is Rahner's major philosophical work, compared with which HW, though adding much on freedom and love, and explicitly using the term person (absent from SW), is a series of talks employing and adapting ideas already worked out in greater detail in the earlier work.

But what in fact do we find in SW? We find that Rahner's approach is not the contemporary one. The subtitle of that work is: Towards a metaphysics of finite knowledge in Thomas Aquinas. Thus it is a metaphysics, as expected (rather than an epistemology or Kantian style critique),[6] but it is a metaphysics of *cognition,* and thus an approach to man through his mode of knowing rather than a metaphysics of freedom and relation.

Why did Rahner use this approach? This question would betray our falling into the mistake of judgment by hindsight were

son person, what distinguishes persons from things in the first place. The eminent value of the person, his dignity which forbids his being made a pure means, as well as his opening to the other, his capacity of welcoming and of giving, are founded upon this opening to being by which spirit is spirit. They too therefore develop the element: rational nature [nature raisonable], in the scholastic definition " (482-483, my trans.). In his *L'affrontement de l'autre* (Rome: Gregorian University Press, 1973) de Finance reiterates this position. This is to say that to do a metaphysics of person, and not merely a phenomenology, is necessarily to come, at the end, to speaking about spirit, and thus to speak, at least traditionally, of cognition.

[5] Three works of Rahner that also take the concept of person as central are J. Speck, *Karl Rahners theologische Anthropologie.* Eine Einführung (München: Kösel-Verlag, 1967), and the works by Eicher and Fischer mentioned above.

[6] GW1, xiv, 7; GW2, 14, 33; SW, liii, 19.

it not for Rahner's own use of person, freedom, and relation vigorously, beginning already with HW. So the question is legitimate and perhaps its answer will be instructive.

One answer would be that since this was Rahner's doctoral dissertation, on Aquinas and under a strict Thomist, he had little or no choice in the matter. Vorgrimler in fact suggests that Rahner was under a certain amount of external pressure to work on Aquinas's noetic.[7] Even were he not, however, it is clear that Rahner understands himself to be a Thomist and has not claimed to find his principles in Aquinas merely to escape ecclesiastical censure. Rahner's personal and philosophical disposition toward Aquinas's ideas was further nurtured by his study of Maréchal and Rousselot, and he readily acknowledges that both of these Thomists influenced him considerably.[8] Now they both approached man from the viewpoint of his mode of knowing (although Rousselot also wrote brilliantly on love).[9] As a philosopher used to working very much from within the heart of his tradition,[10] Rahner would feel at home following such a precedent. Furthermore, as a Thomist, he would hold that freedom ultimately depends on the transcendence of the particular good known as such by intellect and thus he would recognize the value of treating intellect and its transcendence as a prerequisite to any study of freedom and, in fact, freedom does come up in SW, and precisely as the result of intellectual transcendence.[11]

Whatever the reason or reasons, the approach in SW is cognitive rather than dialogal or intersubjective. Now this could lead one to the judgment that it is therefore a static (individualistic, abstract, relationless) approach, to be likened to the approaches

[7] See H. Vorgrimler, Karl Rahner. His Life, Thought, and Works (Glen Rock, N. J.: Paulist Press, Deus Books, 1966, trans. by E. Quinn), 21-25. See also C. Muller and H. Vorgrimler, Karl Rahner (Paris: Fleurus, 1965), 15-16.

[8] See GW1, v; GW2, 9; SW, xlvii.

[9] P. Rousselot, Pour l'histoire du problème de l'amour au moyen âge (Münster, 1908; Paris, 1933).

[10] See F. Fiorenza, "Karl Rahner and the Kantian Problematic," (i. e., the Intro. to SW), SW, xiv.

[11] See GW1, 214-215; GW2, 298-299; SW, 295-296.

to person as substance or as consciousness, approaches that have turned out to be, for the most part, static. This would be a rash judgment. If the approaches through substance or consciousness have been *de facto* static, such was not necessary *de jure*; it seems possible to redefine substance itself in such a way that this concept can do justice to its dynamics.[12] There is thus a way of approaching man's cognitive life as a life, as something dynamic, intentional in the richest sense, radically relational,[13] and it is precisely this dynamic conception of human knowledge, as an activity with the emphasis more on act than on form, that Rahner owes to Maréchal. This is not to say that Rahner's " proof " for the objectivity of human cognition (knowledge of particulars, knowledge of concrete being) is the same as Maréchal's "; it is well known that they are different. Despite Maréchal's considering Blondel's philosophy of action a bit too voluntaristic (no matter what Maréchal himself may have owed to Blondel), Maréchal himself was in turn considered a bit too voluntaristic by Rahner, at least if one can judge by the differences between their uses of dynamism.

Let us be clear, therefore, about how to study SW in search of a theory of person and becoming. One way would be to say, after a less than thorough reading, that all we can salvage is his definition of intellect (and thus of spirit, from the viewpoint of cognition) as self-presence and of sense as presence to another, or self-absence, two definitions which when joined could constitute the complex definition of man as finite (and *thus* intentional) spirit in the material world. Now in a sense this way would be legitimate; one would have a nice definition, perhaps more Hegelian-sounding than Thomist, but not altogether unrecognizably traditional. But it does not take much

---

[12] See F.-J. von Rintelen, *Beyond Existentialism* (London: George Allen and Unwin, 1961), 65-68, and J. Somerville, " Toward a More Dynamic Understanding of Substance and Relation," 218-234 in V. Daues, *et al.*, eds., *Wisdom in Depth* (Milwaukee: Bruce, 1966).

[13] E. g., as S. Strasser uses intentionality in *The Idea of Dialogal Phenomenology* (Pittsburgh: Duquesne University Press, 1969), p. 53.

thought to recognize that a definition is the end-product of a line of analysis without which it could not be understood, or, if the definition be viewed from another direction, the starting point for a series of analyses aimed at understanding everything implied in the definition. Essentially, at least *prima facie,* this is the way Rahner approached the Thomist article whose analysis and interpretation constitute Part One of SW, i.e., the article on the necessity of the intellect to " turn to phantasms " in order to know.

Another way to approach SW would be to begin with one's own experience of knowing in general and of contrasting abstract concepts with concrete perceptions in particular, and then gradually to develop a theory of how we know real beings in both these ways, i. e., abstractly and concretely. We would thereby arrive at a sort of triple hylomorphism: i. e., first, a duality of principles in the *object known* (thus permitting its being known in these two ways) ; second, a duality of principles in the *act of knowing* (thus explaining the two ways of knowing the object) ; and third, a duality of principles in the *knower* (whose act it is, and who also is a possible object to be known). Now in all " three " cases one would arrive at the traditional enough one hylomorphism. Thus, in the first case, form would be the basis of the abstract concept, matter its principle of individuation; in the second, intellect would be the power of abstracting and objectifying, sense the power of knowing individual particulars; in the third, soul or spirit would be the human form, and matter the human body.

Now it is clear that Rahner, although he ostensibly took the first of these two ways, i. e., an analysis of a text rather than an analysis of experience, also brought some ideas of his own (and Hegel's, and Heidegger's) to the analysis and interpretation he made of the Thomist texts. He approached Thomas with his own particular questions and viewpoints, very much conditioned by contemporary philosophy. Rahner, like Thomas, was ultimately interested in the relevance of a metaphysics of knowledge to theology. As a theologian Thomas was more in-

terested in man's spiritual soul than in his body, since he saw
it as the seat of that consciousness and freedom that constitutes man as an apt subject for a theological event, for a divine
revelation.[14] Rahner's aim was broader; he did not seek a mere
means to the apologetic end of defending Thomas's position.[15]
What Rahner offers is a metaphysics of human knowledge, one
that has been considered a real contribution,[16] one that founds
a metaphysical anthropology, a philosophy of religion, and a
whole theology.

That Rahner's approach to Thomas shows the effect of his
concern with Kant and the problem of metaphysical knowledge
is clear from an external as from an internal examination of
SW. And since to raise the question of the possibility of metaphysics conceived in Kantian terms is to raise the question
of the human knowability of God, this one complex question
would naturally become the concern of one whose approach
began with philosophy, i. e., with man as he can be considered
before (logically if not temporally) he is one whom God ad-
dresses in a revelation. So we see that the approaches of Rahner
and Thomas are quite similar, but differ in that Rahner, perhaps due to the influence of Kant and his emphasis on sense
as man's sole intuition, is even more conscious of the contribution of matter to the becoming of the human spirit than
Thomas, who is, of course, quite emphatic about matter's contribution to knowledge, but is much less detailed and developed
in his doctrine on the relation of matter to the constituting of
the total human person.

Of course not all is good in Kant, who made the realm of
metaphysics something like the realm of pure, intelligible,
Platonic forms, a suprasensible world available only to an intellectual intuition. Once he excluded from man's equipment
any such intuition,[17] then it was an open and shut case against

---

[14] GW1, 4. 5; GW2, 30, 32; SW, 15, 17.

[15] SW, xix.

[16] The works by W. Brugger, C. Cirne-Lima, and G. McCool, among others
explicitly attribute to Rahner the theory of objective intuition which they understand to be a better interpretation of Aquinas.

[17] I. Kant, *Kritik der reinen Vernunft* (Hamburg: Felix Meiner Verlag, 1856),

metaphysics as possible (at least for theoretical, if not practical, reason) for man. It would do no good to fall back on the easy solution of reaffirming, with Plato and the idealist tradition, that man does have some sort of special, quasi-mystical intuition, often expressed in oracular language and presented as the prerogative of philosophers supposedly endowed with more powerful intellects. But it is just as facile a solution to deny, usually with a disdainful flourish, that anything corresponding to such a realm called the metaphysical exists at all. For even granted that the realm, conceived as Plato or Kant seemed to conceive it, does not exist, nevertheless something in experience does correspond to it, and thus we are forced to reject both of their solutions. As is often the case, the most difficult position is the true and unavoidable one: we must accept (from experience if not from Kant) that we have only sense intuition, and this is the position taken by Aristotle, Aquinas, Kant, Maréchal, and Rahner; [18] it is the main point of the article the analysis of which constitutes Part One of SW; but we must also accept that metaphysics *is* part of experience and then try to explain *how* it is, within the limitations of a power of knowing based on sensation.

It is in the context of this problem of the possibility of metaphysics, along with its accompanying problem of the possibility of knowing of the existence of God, that Rahner elaborates his first definitions of spirit and matter and thus of man as finite person. Because our concern is with person, we need treat that problem of knowledge only to the extent that it helps us define person. Person is called (implicitly, not explicitly) incarnate spirit in SW. Two constituents, spirit and matter, emerge as irreducible (actually, if not in origin) to one another. They

A19, B33 and A51, B75; in English: *Immanuel Kant's Critique of Pure Reason,* trans. by N. K. Smith (London: Macmillan, 1964), 65, 93; often elsewhere also.

[18] J. Maréchal, *Le point de départ de la métaphysique,* Leçons sur le développement historique et théorique du problème de la connaissance, Cahier V. Le Thomisme devant la philosophie critique (Paris/Bruxelles: Desclée de Brouwer/ L'édition universelle, 1949, sec. ed.), 128, 153-155. See GW1, **23**, 78; GW2, **55**, 128; SW, 41, 116.

emerge from an analysis of the problem of knowing not only the physical but also the metaphysical. This problem has a long history, beginning with the beginning of philosophy itself. Maréchal took the historical approach to this question, which he saw as the question of where to begin metaphysics. He saw the two constantly recurrent streams, which we can call empiricism and idealism, as onesided emphasis; empiricism overemphasized sensation and thus matter, and then reduced spirit to an epiphenomenon of matter, while idealism overemphasized intellect and thus spirit, and then reduced matter to an illusion of spirit. Oversimplifications like these, call them monism or reductionism or whatever, fail to do justice to experience because they neglect one side while attending to the other. Kant was well aware of this and presented himself as the synthesizer of these two streams. Maréchal accepted Kant's self-appraisal but saw Kant's attempt at synthesis as a good beginning gone astray; he offered the hylomorphic synthesis, first stated by Aristotle and developed by Thomas, as a corrective to Kant. The correction is mutual, however, for Thomism has much to learn from Kant (as Pierre Scheuer, a contemporary of Maréchal, delighted in repeating [19]).

It is clear that this view of the two streams of philosophy, corresponding to spirit and matter, the two constituents of man, is the position of Rahner. It is true today that when one takes a philosophical stand, whether atheistic materialism, positivism, sensism, spiritualism, intellectualism, or any of the other isms, that stand often represents either a one-sided overemphasis of the experience of matter and sense, on the one hand, or of idea and intellect, on the other, a third position, which can be viewed as the attempt to balance these two but which really precedes them in experience, completes the picture. There seem to be only these three positions historically, each having its ethical and political consequences, often de-

---

[19] P. Scheuer was the relatively unknown and only recently acknowledged influence on Maréchal whose admiration for Kant knew almost no bounds; for him "Kant was the Newton of the universe of ideas." See D. Shine, *An Interior Metaphysics. The Philosophical Synthesis of Pierre Scheuer* (Weston, Mass.; Weston College Press, 1966); see 181-198.

generating into ideologies. Dondeyne has also called attention
to the constant interplay of these two currents not only
throughout the past history of philosophy but also as constituting the polarities of the contemporary scene.[20] And as
Maréchal's dialogue was with critical philosophy that of
Rahner has been with existentialist and phenomenological
philosophy. In both cases Thomism is offered as the synthesis
of the two streams, not as a synthesis made a *posteriori* to the
prior existence of the two streams, but as the *a priori* synthesis
always and already given before any later distinction into two
constituents; only the synthesis really exists, the constituting
elements being distinguishable but not separable. What pass
for two streams of thought are based on reified abstractions
corresponding to the two polarities constituting all the reality
of our experience. It is dualism (of principles, not beings) that
precedes monism and makes monism possible as a false position.

Now how does this come to light in SW? It comes to light
as an attempt to understand the meaning of Thomas's *turning
to phantasms*. In his *Summa Theologiae*, I, q. 84, a. 7, Thomas
uses this expression to characterize the need of the human intellect for sensation in order to know anything and even to be
in act at all. For our purposes, seeking the meaning of person
as spirit and matter, the important passages are those which
do not remain within the relatively narrow limits of an analysis
of the act of cognition but go on to a definition of the agent
or actor. In a. 7, however, Thomas does not deduce man's
nature from an analysis of his actions, as one might expect,
mindful of the axiom: actions reveal natures, but disconcerting-
ly seems to do just the opposite, appealing to the hylomorphic
nature of man to explain why man must use phantasms (i. e.,
images, sense, imagination) in order to know, even to know
intellectually. Actually what he does is point to the simultaneity of statements about man's acting and man's being.

[20] See A. Dondeyne, *Contemporary European Thought and Christian Faith* (Pittsburgh: Duquesne University Press, 1963, trans. by E. McMullin and J. Burnheim).

There is no need here to get involved in priorities; of course the hylomorphism of the nature precedes that of the act of knowing, which is only this kind of act because it is the act of this nature, this nature's second act. But the point is that it is the act itself of knowing that reveals the dualism of the knower. There is an isomorphism of the knowing and the knower, revealed in the act of knowing: just as the knowing requires phantasms, so also the spirit requires matter. There is an isomorphism of the knowing and the known as well: corresponding to the duality of principles in the known object, there is a duality of principles constituting the act of knowing that object as it really is.

Again, we have here three parallel hylomorphisms. They can be seen as constituting the possibility of—and therefore as deducible from—our experience of knowing some object both abstractly and concretely, i. e., of knowing both the universal and the particular as having their one source in reality. The question: Whence this duality?, leads to a hylomorphism in the known object, a hylomorphism in the act of knowing, and a hylomorphism in the knower as performer of the act. In the known we call the hylomorphism a union of form (considered always universal in itself) and of matter (principle of individuation); this dualism grounds and permits knowledge of the object intellectually, according to its form or idea, and sensibly, according to its spatio-temporal concretion. In the act of knowing we call this hylomorphism a union of intellect and sense (in terms of faculties or powers) or a union of abstraction (or objectification) and intuition or *turning* (in terms of the acts that flow from these faculties or powers). In the knower we call the hylomorphism a union of form and matter, the same terms used for the known (the knower is also a possible known); for living beings the traditional terms become soul and matter, and, for man, spirit and matter.

This isomorphism of hylomorphisms is reached in Part One of SW more through an analysis of the act of knowing than through an analysis of the object known or of the knower. It is true that Aristotle preferred to study the object, to take the cosmocentric approach, i. e., to see hylomorphism first as a theory to explain physical change; the act of knowing then conformed to the known, on the principle that truth is the conformity of mind to reality, and thus we have an isomorphism of hylomorphisms. It is also true that at least since Kant and his Copernican revolution, which set out from the principle of reality conforming to mind, the approach has been to begin with the act of knowing and then make the object known conform to it. But a law of conformity, no matter what its direction, remains a law of isomorphism and thus the same conclusion is predictable. The brief synthesis achieved, at least in intention, in Kant, promptly dissolved insofar as one successor of Kant emphasized intellect and another emphasized sense in the act of knowing, and then logically each went on to describe reality monistically. And yet the post-Kantian approach remains superior to the Aristotelian, despite the danger that one might get no further than Kant did,[21] for the important reason that to study the act is to be able to catch the dynamism of spirit itself, appetitively as well as cognitively, as act and not just as form and structure, and to be able to become conscious of that dynamism as transcending every known object and opening out toward an undefined and unobjectified horizon. It is doubtful that the cosmocentric approach could succeed in leading the individual person to the vivid interior experience of dynamism, important to a grasp of the metaphysical basis of freedom of choice.

Rahner's particular variation of this anthropocentric approach in SW is to assign roles to spirit (intellect) and matter (sense), roles performed in the process of objectification, roles described in terms of presence. The role of sense is intuition, a perfect identification of two acts (forms) in one matter. The role of intellect is objectification of what is given unobjectively in the senses. It will be useful to approach Rahner's meaning

---

[21] See E. Gilson, *Réalisme thomiste et critique de la connaissance* (Paris: Vrin, 1939).

of presence by a brief review of these roles of intellect and sense in human cognition.

Rahner accepts the traditional characterization of knowledge as first of all intuition, i.e., the identity of knower and known. All knowledge is first intuition or identity, or it is never knowledge. In human knowing, this necessary role of intuition is filled by the senses: sensation is precisely this identity of knower and known because the act of the sensed object takes place in the matter of the sensing subject and becomes simultaneously the act of the knower and of the known. There is a relation of dependence by the sense on the object; i. e., the object is a cause. The act (or form) of the object is now the property of the subject insofar as the act now at work in the matter of the sense is the act of the object. The problem is, of course, to explain objectification; i. e., beyond the ability of the knower not only to lose himself in the perfect identity of sense intuition, an identity that overcomes differentiation between subject and object, he can also distinguish himself from the known object, set himself off from it, make it an object. The point is always that it is the combination of sense and intellect that effects what we experience as finite human knowledge. Rahner calls it an objective intuition: sense intuits, intellect objectifies. Aquinas puts it in terms of *turning* and *abstraction*: turning to phantasms means sense intuition: since man is always already united to matter, and thus always already in and of the world, he is always and already turned to phantasms; abstraction means objectification: the intellect, because it is spiritual, is able to remain not given over, as is the matter of the senses, to the act of the object, but can perceive a distance between itself and the known, can distinguish itself from what is not itself. Of course no reification of intellect and sense is intended; to speak of their respective roles always runs that risk. The one man intuits insofar as materially he senses; the one man objectifies, abstracts, universalizes, etc., insofar as intellectually he never is exhausted in knowing but always is other than the known.

Let us allow the above to suffice for a look at SW Part One, and turn immediately to an interpretation of Part Two of that work. Here we find the metaphysical principles of person as spirit, matter, and becoming. Then we continue the search into HW, adding those advances of Rahner's thought on person, freedom, and love, and then into his STh.[22]

---

[22] Because William Dych's translation of GW is generally good and faithful, it is used in place of actually quoting the German, this practice being permissible also because the second edition was, except for additions, left relatively intact by its editor, J. B. Metz. Unfortunately the same cannot be said either of Metz's version of HW or of M. Richards's (and unnamed associate or associates) unacceptably poor translation of that second edition; thus I have always referred to the German and made reference to the extremely useful French translation while making grateful use in the body of the text of the unpublished Donceel translation of the first edition. In all references care has been taken to locate passages in all editions likely to be used by students of Rahner. For STh I use, occasionally modifying, the published translations now available.

PART ONE: PHILOSOPHICAL ANTHROPOLOGY

I

Spirit in the World: Metaphysical Principles of Personal Becoming

PART I OF SW ends with three implicit questions: what do matter, spirit, and becoming mean? But these three make the one question of personal becoming, for the human person is an incarnate spirit, a finite spirit becoming spirit in matter. This is not so explicitly put in SW. One could say that Part I ends with only one question, viz., the meaning of Aquinas's *excessus* and Rahner's *Vorgriff*, i. e., transcendence. Indeed even this question is not so explicit as one might wish. But even if it were, it would still have to be said that the notion of transcendence (*Vorgriff, excessus*) implies matter (sense), spirit (agent intellect), and becoming (possible intellect). All one need do is look at the arrangement of Part II to notice that the three major chapters (2, on Sensibility; 3, on Abstraction; and 4, on Turning, or Conversion) become clear when viewed according to this interpretation. In terms of cognition, sense and agent intellect achieve human knowing in the possible intellect. Possible intellect is for Rahner the most apt summary expression for human knowing. That this means *becoming* is clear from the very term *possible* intellect. Hence to say that Part I ends with the question of the meaning of *Vorgriff* is to say that Part II must *first* take up the meaning of sensibility's intuition transcended (reached beyond) by the *Vorgriff* (i. e., Chapter 2, Sensibility), must *second* take up the meaning of the agent intellect that does the reaching out, without grasping (otherwise it would be an intellectual intuition), toward the horizon of the fullness of being (i. e., Chapter 3, Abstraction), and must *third* take up the meaning of the way intuition plus the reaching beyond intuition constitute together the hylomorphic act of human knowing (i. e., Chapter 4, Turning), a process Rahner describes in terms of spirit's becoming itself through letting matter emanate from itself: the becoming of spirit in matter.

All this is presented as the question of how metaphysics is possible for knowledge limited to sense intuition. To answer that man has a transcendence or *excessus* beyond sensation would be to evade the question if by *excessus* is meant an intellectual intuition. But it does not. It does mean a genuine transcendence of the world,[1] but only as an act proper to the very nature of the intellect present in every act of knowing anything. This concept of transcendence (*excessus, Vorgriff*) is the key to understanding the meaning of spirit from a cognitive viewpoint.

Before we study Part II, let us summarize very briefly what can be gleaned from Part I. In Aquinas's S. Th. I, q. 84, a. 7, duality in the knower, in the knowing, and in the known is affirmed. The intellect is said to need to turn to phantasms because it is joined to a receptive body (*corpus passibile*). This is considered easily verified by referring to common experience (the need to think with images, the fact of senility, etc.). The second step consists in assigning roles to the two principles involved in the experience of knowledge. The experience itself is described as both an intuition (sense's role), by which knower and known achieve identity, and objectification (intellect's role), by which knower and known are distinguished. The explanation of how sense and intellect can fill these roles uses the term presence. Thus knowledge is a being's presence to being. A pure spirit's knowledge would be pure self-presence. An incarnate spirit's knowledge is dual, corresponding to its dual nature: as intellect it is self-presence or presence to self; as sense it is self-absence or presence to other. Thus man is a spirit whose self-knowledge is mediated by knowledge of other. Man must find himself in the world, must come to himself from

---

[1] GW1, 33; GW2, 68; SW, 54.

the world, where he always already is. Man exists, is intentional, embodied, temporal, spatial because finite. So much for a summary of Part I. There is, of course, much more than this, but Rahner repeats the essentials in Part II.

Naturally Part II, which constitutes four-fifths of SW, is far more detailed than my treatment here can be. There is no reason to repeat all those details; it suffices for the meaning of person and becoming to present the basics of Rahner's metaphysics of human knowledge.

The initial section of Chapter I, on the metaphysical question, shows man's finitude, and again in terms of *presence* to being (as questioning *being*) and *absence* from being (as *questioning* being). The following sections of that chapter repeat and develop the notion of knowledge as presence. Immateriality (spirituality) is the principle of self-presence and the measure of a being's power to be and to know.

An essence that has no intrinsic relatedness to matter is by that very fact already actually present-to-itself: it is knowing and actually knowable. Therefore, this actually knowable by no means expresses in the first instance a relation to another knowing but is a determination of the essence of being in itself; it has no intrinsic relatedness to matter. If it were in and at matter, the being of an existent would exhaust itself. By the fact that it is without matter, it is therefore present-to-itself, knowing and known by itself. What is only potentially knowable is such not because accidentally and as a matter of fact it is not known by anyone, but because its being is the being of the empty ' other ' of matter in such a way that it in no way belongs to itself, is not present-to-itself, and in this mode of existence it cannot in principle be present-to-itself; it remains and must remain essentially potentially knowable.[2]

Something purely material could not know, nor could it be known in itself. But nothing purely material is given, only matter and form as one being. The form is the known, the matter that wherein the form is and is known. To the extent that any form is not matter, it is non-material; but by *immaterial* is meant a being with no intrinsic relation to matter.

[2] GW1, 45; GW2, 87; SW, 74.

The forms of material things, intrinsically related to matter, are not immaterial in this strict sense. They exist in matter; the matter itself is not known as such but only as the " wherein " of the form. Put again in terms of presence, a purely immaterial (spiritual) being, precisely because free from the principle of non-knowing (matter), is perfectly self-present; there is nothing within it to keep it distant from itself; it is its own proper object of knowledge.[3] A purely immaterial being can be. It is not self-contradictory and provides a useful limit-concept representing one pole of possibility. The other pole, a purely material being, as self-contradictory, cannot exist. As a limit-concept it is useful but difficult to manage, leading to expressions like " non-being," " relative non-being," " total self-absence," etc. Let's be tolerant of such an admittedly makeshift way of speaking until it's replaced by a better expression. The words " wherein " or " whereto " of the form, or the " empirical residue " of knowledge,[4] shed some welcome light on the experience named by the word " matter," at least from the viewpoint of knowledge. Neither pure spirit nor pure matter is given as such but mixed. Hence the familiar concept of hierarchy in the beings of the world. Rahner variously uses the terms *Seinshabe, Seinsmässigheit,* and *Seinsmächtigkeit,* but the idea is the same: the " more " being a being has, the more knowing and knowable it is in itself. Aquinas found the concept of hierarchy useful and saw an obvious continuity from minerals, to life in plants, animals, man, and pure spirits.[5] There is no need to belabor so well-known a concept. For our purposes it suffices to say that the composition of spirit and matter in man, uncovered by an examination of human cognition, is relevant to human freedom, love, and personal becoming.

[3] GW1, 46; GW2, 88; SW, 75.

[4] B. Lonergan, *Insight,* A Study of Human Understanding (New York: Philosophical Library, 1958. rev. ed.), 25-32 and 516-517.

[5] Thomas Aquinas, *Tractatus de Spiritualibus Creaturis* (Rome: Gregorian University Press, 1937, 1959, ed. by L. Keeler), 28-29 (i.e., art. 2, corpus). See *On Spiritual Creatures* (Milwaukee: Marquette University Press, 1949, trans. with an intro. by M. Fitzpatrick in collaboration with J. Wellmuth), 36-37.

1. *Matter*. Throughout the thought development of SW there are two complex ideas essential to understanding Rahner's view of man as finite spirit. The first is what matter "does" to man: the second is what spirit "does" to man, i.e., what the undefined openness of the intellect and will becomes when embodied. Man is what matter makes him, what spirit makes him, and what he makes of them. Thus to know the full meanings of matter and spirit, we must know the full meaning of man as openness in itself (spirit) and as openness in and through time and space (matter). But this is to define man as becoming, as potential to be actualized in time, for spirit names the power to know and to love, and matter names the way spirit knows and loves in the world. Rahner finds in Aquinas the doctrine of emanation of sense from intellect; the reason for emanation is that the human spirit is such that it cannot become itself except by incarnating.[6] "Human knowing is first of all being-with-the world, a being-with-another in sensibility; and therefore knowledge of this other in its in-itself as proper object is only possible by setting the other opposite and referring the knowledge to this other which is set opposite and exists in itself."[7] He affirms that though knowledge *as such* is self-presence, *human* knowledge is first self-absence (as matter), presence-to-other (as sense), and only *becomes* self-presence in and through this other.[8] The human intellect is totally incapable of self-presence on its own.[9] It must incarnate in order to be itself. This is the meaning of the need of intellect to turn to phantasms. Put negatively: the main effect of matter is to make human becoming *necessary*, since by being material man is spread out in space and time. But it is better to put this positively: the main effect of matter is to make becoming *possible*, because the human spirit as finite is such that becoming is *already necessary* to it in order for it to be itself, and matter is its way. The human spirit is given to itself only

---

[6] GW1, 68-91; GW2, 116-119; SW, 104-107.

[7] GW1, 89; GW2, 142; SW, 133, 229.

[8] GW1, 91, 163; GW2, 144, 235; SW, 133, 229.

[9] GW1, 92; GW2, 145-146; SW, 134-135.

as potential (in terms of intellect we speak of the *possible* intellect, i. e., receptive intellect joined with matter). That matter makes the becoming of the human spirit possible is treated by Rahner under the notion of emanation: spirit, in its effort to become itself, lets matter emanate from itself.

The considerations just expressed place us in Chapter 3 of SW. Not much has been made of Chapter 1; what is said there is general and holds up only in the light of later chapters. Nor have we dwelt on Chapter 2 (sensibility), for a good reason. According to the interpretation of SW presented here, sensibility is Rahner's cognitive way of speaking (Thomistically as well as in the Kantian tradition) of the material component of man. Hence, since matter is the human spirit's mode of becoming itself, discussion of matter cannot be divorced from discussion of becoming; but becoming is more explicitly and fundamentally treated later, in Chapter 4, under the headings of emanation and inner-worldly causality; thus a more metaphysical treatment of becoming and matter is best left until we deal with Chapter 4. Chapter 2, furthermore, where one might expect the most explicit treatment of matter, comes too soon in Rahner's analysis to allow us to move from the specifically cognitive context to the more basic metaphysical treatment of matter in general which we want. And so it happens that the fourth (and last) chapter of Part II becomes the place for this move. Thus we turn to Chapter 3 (abstraction), i. e., agent intellect, the Thomist expression for spirit as dynamic and active (as contrasted with possible intellect, spirit as receptive and incarnate).

2. *Spirit.* We can best relate Chapter 3 to our search for a metaphysics of person by considering it the place where Rahner speaks of the human spirit *as* spirit. Naturally the explicit context, as always, is cognition, and thus he treats spirit under the name of agent intellect. Previously he treated intellect without this distinction being made between agent and possible intellect. At that time he attributed to intellect the general role of abstracting and objectifying. As spirit the human intellect can

fulfill this role. As spirit it can be self-present, can "return to itself" (*reditio in* or *super* or *ad seipsum*). Because spirit can return to itself, man can come from the world in which he always is as sensibility and can thus distance and distinguish himself from the other present in his senses by intuition. This is the way we have seen objectification described up to now. In Chapter 3, Section 4 (Nature of the Agent Intellect), Subsection 3 (Agent Intellect as "pre-apprehension" [*Vorgriff*]),[10] Rahner presents objectification as the effect of the transcendence of the intellect driving right past every object it knows and continuing on to an undefined horizon; the transcended object appears finite because it does not fill this horizon. Imagine a wide beam of light shining past all objects upon which it falls, projecting a background—light outlining each object, making it stand out as an object—and continuing on toward a horizon that remains unfilled and undefined in itself. Transcending objects is not knowing objects but a necessary condition for knowledge; this is a traditional enough way of characterizing the effect of the agent intellect. Neither *Vorgriff* nor *excessus* is well translated by cognitive words, for neither means knowing an object: transcendence only reaches for it, stretches toward it. In the stretching, all finite objects are passed by. But man's grasp does not match his reach (in knowing or in loving): he can experience his reaching out as an unsatisfied grasping-after: knowing never rests on an object without thereby falling back from (or short of) its full reach, without placing a distance between the object and the horizon.

Such an image as that of a horizon is useful, but should not be exaggerated or reified; it is vulnerable to the criticism that it betrays a visual bias. But, of course, horizon is not so novel an image; Rahner considers it but another way of expressing the traditional concept of material object as wider than the

[10] GW1, 98 ff.; GW2, 153 ff.; SW, 142 ff. Dych's translation of *Vorgriff* as preapprehension is not useful beyond a cognitive context; transcendence is a term I prefer because it suggests the basic meaning of spirit as both intellect and will prior to as well as after the distinction of spirit into intellect and will. This is consistent with Aquinas and Blondel.

formal object of a faculty. Thus sensation is also said to project a horizon, that of space and time, of *ens mobile;*[11] whether one is comfortable calling any horizon infinite or merely undefined is another question. But the horizon of intellect is that of being itself, a wider horizon than that of space and time.[12] This but repeats the traditional thesis of being as knowable: everything which is, insofar as it is, is a possible object of knowledge.

Now Rahner offers considerable detail concerning the intricacies of the Thomist theory of abstraction and turning. For us the important point is the nature of man as spirit, that aspect which makes possible this restless intentionality, for it opens an unclosable " gap " at the heart of human nature. We can, in fact, speak of two " gaps " within human being, revealed by our having to become. The first gap is constituted by the very composition of man as spirit and matter, because matter prevents—absolutely—the perfect self-identification that is the privilege of pure spirit; this is the metaphysical meaning of concupiscence, man's inability to dispose of himself perfectly and completely in any one act, but rather needing time and space, a whole lifetime, to actualize his potential, to become a person. Embodied spirit needs a whole lifetime to do one thing; this one thing is personal becoming. The first gap, constituted by what we could accept as a result of something " natural," our incarnate condition, need not startle us nor long delay us in thought; if we accept the law of life as ascent and assent to death, we recognize time as gift, comfort, because it " takes time " to learn, to become, to gain oneself. But the second gap is not so readily accepted and perhaps not so self-evidently recognizable. It seems to present us with something totally unattainable, unreachable no matter how much time we're given. It is less easy to accept that our desire to know and be known, to love and be loved, will never be quieted. Yet horizons of truth and goodness toward which the intellect and

[11] GW1, 98; GW2, 154; SW, 143.
[12] GW1, 131-132; GW2, 195-196; SW, 186-187.

will open remain beyond our grasp. Rahner sees this transcendence as affirmed in experience (as well as in Aquinas). Whether this second gap would or did exist in some hypothetical state of pure nature is not in question now (nor whether the horizon has been "changed" by grace; suffice it to say for now that the theory of the supernatural existential is an explanation of just this experience, for this is the first and basic meaning of Rahner's teaching that grace can be experienced). The question of a pure state of nature is a historical question, subject to the conditions of all such questions. Note that the basis for Rahner's teaching on concupiscence is laid here with the notion of the relation of spirit and matter to becoming. The essential point about these two " gaps " is that they do exist and can be experienced now. Personal becoming begins with trying to close these gaps: first, man becomes a person insofar as spirit is more, not less, incarnate, and insofar as matter is more, not less, taken up into spirit; second, the achievement of personhood ultimately coincides with the reaching of those two distant horizons of knowing and loving, by knowing and loving and by being known and loved; here Blondel's philosophy of insufficiency, maintaining the insufficiency of philosophy, keeps the horizons open, listening.

It will be good to pause over the verification of this second gap.

We know philosophically of no human knowledge in which the pre-apprehension [*Vorgriff*] does not go beyond what is 'grasped' (*Griff*), beyond the objective, concretizing knowledge. This human knowledge, about which alone we know anything philosophically, always falls short essentially of its complete fulfilment, which fulfilment is designated by the breadth of its pre-apprehension. Nevertheless, this pre-apprehension towards this ideal with all that it simultaneously affirms as really possible is not an inconsequential supplementation, but the condition of the possibility of any objective knowledge at all. The pre-apprehension can be explained more precisely in the fact that it is the movement of the spirit towards the whole of its possible objects for it is only in this way that the limitation of the individual known can be experienced.[13]

---

[13] GW1, 100; GW2, 155; SW, 144-145.

How is the "reaching without grasping" experienced?

The pre-apprehension . . . is known insofar as knowledge, in the apprehension of its individual object, always experiences itself as already and always moving out beyond it, insofar as it knows the object in the horizon of its possible objects in such a way that the pre-apprehension reveals itself in the movement out towards the totality of its objects. Thus the pre-apprehension has a being which makes it apprehendable, without it needing an object beyond that object for the objectifying of which it takes place, without the totality of the possible objects in their own selves having to be apprehended by the pre-apprehension.[14]

Rahner devotes several long sections to the action of the agent intellect as *Vorgriff*.[15] Significant for our purposes is the relation of spirit to this *Vorgriff*. After making explicit that the judging intellect reaches toward being[16] and not toward nothing,[17] he further explicitates just what this being is. It has already been made clear that this being is not an object in the usual sense, but the undefined horizon of all possible objects, the fullness of being, the non-object non-objectively co-known in the knowing of objects. But what exactly is this fullness of being? It is not nothing, not pure negativity, but pure, absolute being. Rahner offers a provisional statement, based on the above elimination: in its stretching beyond all finite objects,

an object does manifest itself in a way indicated earlier: the Absolute Being, God. This Absolute Being is not apprehended as a represented object. For the *esse* apprehended in the pre-apprehension, as only implicitly and simultaneously apprehended in the pre-apprehension was known implicitly and simultaneously as able to be limited by quidditative determinations and as already limited, since the pre-apprehension, if it is not to be a 'grasp,' can only be realized in a simultaneous conversion to a definite form limiting *esse* and in the conversion to the phantasm. The fullness of being which *esse* expresses is therefore never given objectively.[18]

---

[14] GW1, 100; GW2, 156; SW, 145.
[15] GW1, 101-161; GW2, 156-232; SW, 146-226.
[16] GW1, 119 ff.; GW2, 179 ff.; SW, 169 ff.
[17] GW1, 129 ff.; GW2, 192 ff.; SW, 183 ff.
[18] GW1, 127-128; GW2, 189; SW, 180.

No finite, particular being, but rather the fullness of being is the "objective" of the intellect. Thus nothing less than the fullness of being can fill the scope of the intellect.

An Absolute Being would completely fill up the breadth of this pre-apprehension. Hence it is simultaneously affirmed as real (since it cannot be grasped as merely possible). In this sense, but only in this sense, it can be said: the pre-apprehension attains to God. Not as though it attains to the Absolute Being immediately in order to represent it objectively in its own self, but because the reality of God as that of absolute *esse* is implicitly affirmed simultaneously by the breadth of the pre-apprehension, by *esse commune*. In this respect, grasping absolute *esse* would also completely fill up the breadth of the pre-apprehension. But, on the other hand, insofar as in human knowledge, which alone is accessible to philosophy, the pre-apprehension is always broader than the grasp of an object itself because of the conversion to the phantasm, nothing can be decided philosophically about the possibility of an immediate apprehension of absolute *esse* as an object of the first order.[19]

This orientation to absolute being is not just an arbitrary or peripheral fact about man and his intellect. For Rahner it is the very essence of spirit: man is spirit *because* he is ordered to infinite being.

Human knowledge as pre-apprehending is ordered to what is absolutely infinite, and for that reason man is spirit. He always has this infinite only in the pre-apprehension, and for that reason he is finite spirit. Man is spirit because he finds himself situated before being in its totality which is infinite. He is finite because he has this infinite only in the absolutely unlimited breadth of his pre-apprehension.[20]

We now have another way to describe spirit. Besides the concept of spirit as self-*presence* (which it is because it is immaterial: the comparison is with matter, and sets up the first "gap"), we now have the concept of spirit as *openness* (which it is because it finds itself before the totality or fullness of being: the comparison is with its horizon, and sets up the second "gap"). If we use words more literally rendering

[19] GW1, 128; GW2, 190; SW, 181.
[20] GW1, 131; GW2, 195; SW, 186.

Rahner's German, we can raise doubt whether we really have two ways of describing spirit, or two ways of expressing one way. If we say that knowledge is a being's being with itself, i. e., with being, and then say that for a being to be spirit is to find itself before infinite being (*sich vor das an sich unendliche Sein* [21]), how different are these two expressions? A being can be present to itself only if it is already essentially open to all being in general. Transcendence (the *Vorgriff*) is the essential mark of man as spirit. It is an experience of being *open* to all being that makes possible a *presence* to this being; thus presence and openness refer to spirit, and to this extent the two gaps are one, because the matter (of the first gap) is spirit's way of trying to close the second gap, i. e., by incarnating.

With this last sentence we bridge to Rahner's more detailed treatment of agent intellect, though we need not dwell on his explanation of abstraction. For our purposes it is enough to study it as the faculty of the *Vorgriff*.

If the agent intellect is the highest faculty of man and if it must be understood as the faculty of the *excessus* to *esse* absolutely, and if in it absolute *esse* is simultaneously affirmed, then as a matter of fact the agent intellect is the metaphysical point at which the finite spirit comes upon his openness to, and dependence upon, God. And that is true not merely in the general way in which every finite being points to the Absolute Being, but in such a way that the absolute *esse* is implicitly and simultaneously affirmed in every act of the agent intellect, in every judgment. For this reason, Thomas can understand the agent intellect in a special way as a participation in the light of the Absolute Spirit, not merely because, being dependent on this, it is as a matter of fact similar to it, but because finite spirit is spirit only through the pre-apprehension of absolute *esse* in which the Absolute Being is already and always apprehended.[22]

Thus while the best formulations on the human spirit in its relation to *matter* will predictably come under the heading of possible intellect, those on spirit in its relation to absolute being come under the heading of agent intellect. We therefore can

[21] GW1, 131; GW2, 195; SW, 186.
[22] GW1, 160-161; GW2, 195; SW, 186.

hope to find such formulations in Chapter 4, Conversion (Turning) to the Phantasm, since this expression means the turning of the intellect to the senses, to matter, just as we found the formulations about spirit as *Vorgriff* in Chapter 3, Abstraction, since this expression means the objectification of the particular in stretching toward the fulness of being. In a sense, therefore, Chapter 4 has to do with what I have called the first gap, later linked, e. g., with the notion of concupiscence, while Chapter 3 had to do with the second gap, later linked, e. g., with the notion of the supernatural existential. Even though this talk of two gaps will be superseded, its usefulness for the time being seems manifest, at least as corresponding to the constant duality in man and in Rahner's treatment of man and his knowledge. There is the duality in man himself, as spirit and matter, as intellect and sense. There is also the duality of functions in intellect itself, named by the tradition agent and possible intellects. Actually this duality adds no new quantity; agent intellect refers to spirit as dynamic, active, relatively self-subsistent; possible intellect refers to spirit as receptive, form in matter, form of matter, of human corporeality. In the earlier pages of Chapter 4 we find important statements for this metaphysics of man as incarnate spirit.

The last two chapters proceeded in such a way that the ontological constitution of man was disclosed in certain characteristics of human knowledge. From the question, what are the conditions of a receptive, intuitive knowledge?, we arrived at the essence of sensibility, and thereby, at the essence of man as a sentient knower: act of matter, form of a body. From the insight into the possibility of a judgmental, universal knowledge attaining to the in-itself of the object differentiated from the subject, we arrived at the essence of thought, and thereby, at the essence of man as spirit: *excessus* to *esse* absolutely; a form subsisting in itself. . . . man is at once 'subsisting in himself' and 'actuality of the other' [of matter].[23]

These two formulations are not contradictory. The one human spirit is source of both. Human knowledge as spiritual is

[23] GW1, 170; GW2, 244-245; SW, 239.

agent intellect; human knowledge as material is possible intellect. But there is one human knowing, one intellect in man, despite this duality. The problem again is one of relating intellect (spirit) to sensation (matter). Rahner assigns to possible intellect the role of relating to matter. " If, then, the agent intellect is the spontaneous, dynamic ordination of the human spirit to *esse* absolutely, the ' *quo est omnia facere*,' then the possible intellect as intellect is the potentiality of the human spirit to comprehend *esse* absolutely in receptive knowledge, the ' *quo est omnia fieri*.' " [24] Possible intellect means the specifically human, embodied way of being spirit. If agent intellect means simply the self-presence of spirit, possible intellect means self-presence only on the condition of first being present to other.

In the light of this it becomes intelligible what possible intellect *qua* possible means. It is being, i. e., being-present-to-oneself, complete return, but it is not of itself already and always present to itself. By itself it cannot give itself immediately to itself; it comes to itself only insofar as it receptively allows another to encounter it, and without this receptive letting-self-be-encountered by another it is itself not present to itself. . . . Indeed the essence of the possible intellect can be defined relatively simply from the way it knows; it is that being which is present to itself in the knowledge of another. But as soon as this definition is to be ' translated ' into ontological terms, it can be discovered only as the mid-point between two different definitions: in its being-present-to itself the possible intellect is a form subsisting in itself; in its drive to let itself be encountered by another it is sensibility; form of matter, form of a body. Only in this duality in which both definitions mutually and intrinsically modify each other, is the possible intellect grasped ontologically. Insofar as the drive to let itself be encountered by another, in order to be present to itself, is derived from the fact that the intellect indeed really is intellect, i. e., the intellect is able to be present to itself, but it is not present to itself through its mere existence—which is precisely what is said by the term possible intellect—*possible intellect is the most adequate and most simple conception for human knowledge and for human being altogether.*[25]

---

[24] GW1, 172-173; GW2, 247; SW, 242.
[25] GW1, 173-175; GW2, 248-250; SW, 243-245. Rahner's emphasis.

Rahner treats the precise question of the relationship of possible intellect to sense as one of origin, and his answer to this question is that intellect emanates sense from itself for itself, in order to be itself. This notion of emanation gets considerable space in Chapter 4, much of it devoted to showing that this is Aquinas's position.[26] Kant can also be interpreted as intimating his personal inclination toward a like doctrine of common origin of intellect and sense when he says: " there are two stems of human knowledge, *sensibility* and *understanding*, which perhaps spring from a common, but to us unknown, root." [27] From the specifically cognitive context of this question in SW we can now select what is relevant to our question of person.

The first point to make is that the process of emanation is not conceived as a " once and for all " event.[28] The human spirit exists as a permanent source and cause in relation to its powers:

the emanation of the powers from the substantial ground can only be conceived as one, so that the emanation of several powers (i. e., in our case, the intellect and sensibility) can only be understood as partial movements of the one movement of the metaphysical self-realization of the one human spirit. Wherefore, this one movement is directed towards the fulfilment of the human spirit. Thus it proceeds towards the final goal of its constitution, hence to that which is most perfect in it. For Thomas this is the intellect. In the intellect the one human knowing reaches its full constitution.[29]

Second is the focus on dynamism. We have seen that the question of knowledge is the question of the relation of spirit and matter, of *Geist* and *Welt*.[30] We have just seen that relation characterized as one of emanation: spirit lets matter flow, originate, result, emanate from itself, all Thomist terms, as Rahner shows. He also emphasizes that a static view of this

---

[26] GW1, 171-224, esp. 175 ff. and 201 ff.; GW2, 245-311, esp. 246 ff. and 282 ff.; SW, 239-309, esp. 246 ff. and 279 ff.

[27] I. Kant, *Kritik der reinen Vernunft*, A15, B29; Smith trans., 61.

[28] GW1, 186; GW2, 264; SW, 260.

[29] GW1, 187; GW2, 265-266; SW, 261.

[30] GW1, 201; GW2, 283; SW, 279.

process falsifies it. Only a dynamic interpretation does justice to experience and to the Thomist texts and their contexts. Some of the best pages of SW on spirit and its relation to matter are in section 5 of Chapter 4.[31]

Rahner makes much capital of this concept of dynamism. He has used it as the very meaning and essence of spirit. He now sees it also as the explanation of sensibility:

the active producing, in which the spirit as the 'active principle and end' lets sensibility emanate from itself must be understood as a moment in its desire for absolute being. . . . in producing the complete constitution of its own essence towards which it tends, spirit lets sensibility emanate from itself, bears it permanently in itself as its power, and informs it from the outset with the laws of its own essence, since it produces it in its striving towards its own fulfilment. . . . It must produce sensibility, because in itself it is only desire (possible intellect).[32]

This statement of the relation of intellect and sense (spirit and matter), a relationship we called the first gap, once again

---

[31] There is, e.g., the following passage: "The essence of the spirit is the 'quo est omnia fieri': spirit is in potency for absolute being. It is 'in a certain way (i.e., in potency and in ordination towards) everything.' Its becoming conscious of its a priori reality is therefore the pre-apprehension of absolute being, and vice versa. As transcendent apprehension of absolute esse, this actuality of the spirit is a becoming, a dynamic orientation to the totality of its objects. . . . The human spirit as such is desire, striving, action. For in itself it is possible intellect, i.e., something which reaches its full actuality from its potentiality, and in fact by its own action, since by its own active power (agent intellect) of itself (always in act) it produces its object (the actually intelligible) from something only sensibly given. Desire as a characteristic of knowledge as such is brought out explicitly by Thomas. He knows not merely a mutual inclusion of intellect and will as the acts of separate powers, so that knowledge acts and will acts have a reciprocal priority with respect to each other, but the intellect also has a desire in itself as its own intrinsic drive. . . . every 'movement' of the spirit . . . occurs . . in virtue of the desire for the one end and goal. . . . The final end of the one desire of the spirit, expressed formally first of all, is the 'good of the intellect,' truth as such. But this truth which is the good of the intellect is absolute being. For spirit is the potentiality for the reception of all being and the active desire for it. . . . Every operation of the spirit, whatever it might be, can therefore be understood only as a moment in the movement towards absolute being as towards the one end and goal of the desire of the spirit." GW1, 203-205; GW2, 284-287; SW, 281-283.

[32] GW1, 205; GW2, 287-288; SW, 284.

relates this first gap to the second, i. e., the gap constituted by spirit in striving toward fulfilment. Sensibility is intellect's attempt to bridge the second gap. It seems ironic that in so doing spirit has produced another gap, at least by one interpretation of the meaning of matter in human experience, i. e., that matter is an obstacle to man's fulfilment. Actually matter is the condition of man's fulfilment. It is easy to see that this conclusion emerges from Rahner's analyses. His is anything but a Platonic spirituality, disdaining body and misunderstanding asceticism. An understanding of the positive and essential role of matter in becoming begins here in the metaphysics of cognition, but does not end there; Rahner extends and applies these same concepts later, e. g., when treating the identity of love of God and love of neighbor. In love, as well as in knowledge, matter is not spirit's obstacle but its way to itself and to others, to all persons, including the infinite: " it produces sensibility in its desire for absolute being, which desire it itself is." [33] Rahner's treatment of freedom in SW, as the effect of intellect's transcendence, also shows how traditional his view is, and need not detain us now. Freedom is the most important factor not treated in this section but we will take it up explicitly later.

Rahner's treatment of the cogitative sense is both disturbing and satisfying. " Cogitative sense " turns out to be a way of talking about both sense and intellect at once, of attributing the properties of both powers to this one power, and then calling it the medium between the two, or the place where the two meet and cooperate. If one is inclined to be critical, it is easy to think of Descartes's pineal gland or of the bridge role of imagination in the second edition of Kant's first critique. Any dualism brings with itself the problem of how to get the two principles together. Let's admit that Rahner is not innocent of expressions that sometimes identify cogitative sense and possible intellect. If we look for justification of such expressions, we can find it first in the experience of man as one

[33] GW1, 212; GW2, 296; SW, 293.

substance, one unified whole, the distinction into two principles being a subsequent theory meant to explain certain aspects of that experience; second, there is the theory of emanation, i. e., that matter is, as he will say later, something like solidified spirit, the form spirit takes when separated from its final goal and dynamically trying to reach that goal; spirit must materialize when it is spirit that *becomes* spirit rather than already perfectly *is* spirit. Such a view of the relations of spirit and matter goes so far toward identifying spirit and matter, by calling matter the emanation of the spirit, that the dualism that is a datum of experience runs the risk of being ontologically less original than a monism of spirit. Later we will see that in his study of hominization Rahner sees matter as capable of evolving toward spirit because matter itself has its source in spirit.

Because of the role attributed to the cogitative sense, viz., to the meeting point of spirit and matter, we should examine Rahner's treatment and try to extract from the psychological context the anthropological conclusions. The first useful statement, besides the very name cogitative *sense,* and the just mentioned fact that it is " the unified center of spirit and sensibility," [34] emphasizes that it is a power, not an act; its act is turning to the phantasm, an act attributed to the intellect; thus the cogitative sense becomes the power of the intellect to turn to phantasms, or, perhaps better phrased, the name given the intellect in its role of turning to phantasms: " cogitative sense and conversion say objectively the same thing: . . . the cogitative sense is the power of conversion to the phantasm." [35] One cannot easily escape the impression that Rahner is trying to cover all the bases: and indeed he is trying to take into account all the Thomist statements relevant to the problem he has set himself, that of the Thomist *conversio ad phantasma.* Faced with Aquinas's use of the term cogitative sense, he must account for it. It appears to be no more than a name for the in-

---

[34] GW1, 217; GW2, 302; SW, 299.
[35] GW1, 217; GW2, 303; SW, 300.

tellect itself in its specific function of turning to phantasms;
i. e., cogitative sense is the name for intellect precisely as incarnate in matter, as materialized in sense; put the other way
around, cogitative sense expresses the spiritualization of sense:
" The spiritualization of sensibility and of the cogitative sense
is shown first of all purely extrinsically by the fact that practically all the names of the intellect's functions are transferred
to it." [36]

Cogitative sense is the continuation of spirit into sensibility.
When we remember the medieval enjoyment of naming powers
and their functions, sometimes finding it simpler to multiply
names rather than explain them (which could have helped explain them away), we can appreciate Rahner's simplification
in reducing cogitative sense to a name for one role of intellect
(just as the two names, agent intellect and possible intellect,
are understood as a distinction of functions of one human intellectual power, not as two different powers).[37] Thus he can
say that

the cogitative sense is a sense power only insofar as it forms the
unified center of spirit and sensibility. . . . The cogitative sense
is really the passive intellect; the center of the free spontaneity of
spirit (intellect) and the reception of the encountering other in
sensibility (passive) . . . the cogitative sense is the name for the
point at which spirit lets itself emanate into sensibility and from
which it permeates it.[38]

The simplification extends to the imagination and memory:
" the cogitative sense with the memory and imagination as a
whole is called once ' particular reason, passive intellect.' " [39]

We can see where this process of simplification is going. The
old tradition of four internal senses has long been considered,
even in Scholastic Latin manuals, more a matter of convenience
(convenienter enumerantur quattuor) than anything else, the
very distinction itself of senses into internal and external being

[36] GW1, 219; GW2, 304; SW, 301.
[37] GW1, 172, 233; GW2, 247, 323; SW, 241-242, 321.
[38] GW1, 220-221; GW2, 307-308; SW, 304-305.
[39] GW1, 223; GW2, 310; SW, 307.

problematic. Rahner has here reduced all sensibility to the form spirit takes when it is finite and therefore receptive spirit.

Letting the definitions of the imagination and the cogitative sense merge in this way is not illogical inconsistency, but comes from the nature of the case, which, with all the perhaps necessary objective distinguishing of the two powers, again and again forces one to see them as the unified totality of a single knowing: as sensibility which emanates from spirit. Sensibility is therefore originally and not subsequently the point, always already spiritualized and standing under the spontaneous formative power of the spirit, at which the spirit is able to receive passively, and yet in freedom, the formal limitation and determination of its a priori breadth. This description of sensibility touches at once the imagination and the cogitative sense. A further separation of the two is without any further fundamental significance for a metaphysics of knowledge.[40]

Thus the same judgment applies both to intellect's multiple names and distinctions and to sensibility's. For Rahner, possible intellect is

only the term designating the fact that the spirit produces of itself, and must produce and possess, the power of reception which we call sensibility, so that it itself as produced is called possible intellect. . . . the spirit is possible, i. e., receptive, insofar as it necessarily produces sensibility as its receptive intuition." [41] " Therefore, an intellect which is not already of itself present to itself must necessarily let a sensibility emanate from itself in order to possess it as its own power. . . . sensibility . . . can only come to be by the fact that the spirit of man becomes the actuality of matter—the form of a body.[42]

With these statements we are beginning to wrap up what Rahner has to say in SW about man as spirit and matter. The confusing multiplicity of names and statements for intellect, sense, and their diverse functions has been considerably simplified. Not only have the many " intellects " been unified into one and seen as spirit open to absolute being, but also the

[40] GW1, 223; GW2, 310; SW, 307-308.
[41] GW1, 233-234; GW2, 323-324; SW, 321-322.
[42] GW1, 177-178; GW2, 253-254; SW, 249-250.

many " senses " have been unified and seen as finite spirit's
way of receiving being as it moves toward absolute being. Matter is finite spirit's way of becoming itself. Although it is not
quite proper to speak of man as soul and body,[43] since body
as such already implies soul, nevertheless, keeping in mind this
corrective, and thinking in terms of the familiar use of the
words body and soul, we can speak of embodiment as the soul's
way of becoming itself, of becoming actual, of reaching its perfection and fulfilment.[44]

3. *Becoming.* We have reached a point of transition in our
study of SW: we move from a discussion of *spirit* and *matter*,
as the constitutive principles of the human person, to a discussion of *becoming*, as the metaphysically necessary concept for
a study of personal becoming. As before, since we have to
search out Rahner's metaphysics in a work on cognition, the
immediate context will be man as knower. It is obvious, of
course, that man as person is more than man as knower. It
should not be surprising, therefore, if a metaphysics of becoming derived from a study of cognition left much to be de-
sired were we to try to apply it without further ado to man's
affective and ethical life. To the extent that we would try to
do this, we would err almost as badly as those who apply to
person categories derived from cosmology. It is easy to miss
the properly personal when speaking of persons with words and
categories proper to things. To the extent that Rahner is interpreting Aquinas and is dependent on him, he seems not to
transcend these difficulties. To the extent that he brings to
his interpretation the questions and attitudes of contemporary
philosophy and theology, and brings especially the conception
of spirit as intentional, as existence, i. e., as dynamic, incarnate,
and transcending openness, he manages to overcome some of
the cosmocentric bias.

Now no one should infer that to speak of a transition from
discussion of spirit and matter to one of becoming implies that

---

[43] GW1, 235; GW2, 326; SW, 324.
[44] GW1, 238; GW2, 329; SW, 327-328.

there are two independent discussions. It has been said often that the very relation itself of spirit to matter is one of becoming. Rahner emphasizes that only a dynamic viewpoint is adequate to the relation of intellect to sense, of intellect to phantasm and to intelligible species, etc. The concept of emanation is a prime example of a concept which when taken statically is subject to misunderstanding and rejection. The same is true of the notion of the intellect as *permanently* turned to phantasms; one could mistakenly infer from this a static notion of the relation between intellect and sense, although the very opposite is implied:

It is self-evident that this whole relationship of origin among the powers cannot be thought of as a process that happens once and for all, that ran its course perhaps at the temporal beginning of a human existence and then ceased. Rather the powers are held constantly in this relationship or emanation from the substantial ground and from one another.[45]

Emanation is the spirit's *present* and continual self-*becoming*. "The human spirit exists permanently in letting its powers emanate and only in this way."[46] Becoming is at the very heart of the relation of spirit and matter. The discussion of spirit and matter and that of becoming are therefore metaphysically inter-dependent. Constructing a metaphysics of personal becoming turns out to mean discovering how the human spirit becomes itself in matter, i.e., how the relation of the human spirit to matter is a becoming that is simultaneously a materialization of spirit and a spiritualization of matter, always keeping in mind that, as the lower is for the higher, so is matter for spirit, and thus is emanated by spirit for its own becoming spirit.

a. *Emanation: First Otherness.* Emanation is thus a form of becoming. It is offered as an explanation of how sensibility participates in intellect,[47] of how matter participates in spirit.

[45] GW1, 186; GW2, 264; SW, 260.
[46] GW1, 187; GW2, 264; SW, 260.
[47] GW1, 190; GW2, 269; SW, 265.

There are other forms of becoming, but clearly emanation is an extremely basic and important form. If we are to speak of becoming in some detail, we should begin with emanation and treat it from this viewpoint of becoming. Rahner speaks of emanation in comparison with action, and this must be clarified; he also speaks of emanation in terms of causality, and this must be examined.

The basic nature or meaning of emanation seems to be that of an essence's unfolding into its powers.[48] This recalls the traditional Scholastic notion of essence as remote principle and powers as proximate principles of acts by which a being perfects itself. The being first begins to become itself in the emanation of its powers from its essence; this emanation is a sort of first act. The acts of these powers are the perfections of the powers and of the whole being; it becomes itself only in acting. There are questions of causality involved in these expressions, first of all, and second there is the question of the relation between immanent and transient action.

To understand correctly what follows it is to be noted at the outset that in the question of the origin of one power from another and from the substantial ground of the spirit, we are not at all dealing with the relationship between a finished, complete existent as an efficient cause and an effect produced by it, but remaining extrinsic to it. Rather we are dealing with the intrinsic metaphysical constitution of an individual essence in itself as a single being in the plurality of its powers. Therefore, this unity can neither be conceived simply as the connection of an effect with its productive cause, nor as the subsequent union of powers already constituted in themselves. . . . Therefore, the plurality of powers which intrinsically constitute an existent, if they are not to be disputed away monistically, can be conceived as arising out of a single origin in which the plurality, antecedent to itself, is already and always one. Thomas calls this emanating: *origo, fluere, resultatio, emanatio.* This emanating is situated at the mid-point, hardly able to be further defined, between (1) an efficient causality, in which what is produced is indeed different from the origin, but it really does not have to determine the origin itself permanently; (2) a simple essential determination, which is identical with the

---

[48] GW1, 181-182; GW2, 258-259; SW, 254.

essence as origin and so does not ground any plurality of powers; and (3) finally an accidental determination of an existent produced accidentally from without, which indeed formally determines this existent as really different from itself but does not form any essential unity with it, as is the case in the relationship of the soul and its cognitive powers, and the latter among themselves. Consequently, we are dealing with the unfolding, which is essentially given simultaneously with a unified existent, of its essence from its innermost core into the plurality of its powers in which it is first itself.[49]

Note two things in this passage. First, the causality involved is left undefined, although its resemblance to immanent action is unmistakable. Second, the emanation is said to be already accomplished " essentially " once we have the existing being. Let's take up the notion of immanent action first.

Among all the weapons in the Thomist arsenal, that of immanent action is one of the most potent. In a sense it is the key to the question of personal becoming. If personal becoming were only self-actualization, immanent action would be the whole answer. But since personal becoming is primarily self-transcendence and only secondarily self-actualization, transient action is also essential. The relationships hidden in these expressions are complex. It is sometimes hard to say which is the primary action. It seems to follow, e. g., from what has been said about the human spirit as needing matter in order to become itself, that man's primary action would be transient action, action in and at the world, action that transcends the narrow limits of immanent action, which is action that remains within the agent. And yet the more original and metaphysical view is to see transient action as a deficient form of immanent action.[50] How are these two views to be reconciled? First of all it must be admitted that immanent action should not be understood as action that remains totally within the agent, but rather as action which has as one of its effects the perfecting of the agent. In ethics we readily distinguish internal and ex-

[49] GW1, 181-182; GW2, 258-259; SW, 253-254.
[50] GW1, 183; GW2, 260; SW, 255.

ternal acts, and refer to elicited and "imperated" acts of the will. Recognizing the terminology of external and internal as problematic suggests something about the distinction between immanent and transient action, too.[51]

For an incarnational view of man, we need not a theory of an immanent action as an action that begins in the agent and ends in the patient, but of an action that begins in the agent, goes to the patient where it also takes place, but also has its effect in the agent; this would be an act of the agent perfective of both agent and patient. Insofar as its effect in the agent depends on its being perfective of the patient, it would reflect the essence of finite spirit as necessarily material, as other-needing, and, given the meaning of finite spirit as person, as necessarily social and interpersonal. Aquinas is not very helpful on this point.[52] Lacking a proper concept from him, we could perhaps speak of a transcendent action, i. e., an action both immanent and transient, having an immanent effect only if transient. It would be an action whose effect on the self would depend on its effect on the other. Such actions are given in experience. In ethics they are considered under the heading of motivation: others are to be loved for their own sakes, not for mine; to "love" someone for my sake is to vitiate the effect of the action in the agent.

We only seem to have strayed from the question of emanation as a form of becoming. Let's review briefly. We began examining the concept of emanation because spirit is said to become itself first through emanation. And since we are interested in personal becoming, we began with the question how the two constituents of man, spirit and matter, relate to one another, i. e., how spirit becomes itself through matter. We consequently began to speak of emanation in causal terms,

[51] See E. Coreth, *Metaphysics* (New York: Herder and Herder, 1968, trans, by J. Donceel), 13. Perhaps it will help to insert a word about *Vollzug*. The word has been variously translated as exercise, performance, actualization, achievement, realization, to mention some. *Selbstvollzug* is rendered self-exercise, and so on. Perhaps the best translation would be enactment (and self-enactment).

[52] GW1, 182; GW2, 260; SW, 255.

finding it hard to specify the causality beyond saying it was less than efficient causality but more than the simple essence itself. That something different is given (produced, caused) through emanation is clear. That the giver is received by the given itself is also clear. Thus we were led to the concept of immanent action and the ensuing discussion. Perhaps we haven't shed much light on the causality involved in emanation, and this is something of an impasse. It is a serious question whether the concept of emanation is worth pursuing. Rahner does not devote much more time to it than indicated above. Perhaps another tack is indicated. In later writings, Rahner speaks, e. g., of the evolution of spirit from matter, and introduces the concept of becoming as self-transcendence. Speaking of the evolution of spirit from matter, Rahner seems to contradict the very notion of emanation, i. e., the coming of matter from spirit. Perhaps the stark opposition of these two expressions (matter emanating from spirit, spirit evolving from matter) is a clue. It is unlikely that the apparent contradiction will turn out to be a real one; more likely it hides not only a harmony of viewpoints but also an access to the meanings of both. Personal becoming has already been called an effect of self-transcendence; becoming *is* a self-transcendence. To be taken seriously becoming must mean becoming other, if not becoming more. I succeed in becoming a person because I am capable of self-transcendence, because true becoming is self-transcendence (emanation would be a true becoming because the essence can be considered to have transcended itself in the production of its powers as something new and not simply identifiable with the essence). If we understand becoming as self-transcendence, we could then say that to become a person, i. e., for potential person to become actual person, is first of all for finite spirit—potentially itself, but not yet itself—to become itself, which it does first of all through the incarnation in matter that Rahner calls (after Aquinas) emanation. In its active reaching for the horizon of its full possibilities, for the horizon of the absolute being, a being actualizes more of its own latent potential (the a priori conditions for the possibility of its very reaching out) ; it does this *first* in the emanation (incarnation), which is its first kind of self-transcendence (becoming), and *second* in its incarnate acts of knowing and free self-disposition (acts Rahner also sometimes calls emanation). Self-transcendence is only self-contradictory if it means that a finite being can be more than it can be. If it means simply that it can become eventually (in time and space) more than it is here and now, then it is not contradictory but self-evident, the meaning of *finite* being. In the most basic experience of life, growth, this is obvious: seed becomes tree, child adult. Self-transcendence means that a future state of a being exceeds a present state in actuality, not in potentiality, e. g., from the potentiality of thinking reasonably (in a child) to the actuality of rational thought (in an adult). Thus self-transcendence is actualization of one's own potentiality, and is thus self-actualization, not in the sense that I actualize myself without any relation to others but in the sense that it is I who am actualized in transcending from present potentiality to subsequent actuality.

Now how does this relate to the above opposition of evolving from matter and emanation of matter? To look at the terms *becoming, matter,* and *spirit* and to say that the decision whether the proper sequence is matter becomes spirit or spirit becomes matter depends solely on your viewpoint, is to express the opposition at its strongest. Rahner appears to want to affirm both. Here, in SW, matter is said to emanate from spirit: spirit becomes matter (incarnation as emanation of matter from spirit). Yet later, in the *quaestio disputata* called *Hominisation* and in the essay of the unity of spirit and matter,[53] spirit is said to evolve from matter: matter becomes spirit (spirit comes from matter). I mention this difficulty now rather than later to emphasize that the correct position is that spirit is primary; spirit can come from matter in evolution only because matter came first from spirit. This last mentioned spirit must, of course, be the infinite spirit, the creator. As Rahner

[53] STh VI, 185-214; ThI VI, 153-177.

explains in the two works just mentioned, since the greater cannot come from the lesser, spirit must precede absolutely; this recalls the basic Scholastic thesis that act precedes potency absolutely. In both cases, absolute pure act is meant, the fullness of being, God. If *per impossibile* potency were first absolutely, nothing would come to be, for potentiality is " reduced " to act only through act, and therefore act must be first absolutely for anything at all to be, including potency. Thus that matter can evolve into spirit in the temporal history of our world is possible only if spirit was already there as the source and " support " of matter. So we find ourselves with an uneasy couplet saying that matter, the emanation of the spirit, does not become itself by ridding itself of matter but by incarnating ever more in matter. Spirit does not evolve or emerge from matter to leave matter behind, but to become itself. But spirit is most itself when it is most free; and it is most free when it can best control matter and make matter serve spirit. Thus the evolution of spirit from matter is the history of our increasing freedom not *from* but *through* matter *for* spirit, and our responsibility for that process. All this may sound very Hegelian, even Marxian (and Sartrian) and Rahner himself is not loath to make comparisons, in another context, between Aquinas and Hegel.[54] It is always necessary to guard against the tendency toward pantheism, ever present in Thomism. We must regard all this as happening (Sartre would concur) in individual, personal existence and not in some cosmic spirit, and regard the general event of evolution as the cumulative effect of individual events. Even teleological explanations of mass orientations can and should be based on explanations of what occur in individuals.

But let's stop looking ahead to later difficulties and complete the present analysis. We have been examining the notion of emanation under the heading of becoming, since Rahner clearly views it as one of the ways in which spirit becomes. In-

---

[54] See K. Rahner, "A Verdade em S. Tomás de Aquino," *Revista Portuguesa de Filosofia* 7 (1951), 353-370.

sofar as this is a study of becoming, we will necessarily return later to whatever remains incomplete in our analysis of emanation as a form of becoming. But now we ought to move on to other forms of becoming. For all practical purposes this means moving to section 9 of Chapter 4, where Rahner takes up the question of efficient causality and relates it directly to the problem of becoming. The last word (for now) on the subject of emanation relates to what was called above " the second thing to be noted," viz., that emanation is " essentially " accomplished once we have an existing being. If emanation has already taken place, given with the nature of the being, then to that extent it is not free choice and does not enter the realm of responsibility. But to the degree that we *can* do something about it, even if only to take up an attitude toward embodiment, no matter how shallow theoretical understanding of it may be, emanation becomes a practical concern. For the time being we can relegate it to the realm of things of only speculative interest. There *is* a realm of high practical interest connected with embodiment and here again we will encounter a question Rahner takes up later, namely the question of man the experiment, i. e., man's self-manipulation, our making and remaking of man through physical, chemical, and biological changes. The last word has not been said on this question either: Rahner has raised new questions as well as left old questions open. But first let's complete our view of the limited extent to which he has elaborated a metaphysics of intersubjective becoming here in SW.

b. *Innerworldly Causality: Second Otherness.* As Rahner states the questions, we are placed in a context *apparently* different from that of emanation:

the problematic of inner-worldly becoming . . . is the coming to be of new determinations in an existent through the influence of another existent, a becoming of such a nature that both existents are already presupposed in their being antecedent to and independent of the causal relationship.[55]

[55] GW1, 240; GW2, 333; SW, 331.

Obviously this description does not apply to emanation proper, which must be conceived, at least according to what we have seen up to now, as a process taking place totally within the limits of one same individual as the unfolding of its essence in its first self-becoming.[56] Insofar as the remark just made about emanation's taking place outside the realm of free action eliminates emanation from practical consideration on the question of personal becoming, the present context, which is that of causality *between* beings (rather than, as is apparently the case with emanation, of causality entirely *within* one being) — is the arena wherein the real debate about becoming persons takes place. We hope to find a metaphysics of the between (as Buber would say), i. e., the realm of interpersonal causality (or dialectic, as Merleau-Ponty would say). And yet we must leave open the possibility that emanation does not mean only intrapersonal becoming; this is why the word " apparently " was used above; as it turns out, Rahner, following Aquinas, sometimes does use the term emanation for a causality extending beyond the agent, and so we must be ready to interpret such uses.

Again let's make the context clear: Rahner is talking about knowledge. Thus, when he says: " Consequently, we must begin with the fact: one existent produces a new determination in another," [57] he is talking about how one being knows another. But isomorphism of knower, known, and knowing allows us to work from a metaphysics of one being's producing a new determination in another *cognitively* to a metaphysics of one being's causing becoming in another *in general*. In the second edition of SW Metz inserted a passage explicitly clarifying this.[58]

Rahner's method in developing his metaphysics of becoming is to interpret and compare all the relevant Thomist texts. Becoming (most often called motion because of the context in which it's treated) shows two aspects, active (insofar as an

[56] GW1, 182; GW2, 259; SW, 254.
[57] GW1, 241; GW2, 333; SW, 331.
[58] GW2, 323-324; SW, 331.

agent is required to bring about the becoming) and passive (insofar as a patient is required as subject of the becoming). Active becoming is called action; passive becoming is called passion. The problem arises when Aquinas says, on the one hand, that action is in the agent and passion in the patient, and, on the other hand, that the act of the agent takes place in the patient and not in the agent: action is the perfection of the patient, not the agent. These statements are either contradictory or reconcilable. They become reconcilable once a correct concept of efficient causality is applied. Essentially this means understanding causality as a relation of dependence rather than as some sort of influence in the literal sense of a flowing-in or influx of being. Although the terminology used by Aquinas and even by Rahner does not always avoid the word influence and its derivatives, the essence of causality for both is that of a relation of dependence, a position shared by Lonergan.[59] Let's examine this important point more closely.

The rest of Chapter 4, which means, for all practical purposes, the rest of the book, is concerned with becoming and its consequences. Becoming, as a phenomenon of finite beings, is partly something received by the becoming being, a fact we would expect just from its being finite and therefore unable to create itself and give itself its perfection. Becoming is also something active: a finite being is endowed with powers through the actions of which it becomes itself. Now this second kind of becoming is most interesting to us because it can be related to the freedom of the becoming being. However, even the first kind of becoming reveals an active side: reception of a perfection from another being can be either passive or active. There is conceivably, e. g., a hearing-by-the-ear (passive reception) that is not yet but can become a listening-by-the-subject (active reception). In the first case an effect is taking place in the ear as long as the causing source is at work, but for only that long; in the second case there is all the first provides plus my appropriation of the sound which I make my own by the

---

[59] B. Lonergan, *Collection* (London: Darton, Longman, and Todd, 1967), 54-67.

activity of harkening to it, i.e., by my own act. There can obviously be an element of freedom in this listening, as shown when I open out to a sound not yet there to be received. Thus there is a range from pure passivity up to pure activity, from "hearing" (by the ear) without listening (by the man), up to listening (by the man) without hearing (by the ear and the man). And all this activity, be it noted, is geared to reception.

The activity is all the more noticeable, of course, when it is not just an active receiving but an active giving. Here, instead of being affected by another, I affect another (and myself). What exactly happens when one being affects another? Let us say that "something new takes place," "comes to be," "happens," etc., in the patient that depends on the agent, not merely as a condition necessary for the "happening," a condition which even when fulfilled would still not be enough to explain what happens, but as that alone without which the "something new" would not come to be. Thus there is a potentiality for act, which must be granted the agent, plus a potentiality for being acted upon, which must be granted the patient, plus actualizations of these two potentialities, this last stage verified by the advent of a new determination in the patient known to depend on the agent. We can also distinguish moments of logical sequence: the agent acts and its activity begins to take place (in the patient) supported (as an act) purely by the agent and yet occurring in the matter of the patient; then the patient begins to react or respond and now the activity begins to be supported by and as an act of the patient also and becomes its own received and self-possessed determination.[60] Note that there is a mutual relation of dependence obtaining between agent and patient: the agent requires the matter of the patient as there where it can "place" its act; the patient requires the act from the agent in order that it receive this new determination. Rahner uses the terms emanation (recall the above word of caution on this) and *emanated* influence for the determination as produced by the

[60] GW1, 241-246; GW2, 335-340; SW, 333-339.

agent in the patient but not yet actively received by the patient, and presents texts from Aquinas to support this; he calls the determination actively received by the patient the *received influence*.[61]

So how are we to reconcile emanation and causality? The first use of emanation referred to the origin of the powers of an essence from that essence in its becoming itself. The second refers to the " influence " of the agent on the patient as something that " flows " from the agent to the patient. Insofar as the first use also meant an " outflowing " of the powers from the essence, the two uses have a common ground of meaning, viz., the activity of a being prescinding from the details of the reception of that activity (whether received in the same being itself, as is the first case, i. e., emanation of the powers of the essence, or, in the second case, received in a patient distinct from the agent, such as with sense cognition). Once granted this common basis, we could logically go on to reduce all causality to emanation, the first being an emanation where the agent is identical with the patient (immanent action), the second being an emanation where the agent is different from the patient (transient action). Action that goes beyond the agent to another can be viewed as an emanation not fulfilled by remaining within the agent but requiring another in, with, and through whom (which) the action will find fulfillment. Rahner seems to say this: " the Thomist concept of emanation means the same things as self-realization [*Selbstvollzug*: self-enact-

[61] Provided we avoid imaginative representations of an influx of being from agent to patient, this terminology is fine. It is innocent enough when the context remains cognition, which is Rahner's only explicit context, as he is careful to emphasize (GW1, 264; GW2, 362; SW, 362). But we are not here interested in stopping at his metaphysics of becoming as derived from and applied to knowledge, but in applying that metaphysics to the larger question of personal becoming, which, as we have seen, is the question of how spirit becomes itself through matter (up to now this is the rather asocial—*sensu aiente*—formulation), its own matter first and then other embodied beings. Rahner himself undertook his examination of knowledge not for its own sake but for an ontology of man; we are thus justified in applying what he himself considers a general metaphysics of becoming to other cases of becoming.

ment]," [62] and "exercising influence on another was shown earlier to be first of all the self-realization (*Selbst-vollzug* [self-enactment]) of the agent from out of its formal ground. Now it has been shown that the self-realization of a merely material being as such is the realization of the potentiality of matter, but this is always and essentially quantitative. Therefore, if there is to be a self-realization of a formal ground which goes beyond the expansion of its qualitative, substantial essence in the quantity corresponding to this, it can be conceived only as an expansion via further spatiality. But this is the spatiality of the other. The emanating influence expands in the medium of the other, in the matter of the other, precisely because it is the self-realization of the agent, and this self-realization can be in the matter of the other because the real spatiality of patient, because of the unity of matter, is already and always the greater potentiality of the agent." [63]

In this important passage Rahner clarifies the relation of *Selbst-vollzug* to emanation. Let's not be misled by the word self-realization (not the best translation of *Selbst-vollzug*) into thinking that a complete and full realization of the person is implied. Actually the term self-realization itself cannot be accused of implying this meaning, although it is easily mistaken to imply it. Let's say self-en*act*ment and mean that in any one instance the self is put into act, is to some determined extent made actual; on the level of person we would say "is made person," personally becomes. Thus *Selbst-vollzug*, self-enactment, is "the unfolding of its essence." [64] A patient enacting itself through actively receiving a determination from an agent has, for Rahner, enacted itself through another's emanated influence, thereby making it received influence.

At this point we meet one of the most important consequences of this human need of matter for self-becoming. It is the metaphysical basis of the study on concupiscence Rahner

[62] GW1, 254; GW2, 350; SW, 349.
[63] GW1, 254; GW2, 349-350; SW, 349.
[64] GW1, 256; GW2, 352; SW, 351.

wrote soon after SW. The clearest way to present this concept is to contrast the human situation with that of a " free form," or angel, used as a limit-concept. As Rahner puts it, in the text and its accompanying note: [65]

In its formal, operative ground, the substance is originally inclined towards two contraries which it is able to let emanate in its otherness in matter, as the unfolding of its essence. But the contraries are not able to be really actualized in matter together at the same time.—Note: the free form can actualize its whole essence at once in the decision for one side of the ' contraries.' So an ' angel ' decides essentially with the whole *virtus* of its essence, and in fact all at once, and therefore irrevocably . . . the self-realization of something immaterial as such takes place essentially all at once.— If, therefore, the substantial form seeks to realize the breadth of its possibilities, this happens on the one hand in an ordination towards the total breadth of its possibilities, and on the other hand, this realization is always possible only in determinations which in principle never realize the whole breadth of these possibilities at once.

Our inability to match the self-disposability of the angels is rooted in materiality, i. e., in the fact that finite spirit's mode of reaching for the horizon is materiality: multiplied spatiotemporal acts, which construct habits and stable attitudes, acts which " take place " and " take time," are our attempt to match the self-enactment of an angel, which happens all at once, beyond space and time. Man cannot measure his being with his act because he is becoming. Nowhere is this more true than on the level of person, i. e., on the level of free self-disposition, completed only in death.

We are obviously beyond the context of cognition and the way the senses receive their *species*. Rahner's metaphysics of becoming applies not only to knowledge but to freedom. In a passage immediately after the one just given, he concludes that an agent's openness to its full breadth of possibilities exists because " it remains with being in its totality, hence is spiritual and thus free." [66] The limitations placed on this freedom, due

---

[65] GW1, 256; GW2, 352; SW, 351-352.
[66] GW1, 257; GW2, 353; SW, 352.

to the metaphysical composition of man, of which the inertia of concupiscence speaks (in part), should be evident, although this inertia should not obscure recognition that matter—embodiment (first otherness) and world (second otherness)—is man's means of becoming free at all.

There is one last important precision needed before the relation of self-enactment to emanation is clear. We find it in the context of a distinction between being and becoming. Rahner treats this distinction when emphasizing that Aquinas considers the agent the cause "merely" of the becoming of the patient, not of its being. Thus he says of agent with respect to patient:

> It is not the ground of the ontological unfolding of the patient as such; it does not provide the determination of the patient in its being and from its ground, but only determines, in which of the ways, possible to the patient itself, the patient realizes its own being, and is also, therefore, only the ground of the becoming of the determination produced, not the permanent, productive ground of its being. . . . Thomas ascribes to the innerworldly cause only the 'determination,' the 'specification' of what comes to be, but not the production of its being. . . . the external agent is the reason why the patient as such, to whose constitution belongs a continual self-realization and which stands continually under the intrinsic influence of God, unfolds precisely in this way rather than in another in its accidental determinations.[67]

Now it has never been my contention, of course, that personal becoming was more than the enactment of potentialities already there. Our constant question has been how these potentialities become enacted, which is the question of personal becoming, in space and time, through the agency of innerworldly causes (primarily other persons, but also things), and not the question of the absolute placing into being of the person. Therefore this passage retains its usefulness. Despite what it says the other (the agent) is *not,* it also says that the other *is* the reason why I (the patient) can become at all, and why I can become who and what I can become. Here is clear con-

[67] GW1, 257-258; GW2, 353-354; SW, 353-354.

firmation that becoming is through others, and thus an indication that we are on the right track in our interpretation. Now
let's resume the question of *how*.

The next pages of Rahner's metaphysics of becoming are
difficult, not so much because of the profundity of the insight
toward which he is slowly trying to lead us, but because of the
constantly shifting viewpoint as he speaks first about the agent
from the agent's viewpoint, next about the patient from the
agent's viewpoint, then about the agent from the patient's
viewpoint, and finally about the patient from the patient's
viewpoint.[68] In the terminology of SW, Rahner simplifies the
question of emanating influence and received influence by
identifying them in their actuality despite the duality of their
origins.[69] He also simplifies the question of causality by reducing efficient causality to emanation.[70] The essential in all
this is the absolute interdependence of agent and patient in
" innerworldly " becoming. We will descend to details shortly,
but let's not slight this conclusion for being so briefly stated.
It is the most " physical " basis for a metaphysics of the social
nature of personal becoming. Rahner arrives at a strict and
inevitable metaphysical basis for all human activity, derived
not from a priori notions about the human nature, but from
analyses of the acts involved in human sensible-intellectual

---

[68] Pedagogically it reminds me of Part I of SW, where, as here, several texts are
worked for all they're worth and pushed to their ultimate conclusions before other
texts are introduced to resolve the difficulties generated by interpretation of the
first texts. Such a method, characteristic of Rahner, demands that we keep several
notions in suspension at once while constantly trying to see where it's all going,
i. e., where Rahner is leading it. In most cases his interpretation of Aquinas results
in reducing the plethora of terms Aquinas, in accord with his method of taking
over others' terminology (but with his meanings!), allowed himself to increase rather
self-indulgently. But as is usually the case with simplified explanations, full understanding comes only in following out the steps by which one arrives at simplification. The present metaphysics of becoming in general is a case in point. We have
followed many of the steps with Rahner and the conclusion is in sight. We can,
as before, omit the specifically cognitive details and go directly to the metaphysics
derived from them.

[69] GW1, 261-267; GW2, 358-366; SW, 358-366.

[70] GW1, 259-261; GW2, 356-358; SW, 355-358.

knowledge; the accent (for the present consideration of becoming) has been on the activity and passivity of sensibility. Later we will have to apply this interdependence of agent and patient to freedom, love, and ethics.

The interdependence of agent and patient in all becoming, in the dependence of one person on another in their both becoming persons, in their mutual interpersonal becoming, cannot be understood as though agent depended on patient because the patient merely provided the matter wherein the agent could act (some expressions used to describe sensation seem to contribute to this minimalist interpretation), nor as though the patient merely reacted to the agent, its reaction constituting the sum total and content of its activity, in which case the dependence of patient on agent would be a passive being-affected. Rather, " the determination of the patient from without is strictly identical with its own act from within." [71] " To act on another is for Thomas a ' bringing self as realizing self [enacting self] into the medium of the other; ' what is ' in ' the patient is therefore the agent in its completed essence, the emanation of the agent's own interior, its self-realization [self-enactment] in that interiority which alone is possible to an essence which is exterior to itself." [72] To speak of the enactment or actualization of potentiality cannot mean, therefore, that another somehow " turns me on " or " gets me going " by a sort of triggering or putting into gear or other such passively conceived " actualization." If anything has become clear from our study of becoming up to now it is that all enactment (actualization) is self-enactment (self-actualization). Rahner's analysis of emanating influence (as the agent's action, prescinding from the patient's) and received influence (as the emanating influence *plus* the patient's receptive act) shows that there is no enactment of the patient without the patient's own act. As Rahner points out, the distinction between emanating and received influence can now be abandoned; its pur-

[71] GW1, 260; GW2, 357; SW, 357.
[72] GW1, 261; GW2, 359; SW, 358.

pose was only to emphasize the patient's need of the self-enactment for the appropriation of the agent's action upon it. As he states, " what emanates from the two substantial grounds is one and the same actuality in spite of the dual origin itself. . . . the influence is also strictly identical with what emanates from the productive, substantial ground of the patient itself, however much this emanation is determined in its quiddity by the external agent." [73]

Note well: the patient is not so much enacted by the agent, but the patient enacts itself through the medium of the agent. And this is also what the agent does: the agent enacts itself in the patient, nor can it reach this particular self-enactment except in the medium of the patient. Later, in his profound study of guilt,[74] Rahner gives his best analysis of this " medium " as person. Neither agent nor patient is self-sufficient; neither is able to enact itself alone, but depends on the other. All becoming reveals this structure, not only that of sense knowledge. All becoming reveals active and receptive sides, but activity and receptivity are characteristics of both agent and patient. In the case of the agent, its activity is clear; its receptivity is its dependence on the other as where it acts. In the case of the patient, its receptivity is clear; its activity is in its appropriation of the act of the agent, which it effects by enacting the agent's act as its own, by supporting the agent's act with its own substantial act of being. Rahner puts it thus:

Our general consideration of efficient causality showed that the reason why the substantial, formal ground of a material existent produces the emanating influence of the agent as its own determination lies in the fact that this formal ground is actively ordered to such a determination as to its own self-realization [self-enactment], and so for it to produce this determination there is need only of a delimitation of its greater potential breadth.[75]

This is about as far as Rahner takes us in SW, insofar as a metaphysics of becoming is concerned. The rest of the book

[73] GW1, 266; GW2, 365; SW, 365.
[74] STh II, 279-297; ThI II, 265-281.
[75] GW1, 269; GW2, 369; SW, 369.

consists of applications and conclusions. Of these only a few are directly relevant to a search for the meaning of person. Part 3 of SW is entitled: The Possibility of Metaphysics on the Basis of the Imagination. The fourth and last of its brief sections is entitled: Man as Spirit in the World. Since we never meant to deal with everything in this work, let's again restrict ourselves to what Rahner concludes about man as spirit becoming itself in matter. We previously put human becoming in terms of a double gap to be bridged or closed, the gap separating spirit from matter, bridged in the manifold incarnations of the human spirit, and the gap separating man from God, a gap of which we become aware when the objects of intellect and will are experienced as falling short of distant horizons of possibility. We saw too that both gaps are one, matter being interposed between man and his infinite horizon precisely as mediating that horizon. In Rahner's words:

For strictly speaking, the first-known, the thing encountering man, is not the world in its ' spiritless ' existence, but the world—itself— as transformed by the light of the spirit, the world in which man sees himself. The world as known is always the world of man, is essentially a concept complementary to man. And the last-known, God, shines forth only in the limitless breadth of the pre-apprehension, in the desire for being as such by which every act of man is born, and which is at work not only in his ultimate knowledge and in his ultimate decision, but also in the fact that the free spirit becomes, and must become, sensibility in order to be spirit, and thus exposes itself to the whole destiny of this earth. Thus man encounters himself when he finds himself in the world and when he asks about God; and when he asks about his essence, he always finds himself in the world and on the way to God. He is both of these at once, and cannot be one without the other.[76] " Thus every venture into the world shows itself to be borne by the ultimate desire of the spirit for absolute being; every entrance into sensibility, into the world and its destiny, shows itself to be only the coming to be of a spirit which is striving toward the absolute. Thus man is the mid-point suspended between the world and God, between time and eternity, and this boundary line is the point of his definition and his destiny: ' as a certain horizon and border

[76] GW1, 294-295; GW2, 405; SW, 406.

between the corporeal and incorporeal.' Man: ' existing as it were, at the horizon between time and eternity.' [77]

The last page of the book reminds us that although all that has gone before is philosophy, it can ground a philosophy of religion which opens man to revelation:

Man concerns Thomas the theologian at the point at which God manifests Himself in such a way that He is able to be heard in the word of His revelation: ' From the viewpoint of his soul.' In order to be able to hear whether God speaks, we must know that He is; lest His word come to one who already knows, He must be hidden from us; in order to speak to man, His word must encounter us where we already and always are, in an earthly place, at an earthly hour. Insofar as man enters into the world by turning to the phantasm, the revelation of being as such and in it the knowledge of God's existence has already been achieved, but even then this God who is beyond the world is always hidden from us. Abstraction is the revelation of being as such which places man before God: conversion is the entrance into the here and now of this finite world, and this makes God the distant Unknown. Abstraction and conversion are the same thing for Thomas: man. If man is understood in this way, he can listen to hear whether God has not perhaps spoken, because he knows that God is; God can speak, because He is the Unknown. And if Christianity is not the idea of an eternal, omnipresent spirit, but is Jesus of Nazareth, then Thomas's metaphysics of knowledge is Christian when it summons man back into the here and now of his finite world, because the Eternal has also entered into his world so that man might find Him, and in Him might find himself anew.[78]

4. *Concluding Summary*. In SW we have had to follow some interesting and suggestive analyses. We have not paused long to make detailed applications to person and becoming, but only sought to lay foundations. It is far too soon to stop, of course: no metaphysics of personal becoming is complete without treating love and freedom. We do, however, have some solid indications and can continue the search in HW (and later in Rahner's other writings) with increased familiarity.

The terms spirit, matter, and becoming are the basics; self-

---

[77] GW1, 295; GW2, 406; SW, 407.
[78] GW1, 296; GW2, 407; SW, 408.

enactment, self-transcendence, and emanation have been added to these. Finite spirit becoming himself in, by, and through matter is person enacting himself in, by, and through emanation and self-transcendence. The initial becoming is called emanation and refers to the most basic constitution of the incarnate spirit (i. e., in its active powers, the powers to be used for self-enactment through self-transcendence). Although the term emanation is used by Rahner (after Aquinas) for all becoming, we can consider it the origin of the basic " starting " essence given already as incarnate before that free action proper to personal becoming. Thus we are left, having relegated the terms spirit, matter, and emanation to the pre-free grounding of the essence as potentiality for action, with the terms person, enactment (self-enactment), and transcendence (self-transcendence), and becoming. These terms constitute the working concepts of personal becoming. We can thus provisionally say that personal becoming is self-enactment through self-transcendence. Banal enough when put so abstractly. Banal enough when unrelated to the foregoing grounding that makes stating it so banally possible. But we are not through until we work these working concepts. It is not enough to say that spirit-in-matter (*Geist in Welt*) *becomes* (the name for their interrelation) in self-enactment through self-transcendence, without further explaining what these terms mean. Clearly these are the questions to be carried forward, especially the meanings of enactment and transcendence, since to know them is to know the meaning of finite spirit. That enactment and transcendence must lead us to study freedom and the personal " self-construction " effected in ethical activity, should not be surprising. Let us open HW with these needs in mind.

II

LOVE AS WILL-TO-PERSON: PERSONAL BECOMING
AS FREEDOM IN *HEARERS OF THE WORD*

WE ARE SEARCHING for a metaphysics of personal becoming, and since there is more than that
in HW, we can limit full analysis to two chapters,
or lectures,[1] from that work. Before that, there are two other
chapters meriting partial analysis as a review of SW, as a bridge
from SW to HW, and as an introduction to HW. For our purposes HW falls into four divisions corresponding neither to the
five parts in the two German editions [2] nor to the three parts
proposed by Hofbeck.[3] The first division we can call introduc-
tory,[4] the second, ontological,[5] the third, anthropological,[6] and
the fourth, philosophy of religion.[7] Of these four divisions, the
third, on a metaphysical anthropology, is our main source for
a metaphysics of man as person. There are four subdivisions in
thát fourth division: man as spirit,[8] free,[9] material,[10] historical.[11] Of these four, two (spirit and matter) will serve as
the review of and bridge from SW just mentioned. The other

---

[1] HWF, 318-319.

[2] HW1, 5; HW2, 7.

[3] HWF, 319-327.

[4] HW1, 9-50; HW2, 15-55; HWF, 25-80; HWE, 3-38; LW, 1-30.

[5] HW1, 50-67; 88-102; HW2, 55-70; 91-104; HWF, 80-102. 131-149; HWE, 38-
52, 71-82; LW, 30-44, 59-69.

[6] HW1, 68-87, 116-137, 150-162, 162-175; HW2, 71-88, 117-134, 150-160, 161-172;
HWF 102-127, 167-191, 211-225, 226-242; HWE, 53-68, 94-108, 121-129, 130-139;
LW, 44-58, 80-95, 105-113, 114-123.

[7] HW1, 103-116, 138-149, 175-229; HW2, 105-116, 137-149, 173-221; HWF, 150-
166, 195-210, 243-312; HWE, 83-93, 111-120, 140-163; LW, 70-79, 96-104, 124-163.

[8] HW1, 68-87; HW2, 71-88; HWF, 102-127; HWE, 53-68; LW, 44-58.

[9] HW1, 116-137; HW2, 117-134; HWF, 167-191; HWE, 94-108; LW, 80-95.

[10] HW1, 150-162; HW2, 150-160; HWF, 211-225; HWE, 121-129; LW, 105-113.

[11] HW1, 162-175; HW2, 161-172; HWF, 226-242; HWE, 130-139; LW, 114-123.

two, to be studied in more detail, constitute HW's advances
over SW in Rahner's philosophy of person.

1. *Man As Spirit.* In this section,[12] Rahner explains that the
first statement of a metaphysical anthropology—" man is spirit "—means that ". . . the essence of man is to be absolute
openness to the fullness of being . . . ," [13] to the undefined horizon of being known in his dynamic reaching for it without
grasping it (*Vorgriff*). Man is spirit because present to being
in its totality, and is finite spirit because present in this particular way, i. e., as absent, as questioning.[14] Transcendence
toward being in general is the fundamental proposition about
man's essence.[15] We need not dwell on " proofs " for man's nature as spirit. The *reditio completa in seipsum* or self-presence,[16]
the self-revealing work of spirit, was analyzed in detail in SW;
Rahner merely recalls it here: objectification is attributed to
spirit which, in its return to itself, distinguishes itself from its
objects. But this was only one of two ways to explain objectification. The other involved the concept of *Vorgriff*: the object
is known as such (*as* an object) in the sweep of intellect toward the unlimited horizon of being. Rahner repeats this in
HW: [17] the concept of *Vorgriff* and its applications to questions
of man as spirit, of God and transcendence, in general, i. e., to
the philosophy of religion, constitute the contents of this section. Metz's notes are excellent, and some clarity is gained over
the first edition, at least in terms used in SW; but there is no
advance over SW in the general doctrine of *cognitive* spirit (ex-

[12] HW1, 68-87; HW2, 71-88; HWF, 103-127; HWE, 53-68; LW, 44-58.

[13] HW1, 50; HW2, 55; HWF, 79; HWE, 38; LW, 30: ". . . man's nature is absolute openness for all being or, to put it in one word, man is spirit."

[14] HW1, 65-66; HW2, 69; HWF, 100; HWE, 51; LW, 42: ". . . he is not absolute
consciousness, but, precisely in his metaphysics, hence *as* ' transcendental consciousness,' a *finite* spirit. . . . when man feels that he has to inquire about being, he
shows the finiteness of his spirit, in such a way, however, that the question itself
reveals that being is, of itself, self-presence, luminosity, the original unity of
knowing and of being known."

[15] HW1, 69; HW2, 69; HWF, 100; HWE, 51; LW, 45.

[16] HW1, 68-77; HW2, 72-77; HWF, 104-112; HWE, 54-59; LW, 44-50.

[17] HW1, 77-87; HW2, 78-88; HWF, 113-127; HWE, 59-68; LW, 51-58.

cept that love is said to be the light of the intellect; the advance comes in the realm of freedom and love). Thus man is spirit because he conceives everything *sub ratione entis*,[18] because he is *reditio completa subjecti, abstractio*, [19] is *Vorgriff*,[20] extension toward, stretching out for (*Sichausstrecken*) the absolute: openness toward God.[21]

In the first of five important notes on the subject of a cosmocentric deduction of the nature of spirit,[22] Metz says that because of Rahner's Thomist starting point and orientation, his analyses draw almost entirely on experience of the world of things rather than on relations with persons. Thus it is not that interpersonal community (*die personale Mitwelt*) is less original than the world of things (*die Dingwelt* or *Umwelt*) — indeed a strong case is made for the opposite.[23] We return to this point when treating man as historical spirit.

2. *Man As Incarnate Spirit*. The other section for brief review concerns man as material.[24] Again the context is cognition, with the added focus on philosophy of religion. For us the essential concerns the role of matter in personal becoming. We have already learned to view matter as the effect of finite spirit, not as the cause of its finitude. Thus, in a cognitive context, sense is viewed as effect of intellect which, as finite, and thus as not only agent but also as possible intellect, had to become material in order to perfect itself, to become itself: its *self-enactment* (as spirit) is an enactment of *other* (matter). In HW Rahner repeats this; its application to philosophy of religion is not made here but when treating man as historical

---

[18] HW1, 83-84; HW2, 84-85; HWF, 122; HWE, 65; LW, 56.

[19] HW1, 74-75; HW2, 76-78; HWF, 110-112; HWE, 57-59; LW, 49.

[20] HW1, 77-84; HW2, 78-85; HWF, 113-123; HWE, 59-66; LW, 50-56.

[21] HW1, 85; HW2, 86; HWF, 124; HWE, 66: LW, 57.

[22] The five are: (1) HW2, 88, n. 13; HWF, 127, n. 13; HWE, 68, n. 13; (2) HW2, 164, n. 2; HWF, 231, n. 2: HWE, 133, n. 2; (3) HW2, 170-171, n. 6; HWF, 239, n. 6; HWE, 138, n. 6, (4) HW2 175-176, n. 2; HWF, 247-248, n. 2; HWE, 142, n. 2; (5) HW2, 180-181, n. 3; HWF, 254-255, n. 3; HWE, 146, n. 3.

[23] See HW2, 11; HWF, 20; HWE, ix.

[24] HW1, 150-162; HW2, 150-160; HWF, 211-225; HWE, 121-129; LW, 105-113.

spirit. The conclusion reached is that man is that sort of spirit which, to become spirit, enters matter, and, as far as its "ontic" status is concerned, i. e., as far as its enacted potential is concerned, is already always in matter, in otherness, in the world.[25]

We have spoken, in this review and bridge, of spirit and matter; we have just mentioned becoming, the third term of the familiar trio of spirit, matter, and becoming: ". . . man is spirit and becomes ever more spirit;"[26] not that man ever reaches a point where spirit has no more need of matter, as though thereby he would become a pure spirit and as such have direct access to God as pure being. In the very context of the above quotation, Rahner denies any such "spiritualization" (Geistwerdung) that could obviate the need for revelation. Man is spirit only as and through becoming spirit in matter: matter is an essential part in the very becoming of man as spirit. Man is not first pure spirit who then becomes "finitized" by an unfortunately necessary relation to matter; man is first finite as spirit (material because finite, not finite because material) and thus can become at all only through matter. Under the heading of man as historical more will be said about becoming.

3. *Man As Free*. Let's turn now to the two sections from which we hope to gain an advance over SW, i. e., the discussions of freedom and history. Keep in mind, Rahner says, that any human attempt to construct a metaphysics inevitably turns out to be an analysis of man himself.[27] But if our analysis of man stops short of man as free, then that metaphysics can never be valid for persons, whose very essence is freedom. It's therefore good

---

[25] "Such a conception of human sensibility corresponds fully with a Thomist metaphysics of knowledge, which explicitly conceives sense as a power that originates from spirit; spirit in transcending based upon this sense knowledge is enacting its own essence which is to be an openness to being as such." (HW1, 177; HW2, 174; HWF, 245; HWE, 141; LW, 125.) "Man is spirit in such a way that, in order to become spirit, he enters and has ontically always already entered into otherness, into matter, and so into the world." (HW1, 161; HW2, 159; HWF, 225; HWE, 129; LW, 113).

[26] HW1, 92; HW2, 93; HWF, 135; HWE, 73; LW, 61.

[27] HW1, 48; HW2, 53; HWF, 76; HWE, 36; LW, 28: ". . . human metaphysics is also always and necessarily an analytic study of man."

to keep in mind that Metz felt it necessary to try to transcend
the Thomist concept of a world of objects and replace it with
the more primordial concept of a world of persons.[28] Metz's
attempt is predicated on a lacuna in Rahner's explicit treatment precisely where it is most apt to appear, i. e., on man as
free and historical. We already noted that Rahner did not have
explicit recourse to experience of the *Mitwelt*, but only to the
Umwelt (*Dingwelt, Gegenstandwelt*), in his deduction of the
transcendence of the human spirit. Rahner *can* arrive at a
theory of freedom on the basis of such experience of objectification possible to man transcending the finite. " Human activity
is free," he says,[29] i. e., the agent experiences independence from
objects upon which he acts, and he does this in the very act
of knowing an object as such (i. e., in the judgment, where subject and object are distinguished), because in such knowledge
the subject's complete return to himself sets him off from an
object, thus allowing him to act freely toward it.[30] We could
view this from the other side: that I *do* act freely with the
things of my world proves my consciously experienced independence of them in judgment, my self-subsistence.[31] But this
is still a deduction based on traffic with things,[32] not on community with the world of persons. The point is that as long
as we remain entirely within a cognitive context, i. e., within
a discussion of knowledge, of man as knower—no matter how
dynamic the interpretation—we will never reach a satisfying
understanding of man as person; we must speak of will, of
affectivity, of choice, of freedom. For this reason SW, and
most of HW, yield a metaphysics of that level of personal be-

---

[28] HW2, 11; HWF, 20; HWE, ix.

[29] HW1, 70; HW2, 73; HWF, 106; HWE, 55; LW, 46.

[30] HW1, 70; HW2, 73; HWF, 106; HWE, 55; LW, 46; " But there can apriori be
freedom only where the acting subject occupies a position that is independent
of the position of the object of his action. Because in his judgment man returns
completely into himself, thus occupying a position opposed to and independent
of the object of his knowledge, he is free before this object and he can freely act
upon it."

[31] HW1, 70; HW2, 74; HWF, 106; HWE, 55; LW, 46.

[32] HW1, 70; HW2, 74; HWF, 106; HWE, 55; LW, 46.

coming only speculatively interesting because they deal with personal becoming prior to free self-enactment proper (e. g., with becoming described as the emanation of sense from intellect conceived as already accomplished with the given essence).

Freedom and will indeed enter SW, but only in the classical context, i. e., freedom as proved through the capacity of intellect, in its transcendence toward being in general, to judge a being as finite in order to present it to the will as a limited good and therefore as an object of free choice. In HW the basic approach is Thomist and thus the same, but there are important differences. These first appear in the treatment of God as the free unknown ("general ontology"),[33] and continue to affect the important section of man as free ("metaphysical anthropology").[34] Let us note the main points in that first treatment, then see how they apply to man.

a. *General ontology.* Rahner places will at the very heart of all and every human transcendence toward being, even, therefore, at the heart of knowledge; an act of will is an intrinsic constituent of all openness to being of finite spirit: [35]

"Therefore in the realm of person—spirit and freedom—openness depends on will. It is not a matter of intellect automatically open to the fullness of being; because man is free, even the openness of his cognitive faculties is actualized, enacted, effected by his will, which, as free, can choose to remain closed to being in this or that aspect. In the present context (God as the free unknown), Rahner is quite clear in affirming that this relation of openness to being is a constituent of persons as such, both divine and human. God is free to open himself to man or not, as is man to open himself to God. In this particular context, significantly, Rahner's first unequivocal use of the term person (absent from SW) is found: approaching the climax of this section, he says

[33] HW1, 103-116; HW2, 105-116; HWF, 150-166; HWE, 83-93; LW, 70-79.
[34] HW1, 116-137; HW2, 117-134; HWF, 167-191; HWE, 94-108; LW, 80-95.
ground of human existence we discover within the primordial transcendence towards being the (necessary) act of the will. The fact that being opens up for human existence is brought about by the will as an inner moment of knowledge itself."
[35] HW1, 108; HW2, 109; HWF, 156; HWE, 87; LW, 73-75:

the essential factor in this whole relation of man to God (as the free unknown whom man as spirit unobjectively knows as absolute being, present to him in such knowledge as is proper to finite spirit) is this: man *is* spirit in that he knows God as a free self-disposing Person.[36]

Now we need not dwell on aspects of this or other statements proper to philosophy of religion. We are less interested, for now, in what is said about God than in what is said about man. Statements *can* be made about both God and man because of both it is (at least analogously) true to say they are persons. Openness is free in God because he is personal.[37] Rahner is content to speak only of God here, having already said [38] that man would be the subject of the next section. But let's not miss that what is affirmed here of person applies to man. To speak of freedom and openness is to speak of spirit and person as such, human and divine. Thus Rahner says that we do not call God person because we anthropomorphically attribute to him, after the fact, traits of human personality, but because God shows himself to be person in our encounters with him, in his own opening of himself to human transcendence; i. e., as absolute being, God grants man this access to himself, freely: God is open to man; but human action can no more measure God than it can measure the fullness of being; thus both remain present to man as questions.[39]

The essential is freedom: the openness of persons is a free act, whether on the part of God or man. This remains true when what is opened is one's " mind." Access to persons as

[36] HW1, 110; HW2, 111-112; HWF, 159; HWE, 89; LW, 75: " Central in this whole discussion [is] . . . : Man as a spirit who knows the absolute Being, stands before the latter as before a person who freely disposes of himself."
[37] HW1, 111; HW2, 112; HWF, 159-160; HWE, 89; LW, 76.
[38] HW1, 108; HW2, 109; HWF, 156-157; HWE, 87; LW, 74.
[39] HW1, 111; HW2, 112; HWF, 159-160; HWE, 89; LW, 75-76: " When God thus looks like a person, it is not because, having discovered him, we have afterwards provided him with human features. Rather God appears as a person when absolute being becomes manifest for human transcendence, because this being assumes the form of the totality of being about which man not only can but must inquire."

such depends on freedom: that to which I open myself (or my
" heart "), when I dispose myself to grant to you, the other,
access to me, is another freedom, transcendence; you, the other,
are given a goal for your self-transcendence, a place where your
act of going out of yourself toward others can rest. There is
a parallel here with the analyses of sense in SW. Sense is
described in terms first of the (only) matter wherein the act
of the (sensed) object could and did take place; (second, of
course, the sensing subject enacted this act of the other, taking
place in its senses, as its own act; but this second aspect is not
our concern at the moment). Here we see, more in terms of
willing than of knowing, a similar structure: the human act,
finite, subject to becoming, requires a " wherein," a place or
term wherein it actually " takes place." In love this term is
the personal other, to whom I transcend insofar as that other
opens to me, freely (in his *disponibilité*), and gives me access.
As Rahner states, encounter between free, independent persons,
in relation to their knowing one another, requires that each
leave to the other the decision to remain unknown. The reason
for this is that a person, because free, opens himself to another,
even to be known by him, ultimately only by a will-act,[40] Decision by a person to remain closed to another's wish to know
him would preclude any personal encounter, dialogue, and mutuality of love as well, of course. The effect on the lover would
be rejection, because, without a term of his self-transcendence,
he could not achieve his own self-enactment.

Recall that the aim of HW is to lay the foundations of a
philosophy of religion, as the book's subtitle shows. Thus the
conclusion toward which Rahner is working is that God has
room to act freely toward man, and man can know it; i. e., revelation is possible.[41] This conclusion is based on an implicit phe-

---

[40] HW1, 111; HW2, 112; HWF, 160; HWE, 89; LW, 76: " When the object of
our knowledge is a free, autonomous person, our knowledge turns into a lack of
knowledge. Because of his freedom a person manifests of himself only that which
he wishes to manifest."

[41] HW1, 111-112; HW2, 112-113; HWF, 160-161; HWE, 89-90; LW, 76. Let's
recognize this to mean also that *Christ* is possible.

nomenology of human encounter wherein the same structure
of free self-opening and self-revelation occurs. It should be
clearer than ever now why openness is Rahner's favorite term
for human intellect. Openness is an apt description of persons
qua free, and a useful category for a philosophy of religion,
since it is the category that " allows " the possibility of revelation: God, as person and thus free, can open or close himself
to man, to the human person in his dynamism toward knowing
and loving self-transcendence. Man as spirit stands before God
who, as living and free, can open or close himself.[42]

Now there are aspects of Rahner's discussion of philosophy
of religion that although proper to God throw light on human
encounter. It is true, e. g., that by God's very act of creation
whereby he constitutes a race of beings who, as spiritual, can
know him, he already thereby opens his essence to them in a
limited way. And it is humanly true also that just to find
oneself before another person is already to reveal oneself as
free, as one who can open or close.[43] As Metz points out,[44]
just to stand as a free person before another person already
always implies a certain openness, even though it is the openness of a person who can become closed, and thus is free openness.

Openness as free is essentially related, as mentioned above,
to self-transcendence. Within a cognitive context, *Vorgriff* (already known as transcendence) is the same as openness.[45] And
human personal becoming, i. e., self-enactment as person, depends on self-transcendence. Thus personal becoming depends
on the free openness of other persons, not so much as others
who will love me, but as others who will, in freely opening to
my self-transcendence, give me that access which I need in order
to love them, for personal becoming depends ultimately as

[42] HW1, 114; HW2, 115; HWF, 164; HWE, 92; LW, 78: "As a spirit man
stands before the living, free God, the God who manifests himself or the God who
keeps silent about himself."

[43] HW1, 115; HW2, 116; HWF, 165; HWE, 92-93; LW, 78.

[44] HW2, 116, n. 4; HWF, 165, n. 4; HWE, 93, n. 4.

[45] HW1, 77; HW2, 79; HWF, 114; HWE, 60; LW, 50-51.

much on loving as on being loved. In both cases the other is necessary, and not merely as a passive and arbitrary object of some self-perfecting charity which I perform on an other who tolerates it, but as one who in his free self-disposability actively opens to my will to know and love him. Rahner shows the relation of openness to self-transcendence on the human level to be all the more intimate when, in the next section (i. e., the metaphysical anthropology mentioned above), he places them in apposition.[46] This can only mean that man's very transcendence toward the general other of being and the particular personal other already by that act (transcendence) opens to both; thus later he can show the unity of love of God and love of neighbor.

Now we have often enough linked openness, or free self-transcendence, to self-enactment and personal becoming, to make clear that the most important aspect of personal becoming is freedom: personal becoming is self-enactment; but potential person is enacted only when he opens to others, transcends self toward others, both to know them and let them know him, and to love them and let them love him, all of which depends on free acts. Now we must examine further, as much as HW allows, the essence of the free act, especially in terms of personal becoming as self-enactment.

b. *Metaphysical anthropology.* Rahner begins the important discussion of the free act, and its relation to knowledge, love, value, and especially to ethical (and religious) becoming, by saying that the free act fulfills (enacts) the agent's (the person's) *own* essence, i. e., is an act whereby he takes possession of himself, enacts (appropriates in his own actuality) his own self-creativity, his very power to create himself.[47] In other words, the noteworthy difference with free acts is their effect on the agent. A free act is a *self*-enactment, a certain deter-

[46] HW1, 116-117; HWF, 167-168; LW, 80; deleted from HW2 and thus also from HWE.

[47] HW1, 123; HW2, 122; HWF, 174; HWE, 98; LW, 85: " Now, a free act is . . . the fulfillment of one's own nature, a taking possession of oneself, of the reality of one's own creative power over oneself."

mination of the agent's essence: a free act makes a difference to the person whose act it is. Beyond the sense in which it is true to say that any human act is a self-enactment, there is this properly essential meaning of self-enactment, because it reaches to the deepest source of person, freedom. As the most essential expression of person, the free act is the most decisive enactment of person; the free act *is* the act of personal becoming, of self-enactment through self-transcendence (in a cognitive context this self-transcendence is called *Vorgriff;* in a volitive context, as we shall see, it is called love), i. e., through the other-oriented openness essential to finite spirit as such: a finite being is precisely one who cannot find what he needs in himself, and so must turn to other.

The statements concerning the relation of the free act to knowledge, love, and value (good), which follow the last quotation, culminate in Rahner's clearest affirmation concerning the ethical implications of the free act.[48] Together with that quotation, they constitute the basis of all Rahner's later theological reflections on freedom and man, including his study on death. Very little materially is said, but within the metaphysics of person as spirit becoming itself in matter, elaborated here and in SW, this focus on the free act, as the chief act whereby person is enacted, is completely predictable. It is also completely traditional, insofar as it follows directly from traditional Thomist principles. But without his elaboration of the basic relation of finite spirit to matter in its self-becoming, Rahner's theory of a real, ontological becoming through free, ethical activity could be misunderstood. He is not asserting that there is but an accidental difference between one whose free, ethical decision aligns him with good and one whose decision is an alignment with evil. Rather he is stating that a person, by his free acts, enacts his very self as a person, decides who and what he is as a person, actively forms himself as the person he is.[49]

---

[48] See HW1, 123-132; HW2, 122-130; HWF, 174-186; HWE, 98-105; LW, 85-92.

[49] HW1, 132; HW2, 129; HWF, 185; HWE, 105; LW, 91: ". . . a free decision about a single value is ultimately always a decision about and a molding of the person himself."

In free ethical acts, although they be decisions about particular goods (values), about some action or thing, a person decides about himself.[50] Thus, in his free decisions man (as free, and thus as person) *enacts himself* and so loves, and thus determines his very essence.[51]

This freedom, this self-determination, must not be understood as a passing or atomic phenomenon. No series of isolated acts could constitute of themselves the essential self-determination meant here. There is rather a set of face assumed (taken up) by man in his decisions, an attitude, a law of habitual action. Man structures, constructs *himself* according to his loves and hates, freely making his own laws for himself, either by re-enacting (ratifying) those authentic laws of love to which he has always necessarily assented or by opposing them with his own.[52]

Now such a concept as law (habit, attitude) means more than an external or superficial determination. A person is forming himself in forming his attitudes, taking up his very essence in taking on his habits, establishing and enacting his being as person in establishing and enacting his laws of free activity, of values, of whom and what he loves. Thus Rahner can say that the acts of a person are not just a disconnected series of isolated acts; on the contrary, a person, in every free act, constitutes (enacts) a law for all his action and his whole life; thus it is not a matter of merely *doing* good or evil, but rather of his very self *becoming* good or evil.[53]

---

[50] HW1, 132; HW2, 129; HWF, 185; HWE, 105; LW, 91: "In every decision man decides about himself, not about an action or a thing."

[51] HW1, 132; HW2, 129-130; HWF, 185; HWE, 105; LW, 91: "Thus in his free decision man works back upon himself; he affects the very criteria of his love, which determine his own being."

[52] HW1, 132; HW2, 130; HWF, 185; HWE, 105; LW, 91-92: "He not only *assumes* the basic laws that govern his love and his hatred, but he himself freely *ratifies* anew the right laws, which he always already welcomes unconsciously, or he sets up his own law in opposition to the right order of love."

[53] HW1, 132; HW2, 130; HWF, 185; HWE, 105; LW, 92: "Thus he does not merely string out without any connection single actions one after the other. But in every action he sets down a law of his whole activity and life. He does not simply perform good or bad actions; he himself becomes good or bad."

The personal becoming achieved in free ethical activity is the most important we have seen up to now. The prior becoming involved in spirit's becoming itself through incarnating in matter is of a different level of significance; if it means that as a given (born) essence man, as finite spirit, is incarnate in a world of persons and things, then it is to that extent outside the realm of free decision and ethical activity, except perhaps attitudinally, as mentioned before; if it means that we must not flee the world and try to take the Ideas (heaven) by storm (intellectual intuition), or that we must actually do, materially, physically, economically, in concrete law, etc., what we usually just think and talk, then it means more, in practical terms of social and political life. But the highest meaning so far remains that pertinent to the deeper moral becoming of a person, who creates his very person by the self-enactment effected by his opening or closing himself to value. For Rahner, my self-creation is identified with my forming an order of love of my own, enacted and imposed by myself, according to which I think and act, i. e., according to my own responsible decision.[54]

We are near the end of this lecture (chapter) on man as free, ready to turn to Rahner's treatment of man as historical. We have avoided, because it was not our purpose, statements specifically identified with Rahner's grounding philosophy of religion. We have found it possible, in SW and here in HW up to now, to detach from a context of metaphysics of knowledge and philosophy of religion, respectively, what Rahner says about man as finite spirit enacting himself as person in a world of persons and things. This is no longer possible. Once personal becoming enters the field of the ethical, moral, and practical, then, to fulfill the condition we identified as necessary for all self-enactment, viz., openness (self-transcendence), we must place no self-crippling limits on this openness, but rather remain as open as the horizon of being itself, the unified term of our dynamism toward knowing and loving.[55] If we wish to

[54] HW1, 132; HW2, 130; HWF, 185; HWE, 105; LW, 92: "In this way he constructs . . . his own order of love. Man knows and acts according to his self-chosen order, according to what he himself has freely decided."

[55] HW1, 125-128; HW2, 123-127; HWF, 176-180; HWE, 99-103; LW, 86-88.

call this active remaining open (or active ever opening more and more) an access to the religious, then Rahner's context is rejoined, and, along with it, a strong tradition concerning the dependence of man's ethical maturity on his religious maturity, i. e., on the maturity of his relation to God. For Rahner, the dependence is more the reverse: ". . . man's opening to God depends on his moral (ethical) self-determination . . ." [56] By his " style " of life, in ethical and moral terms, a person is already and always determining his relation to God. God can enter history to meet a man who is historical by nature, and man's openness as one who can know God as a God of a possible revelation is simultaneously and essentially an openness that a man determines in its intrinsic concrete structure by his free behavior.[57]

It is not our intention to dwell on the religious aspect for its own sake, but only in relation to personal becoming. Let's be content to admit at least this much, viz., that the question of personal becoming is inevitably *also* (i. e., in addition to a question of metaphysical constitution in terms of spirit, matter, and becoming, dealt with in the first section of this study) an ethical and religious question. As a question about the becoming of finite persons, it remains open to the eventuality that such becoming, precisely as a becoming of persons, depended on infinite persons. In other words, if openness is the very *conditio sine qua non* of personal becoming, and if one has not through a misguided " love " restricted the absolute horizon of his openness, which of itself opens up for being without restriction,[58] then there is no obstacle placed, by the free act of the created, finite person (who knows quite well his finitude), between himself and uncreated, infinite persons. Again, to do

---

[56] HW1, 136; HW2, 133; HWF, 189; HWE, 108; LW, 94.

[57] HW1, 135; HW2, 133; HWF, 189; HWE, 108; LW, 94: ". . . the openness of man's knowledge for this God of an eventual revelation, which belongs to man's basic make-up, is always at the same time and essentially an openness which, in its inner concrete structure, is determined by man's free attitude."

[58] HW1, 136; HW2, 133; HWF, 190; HWE, 108; LW, 94: ". . . when he has not, on account of a wrongly directed love, narrowed the absolute horizon of his openness for being as such. . . ."

the opposite would be to go against the very essence of person as openness and would thereby be a self-contradictory foreclosure of personal becoming. Rahner insists on this dependence of openness on an act of will, on a free act, on love. Thus the mutuality of persons, and the encounter and dialogue that lead to it, ultimately are rooted in *love*, i. e., in a "*will to person.*" [59]

If love is will-to-person, then we have regained the truth, now based upon a metaphysics, already unequivocally proclaimed by the psychologists and (phenomenological) philosophers, that personal becoming is primarily through love. We are by no means at the end of our study; love is never an end but an eternal beginning. But we have reached a certain stage. A metaphysics is not just a matter of the "labor of the concept," [60] i. e., a working out conceptually of what one has already always *known*, but is also a matter of bringing to concept and word what one has already always *practiced*, loved, acted out in one's being and doing [61] (and vice versa).

[59] *Wille zur Person*—HW1, 125; HW2, 123; HWF, 176; HWE, 100; LW, 86. The full sentence reads: "Denn Liebe ist der gelichtete Wille zur Person in ihrer unableitbaren Einmaligkeit."

[60] HW1, 40; HW2, 47; HWF, 64; HWE, 31; LW, 22. The expression is, of course, Hegel's, as Rahner notes.

[61] HW1, 43-44; HW2, 49; HWF, 70-71; HWE, 32-33; LW, 24-25. It is a slow business, with no place for impatience or a taste for making a sensation (HW1, 40; HW2, 47; HWF, 64; HWE, 31; LW, 22). Rahner has always been happy to show his thought to be traditional, at least in its principles, however much others may have left them undeveloped. But metaphysics, especially, e. g., in Levinas's sense, as more than a matter of conceptually working out what one has already known and done, is also work by someone who is not content just to *talk* about person and becoming, but wills to *do* something about it. It is not enough to be brilliant and have beautiful intuitions; one must be willing to do the work. Rahner is an example of both; capable of original insights, he does not balk at the sheer labor of historical study, systematic reflection, and unsparing writing. If we gain a deeper grasp of what we already knew, or thought we knew, or, more likely, should have known, then it's worth the work. If in addition the result is a conviction that a change is in order, that something is to be done, then all the better. Rahner has, in his many ways, managed both. In his concept of person as becoming, as self-creative, there is a call (see HW1, 125; HW2, 123; HWF, 175; HWE, 99; WD, R86-R87) to man to *do* something about his freedom, about his love, because it is in this way that he possesses himself and enacts his creative power over his very self. (HW1, 123; HW2, 122; HWF, 174; HWE, 98; LW, 85).

4. *Man As Historical And Interpersonal.* We move now to the final section of HW to be analyzed in this section. Note, however, that already in the ninth lecture (chapter) Rahner, in setting up our question, anticipated its answer by saying that man is historical by his very essence as spirit; indeed man is only ". . . spirit as a *historical* being." [62] " The ' place ' of man's transcendence," which is the essential mark of spirit, " is always a historical place." [63] What will be shown, he says, in the eleventh lecture (chapter), is that ". . . turning to his history is an intrinsic constituent of the very spirituality itself of man." [64] Not just de facto but de jure, as spirit [65] man stands in history and possesses as essential his historicity.[66]

Rahner affirms that historicity, though it can be shown to follow from the receptive nature [67] of cognition (human knowledge as becoming), which some might wish to reduce to materiality to try to keep from rooting man's historicity *directly* in his spirit, can also just as clearly be shown to follow from his *freedom* (human willing as becoming). To act freely, he says, is in an essential sense to act historically.[68] To understand the term history not just generally but metaphysically is to be able to say that ". . . wherever there is free activity, there is history. . . ." [69]

When we turn to Rahner's treatment of man as historical spirit, we do indeed find first a summary of man as material.[70] The aim there is to show man's temporality (and to that extent

---

[62] HW1, 143; HW2, 143; HWF, 202; HWE, 116; LW, 99.

[63] HW1, 143; HW2, 143; HWF, 202; HWE, 116; LW, 99.

[64] HW1, 145; HW2, 145; HWF, 204; HWE, 117; LW, 100.

[65] HW1, 145; HW2, 145; HWF, 205; HWE, 117; LW, 101: ". . . he stands in history as a spirit. . . ."

[66] HW1, 145; HW2, 145; HWF, 205; HWF, 117; LW, 101: " . . man's historicity is not simply something which just happens to him among other things, but rather something which he has to be precisely *as* a spirit. . . ."

[67] See HW1, 147-149; HW2, 147-148; HWF, 207-209; HWE, 119-120; LW, 102-104.

[68] HW1, 143; HW2, 143; HWF, 203; HWE, 116; LW, 99: " But free activity is essentially historical activity."

[69] HW1, 143; HW2, 143; HWF, 203; HWE, 116; LW, 99-100.

[70] HW1, 162-166; HW2, 161-164; HWF, 226-231; HWE, 130-133; LW, 114-117.

his historicity) as based on his materiality. Then, after a page devoted to showing man's historicity as based on his spirituality ("directly"),[71] Rahner returns to materiality as basis, this time by relating his ideas to those of a Thomist anthropology.[72] Obviously this results in more focus on things than on persons; at least the deduction of man's social nature is not made through spirit in its material incarnation; Metz calls attention to this fact in two important notes.[73]

What exactly does this term historicity mean, if not simply man's temporality, corollary of his materiality? For Rahner it means more than time, more than that we become persons in space and time. It means that personal becoming happens within *community*, i.e., in, through, by, and with other persons.[74] But let us first briefly relate to historicity the treatment here of man as material.

Becoming, our focus for all discussion of spirit and person, is a phenomenon of finitude. Exemplified in a cognitive context by receptive knowledge, finitude has traditionally been related to matter and sensibility. To speak of becoming in terms of movement or motion is just to use more "material" or physical terms. Thus to say that man as a material being is constantly in movement, never limited to its present actuality, always open to further determinations, oriented toward a future of new enactments, etc., is to say again that man *becomes*.[75] Thus a material being is one whose full enactment of potential is always before him in his future as that toward which he is "moving."[76]

One result of this materiality in relation to temporality, important for Rahner's later doctrine on concupiscence, is man's

[71] HW1, 166-168; HW2, 164-166; HWF, 232-233; HWE, 133-134; LW, 117-118.
[72] HW1, 168-174; HW2, 166-171; HWE, 233-240; HWE, 134-139; LW, 118-123.
[73] HW2, 164, n. 2: HWF, 231, n. 2: HWE, 133, n. 2; and HW2, 170, n. 6; HWF, 239, n. 6; HWE, 170-171 n. 6.
[74] HW1, 167; HW2, 168; HWF, 233; HWE, 133: LW, 117.
[75] HW1, 163-164; HW2, 162; HWF, 228-229; HWE, 131; LW, 114-115.
[76] HW1, 164; HW2, 162; HWF, 228; HWE, 131; LW, 115: "Hence the material being is one which always points towards the totality of the realization of its possibilities as the future of its inner movement and keeps striving towards it."

inability to enact himself full and all at once at any one time; [77]
only in a succession of enactments does finite person achieve
full self-enactment.[78] Through this line of reasoning Rahner
concludes that man's enactment is possible only as community,[79] as interpersonal community. [80] In other words, a
person's orientation to other persons appears as a share in the
dynamism of the whole human species toward its full enactment. History is the working out of this specific self-enactment; and it must be free or it is less than human and personal.
Humanity is a species in search of its identity.

Here we reach the heart of historicity. As we saw before,
man is historical not only because he is material and thus
temporal, not only, i. e., in that he must constantly become
actually who and what he is potentially, because as finite he
is openness to becoming as a material being, but also because
he is more originally spiritual and thus a free person. History
really exists only where person is the highest value, i. e., where
there is freedom; and historicity in the full human sense exists
only where this freedom is exercised together with other free
persons in community.[81]

Rahner reaches the culmination of this line of thought when
he affirms that the human person, as constituted historical by
his very essence as a free person, must freely enact himself, in
space and time, within a community of persons, that community being the full enactment of his essence as person.[82]

---

[77] HW1, 164; HW2, 162; HWF, 228-229; HWE, 131; LW, 115.

[78] HW1, 164; HW2, 162; HWF, 229; HWE, 131; LW, 115: "The total realization of the possibilities of a material being is possible only in the succession of the
latter's inner movement." With Sartre we might speak not of a mere series but
of a detotalized totality; this meaning of totality only partly escapes Levinas's
rejection of person as totalizable.

[79] HW1, 166; HW2, 164; HWF, 231; HWE, 133; LW, 116.

[80] HW2, 164, n. 2; HWF, 231, n. 2: HWE, 133, n. 2.

[81] HW1, 167; HW2, 165; HWF, 232; HWE, 134; LW, 117: ". . . in a together-
ness of free persons in their multiplicity. . . ."

[82] HW1, 167; HW2, 165; HWF, 233; HWE, 134; LW, 117: "And precisely
such a historicity is found in man because he is essentially a free, self-subsisting
person who must freely realize himself through a multiplicity of such persons as
the total realization of the very essence of such a person in space and time."

Man's full self-enactment as person can only happen in his own history as a shared history, in the mutuality of a community of persons, and this self-enactment is precisely the effect of those free acts (love in word and deed, including law) which create and constitute that community. In other words, just as man humanizes himself by humanizing his home, work, city, and world, so also man " personizes " himself in those free ethical acts which enact community as the only space-time wherein persons can become and be persons. This freedom, and its issues, love and law, cause and effect persons; i. e., persons enact themselves as persons in enacting love and justice. Personal becoming is and must be, therefore, interpersonal becoming. Isolationism is suicide for an individual, family, nation, or world.[83]

---

[83] Before ending this section, I should mention the notes added by Metz on person and community. Conscious of the possible misunderstanding that could come from Rahner's speaking (equivalently) of DAS *Andere*, but not of DER *Andere*, or of *Welt*, *Umwelt*, *Dingwelt*, *Gegenstandwelt*, without adding *personale Welt* or *Mitwelt*, or the like, Metz added the five notes. Let's accept both that Metz was reflecting Rahner's own position (of that time, i. e., some twenty years later than HWI) by emphasizing person and community, and that Metz was also reflecting a contemporary critique of Thomism, especially when he suggests that to do full justice to love, freedom, and persons as community, a different approach from the one presented in HW (or SW) is needed, i. e., different from one based on a (Thomist) metaphysics of knowledge more cosmocentric than anthropocentric. To the extent that Rahner's metaphysics of knowledge, while dependent on Aquinas's, transcends it by being more anthropocentric, it would escape this criticism. But to the extent that this even anthropocentric metaphysics of knowledge is applied to man as person, whose mark is less the transcendence (openness) of intellect than the transcendence (openness) of freedom and love, then it would come under the criticism contained in Kern's suggestion that categories coming from a cognitive context (for example, self-presence: *Beisichsein*) cannot, without adaptation, be simply applied to an affective, volitive context. He suggests that spirit cannot be adequately expressed as self-presence (*Beisichsein*) but as the presence to self/other of the self/other: *Bei-(dem Selbst/Andern-) Sein (des Andern/Selbst)*. And he suggests that *bei* (presence) canot be interpreted merely spatially, but must mean in and with and through (*in und mit und durch*); it's not much better but it is the way we have expressed the relation of person becoming person in, with and through other persons. See W. Kern, " Einheit-in-Mannigfaltigkeit. Fragmentarische Überlegungen zur Metaphysik des Geistes," in *Gott in Welt*. Festgabe für Karl Rahner (Freiburg: Herder, 1964, two vol., ed. by J. B. Metz, W. Kern, A. Darlap, and H. Vorgrimler), Vol. I, 207-239; see esp. 232.

5. *Concluding Summary.* To conclude this section we must admit that there is much more in both SW and HW than has been treated here. My purpose was not to treat everything, but to take Rahner's major philosophical works and interrogate them on the meaning of person. The question whether God must be part of my community for me to achieve personal becoming (as well as the question whether God is necessary to man as species for its specific personal becoming) would be answered by Rahner with a Yes; HW clearly works toward that conclusion; quotations meant to substantiate this claim could come from nearly everywhere in that work.[84] But later ideas on membership in the church, on heresy, on the anonymous Christian, etc., would also have to be included. I have not pursued this question further here both because God, as personal, is at least implicitly included in every statement about person made in HW, and because a more explicit and satisfactory treatment can better be made through Rahner's theology.

These remarks suggest at least two tasks, the first of which is taken up in the following sections of this study, viz., to pursue the meaning of personal becoming through Rahner's theological works, with an eye especially open to evolution in his concepts of person, freedom, community, and love. The second would be to undertake an independent study, beginning with interpersonal experience of the heart, of love and freedom, deriving a metaphysics from it directly, rather than starting with a metaphysics of cognition, contrary to Rahner and Lonergan (and Aquinas, Kant, and Hegel) and the whole tradition giving primacy to knowledge. Some of the phenomenology already exists. But Rahner's metaphysics of personal becoming, though an application of a metaphysics of cognition, wherein the categories of spirit, matter, becoming, self-transcendence, openness, self-enactment, etc., were forged, will not soon be replaced.

Now finally since this is meant to be a concluding *summary,*

[84] E. g., see HW1, 204; HW2, 199; HWF, 279; HWE, 161; LW, 144.

and since everything Rahner wrote on person after these two works came from them, I will rapidly run through the essentials. Our most apt terms for becoming on the highest level of person (the free and ethical) are not spirit and matter, or *Vorgriff* and horizon, but transcendence and openness, enactment and community. Man is a capacity to establish (enact) relations. Community is the set of interrelationships enacted in a mutuality of self-transcendences; openness (seen as an active opening, remaining open, and continually opening more) is another name for self-transcendence, effected only in enacting community: to enact person is to enact community. There is no person without community.

Now historicity calls to mind both becoming (in time and history) and community (my history within the species's history). The two go together. As constantly becoming, person can receive only an open definition. Thus the idea of person must remain open to history, for only in history is man working out his own definition. By trying to become a person, a man gradually learns what it means to be a person, and learns who is this person he is. In this effort toward personal self-enactment, each realizes that he is spirit by experiencing openness to personal and impersonal being without restriction, especially to being as goodness and value. He enacts himself as more and more spirit in his free decisions for those values that relate to him on the level of spirit. Second, in his effort toward becoming he also learns his meaning as a material being, whose every act, including the most free and spiritual, is an enactment in, through, and of matter. He distinguishes velleity from will, lip service from religion, sweet nothings from love, and thus learns that he becomes even spirit only in incarnating his intellect and will in concrete, existential activity. In this effort toward becoming, he learns that person, as essentially social and relational, is enacted only in and through the enactment of community. Thus no one is enacted as a person by another: all enactment is self-enactment. But all enactment is also relational; it is self-performed yet radically depends on others, who are not inert or passive means to my self-perfection, but other freedoms opening to me and granting me access to my self-enacting self-transcendence. What are the metaphysical bases for these interdependencies?

In his detailed study of the precise interrelationships necessarily obtaining between sense and its object, Rahner identified and distinguished the object's acts and the subject's and showed their interdependencies. The object needs a " wherein " for its act (a " thing " becomes an " object " only in a subject, one might say to Kant). The subject needs a " wherefrom " and " whereto " for its act, and enacts itself as knower in enacting the act of the other as its own. The lover exemplifies these interrelationships and interdependencies, with the added dimension of freedom. Person as lover enacts himself on condition of basically the same mutual relations and dependencies. Persons emerge and becoming occurs only as the interpersonal. This means that one must be loved in order to love, that one must be loved in order to become a person, and that love exists to become mutual: it means that love is will to person. As will to person, love personizes the lover. As a " transcendent " act, its effect is on the lover (as an " immanent " act) only because it goes to the loved (as a " transient " act), i. e., because it wills the loved *as* (and to be) person, *as* (and to be) free. But for this act of love to find fulfilment (full enactment), it needs another openness to receive it (somewhat as a " thing " needs a " subject " in order to become an " object "). Thus personal becoming is interpersonal becoming as much because a person needs someone to love as because he needs someone who will love him in return. But we must not miss noting that in terms of the enactment of person, the free will to person, i. e., love, reveals as its basic metaphysical structure a need for the other more as one who can freely and actively open to receive love. But neither should we miss that this very opening to accept love from another is also a will to person and thus also love, for I will the other as (and to be) person also in making it possible for his love to reach its term and goal. Thus we regain mutuality, but from another direction. Personal becoming is interpersonal becoming not so much because one appeals for love and responds to love when it is given, as because love as will to person is perfect only when, as a real *will* to person and a real will to *person*, each person freely enacts himself as a lover (in his act of willing the other as person, seen as an act of love for the other) *and* as a beloved (in his act of willing the other as person, seen as an act of freely opening to the other's act of love in order to receive it, an act which makes possible the *other's* full self-enactment by enacting *oneself as* one loved by the other, which one does by enacting the other's emanated act as my received act of love, as an act of love for oneself, as one's own possessed act of received love). Thus both persons enact themselves through the other as both lover and beloved, each enacting himself as a person in loving the other, and each making possible one another's self-enactment as person by enacting the received love from the other. The lover, to be a lover, needs a beloved; but only the person can enact himself; thus the one being loved *is* one being loved only if he enacts himself as one being loved, which he does and can only do by enacting the other's act of love for him as his, as an act from another that is acting upon, in, and for himself.

It should be clear that this description of the interrelations and interdependencies of the acts of bestowing love and accepting love (i. e., opening to love, in the double sense of opening to give love and opening to being loved) is a simple application of elements from SW (especially the analyses of sensation) and from HW (especially the analyses of free acts and historicity). Since our interpretation of Rahner is limited in this part to these two philosophical studies, this is about as far as we can go, on that basis, toward a metaphysics of personal becoming. Next we turn to an interpretation of his theological studies.

PART TWO: THEOLOGICAL ANTHROPOLOGY

III

Person in the Earliest Essays in Theological Anthropology.

1. *Concupiscence: Finitude as Inertia.* The first important theological study we consider is the article on concupiscence, the very title of which, " The Theological Concept of Concupiscentia " (1941, the same year HW was published), makes worth remarking that often what may first seem an unlikely source for a metaphysics of person actually turns out to be essential. In it Rahner advances from a dialectic of spirit and matter to one of person and nature. He is actually making clear the effects of man's being spirit in the world, i.e., the meaning of finitude: man is an incarnate *spirit* who is an *incarnate* spirit. He insists on the *unity* of man, *and* on the *duality* of the principles constituting that unity.[1] Because Rahner is here bringing his metaphysics of the human person to a theological question, his use of the term *concupiscentia* identifies that question, and a certain context, for theologians. But let's not be misled by this technical term. Man in his very metaphysical essence is the subject of this essay, i.e., man in his free, ethical activity, by which he becomes, determines, and enacts himself.

It was to be expected that Rahner would have turned his attention to this question soon after SW and HW, since it follows as a direct application of his anthropology worked out there. I have spoken of two " gaps," the second resulting from the first. Man's distance from the ultimate term of his total becoming as a person is the first gap. Human materiality is spirit's way of trying to close that gap. But materiality, while man's sole way of being and becoming, introduces a duality within his very essence, thus effecting a second gap, between

[1] STh II 254; ThI II 241

95

spirit and matter: *concupiscentia* names experience of the
second gap. Pure spirit, conceived as a limit-idea, would exist
without this second gap (though still with the first).

Now it would be unnecessary repetition to state the main
notions of an essay available in English for so long—and presented substantially (almost ten years before translation) by
John Kenny; [2] furthermore, presupposing the philosophical part
of the present study, I can be brief and direct. Let us, therefore, move immediately to the point:

> . . . man's free decision is an act by means of which he disposes
> of himself as a whole. For originally and ultimately moral freedom
> is not so much a decision with regard to an objectively presented
> value-object as a decision with regard to the freely operative sub-
> ject himself. . . . the free decision tends of itself to dispose of man
> as a whole. For the spiritually knowing and willing subject neces-
> sarily brings to completion [*vollzieht*: enacts] in every objective
> act of knowledge and decision a return upon himself as well (*reditio
> completa subjecti in seipsum*: St. Thomas, IV *Cont. Gent.*, c. 11),
> and in this way is present to himself and himself acts as someone so
> present to himself. In this way the free operation, as a genuine
> operation, and not just a passive experience, arises from the in-
> most core of the subject and exercises a determining influence upon
> this subject. For otherwise the operative subject, insofar as he is
> identical with this personal center, would merely undergo the free
> decision passively and not actively posit it. But that is in contra-
> diction to the inmost essence of the free operation, inasmuch as
> the operative subject is really responsible for it. Now the opera-
> tive subject himself can only be and remain responsible for the
> free decision if he posits this decision in such a way that the de-
> cision becomes a qualification of the operative subject himself.
> Thus the free decision is essentially a disposal of himself made by
> man, and one which proceeds from the inmost center of his being.
> Now if man's free decision is the shaping (or in the terms of con-
> temporary existential philosophy, the 'self-comprehension') of his
> own being proceeding from its *inmost* core—from that core, i. e.,
> from which man's whole metaphysical essence arises and derives
> its unity and identity—then the free decision also tends essentially

[2] See J. P. Kenny, "The Problem of Concupiscence: A Recent Theory of Professor Karl Rahner," *Australasian Catholic Record*, 29 (1952), 290-304, and 30
(1953), 23-32.

to shape and modify this whole essence arising from the center of the person.[3]

Any student of SW and HW knows this conclusion follows from the principles worked out there. The free act is an enactment of the person himself in a certain direction. It is not an accident in any epiphenomenal sense, but issues from and returns to the very center of the person. Man becomes person through such free, responsible acts, originating from and modifying man where he is most person. Rahner thus continues his philosophy of person in this essay. But it is more than a continuation; what was implicit now becomes explicit; he is dealing with *person,* precisely under the aegis of *freedom* as the person's act of *self-disposition* and *self-enactment.*[4]

To what extent does the person's free act really enact him as a person? Rahner is no less explicit.

The question now arises as to how far the freely operative subject when he makes his decision succeeds in actually extending this tendency totally to dispose of himself throughout the whole extent of his being. And here we simply lay it down *a posteriori* . . . that this tendency within man's ordinary free decision never completely succeeds in making its way. There always remains in the nature of things a tension between what man is as a kind of entity simply present before one (as ' nature ') and what he wants to make of himself by his free decision (as ' person ') , a tension between what he is simply passively and what he actively posits himself as and wishes to understand himself to be. The ' person ' never wholly absorbs its ' nature.'[5]

Personal becoming appears here as the enactment of his nature by a person, " nature " being that which, when enacted, is

---

[3] STh I 392-393; ThI I 361-362. Resonances with HW are obvious.

[4] " The concept of *person* as the ontological principle of a free active center . . . self-conscious, present to himself and through himself in being, is a concept which . . . has always played around the edge of the most static and objective concept of *person* (i. e., as substantial unity and distinction involving incommunicability)" (STh I 180; ThI I 159): ". . . freedom remains in its intrinsic ontological root supremely central to the person " (STh I 182, n. 2; ThI I 162, n. 2 [from 161]).

[5] STh I 393; ThI I 362.

that person.[6] Becoming a person is thus enactment of one's nature, is raising to the level of act what is latent in that nature. Rahner uses the term nature here not as it is used in the couplets nature and grace or nature and supernature. He is drawing on the contemporary meaning of person as freedom,[7] as free self-disposability: "man is a 'person' insofar as he freely disposes of himself by his decision, possesses his own definitive reality in the act of making a free decision about himself."[8] Now nature is defined, in the present context, in terms of this self-disposability: "By 'nature' is meant all that in man which must be given (and insofar as it is given) prior to this disposal of himself, as its object and the condition of its possibility."[9] Personal becoming is an essential and ontological "self-con-

---

[6] "Where the person is, there is freedom; this means, however, that there is self-control [*Selbstverfügung*: self-disposition] over the person's own reality and that the person shapes his own being and life as a result of internal decisions. Every finite person, of course, has imposed on it the law of the direction in which these decisions should be taken, so that we must in this sense distinguish in each finite person between its nature (understood as that which is pre-established for free personal control and something which serves as the norm of this decision) and the person (understood as what this being in freedom makes of itself and as how it wants to understand itself). . . . For the finite person itself is at the same time always also a nature. There is no point in the concrete existence of man—call it spirit, *scintilla animae*, ego, autonomous subject, or anything else you like—which is not affected by the fate of the nature of the person. The finite person itself, precisely as a person, is affected by the fate of its nature, since the possibilities of personal existence always rest essentially on the possibilities of the nature. . . ." (STh III 86; ThI III 69-71). "For by reason of his twofold nature of spirit and matter, we must distinguish between man as intelligible person and man as 'nature.' By person we mean man insofar as he can be, and is, freely in command of himself (as nature). By nature we mean here everything which, as condition for its possibility, precedes this free activity of man as a person and signifies a norm which sets bounds to the autonomous sovereignty of his freedom" (STh II 79-80; ThI II 86). A good illustration of person and nature in experience is given by J. Cowburn, *Love and the Person. A Philosophical Theory and a Theological Essay* (London: Geoffrey Chapman, 1967), 3-16; the extension of the idea goes to 49.

[7] ". . . [F]reedom of choice . . . is the presupposition of what is called *responsibility,* and it characterizes what is meant by *person in the modern sense* of the word" (emphasis added) STh II 96; ThI II 90).

[8] STh I 393, n. 1; ThI I 362, n. 2.

[9] STh I 393, n. 1; ThI I 362-363, n. 2.

struction," because free acts touch, change, and make a difference to the very essence of a person. To emphasize this
ontological making-a-difference, Rahner contrasts the effects
of a free act with a " mere moral or juridical imputation " of
an act to a person. We would misunderstand him if we take
this particular (and pejorative) use of the term moral as a
relegation of such acts to the domain of acts that do *not* " make
a difference " to man's essence; he is rather saying the opposite,
viz., that precisely the free act (and the moral / ethical act is
the free act *par excellence*) penetrates through to the very essence of man and enacts him as a person, because such an act is
by its very nature reflexive, self-determining: the free act *is*
the human nature in its self-becoming as person, *is* the nature
enacted by the person's self-disposition.

If my nature is the raw material " at my disposal " for actualization, then I am nature and person: person is enacted nature, and the enactment occurs through and in free activity:

. . . a clear and handy distinction between that in man which is
not open to question and that which he is in virtue of his capacity
to dispose of himself, is of fundamental importance; otherwise the
free operation is going to look like a sporadically occurring activity
of the man in connection with an object distinct from himself, and
this transient operation will then leave the operative subject untouched and at most of significance for him by being imputed to
him in a moral-juridical way. Apart from all else, this is already
excluded by the ontological nature of the spiritual act: the spiritual act (the free decision, above all) is by its very nature reflexive, reflecting back upon the subject; the free act is not simply
imputed to the subject, for the latter has from the first determined
itself through this act.[10]

For Rahner the essence of person is found in the *freedom*
of his becoming; all finite essences (natures) are characterized
by becoming, but human nature (essence) unfolds freely also,
the ideal, as a distant and unreachable horizon, being the full
enactment of all the potential latent in that essence: ". . . the
essence, in its complete unfolding, always remains an ideal

[10] STh I 393, n. 1; ThI I 363, n. 2.

capable of being attained only asymptotically by the concretely existent being, even as regards the freedom through which
it makes itself what it is." [11]

A person becomes a person through enactment of his nature.
Now becoming says both a dynamic momentum toward ever
fuller enactment and a sluggish inertia resisting this dynamism.
We named these two polarities spirit and matter, person and
nature. Nature is both the source and power of personal becoming, yet resists that becoming:

> . . . just as essential an element of the dualism of person and na-
> ture, of the resistance of the entity given prior to the free decision
> counter to the tendency of the free subject totally to dispose of
> his whole subsistent reality, arises from the materiality of the hu-
> man being, from the real differentiation of matter and form, which
> prevents the form from bringing itself fully to manifestation in
> the ' other ' of matter. . . . the whole ' nature ' given prior to free-
> dom offers resistance to the ' person's ' free and total disposition
> of himself, so that the boundary between ' person ' and ' nature '
> stands as it were vertically in regard to the horizontal line which
> divides spirituality from sensibility in man. The specifically *human*
> form of the distinction between person and nature (as distin-
> guished, e. g., from a like dualism which has to be supposed for the
> angels as well) is explained by the dualism of matter and form
> in man. . . . [12]

, We move to the properly ethical aspect of Rahner's discussion, where person is viewed as enacting his nature through an
act that determines him as morally good or evil, through a free
decision. As we just saw, ". . . to the nature (as opposed to
the person) belongs everything which must be given prior to
the person's free decision, as a condition of its possibility." [13]
The natural dynamism of human nature is one of these givens;
without it there is no activity at all. When this basic dynamism, already naturally oriented toward what accords with it,
enters the realm of conscious choice, the person takes up this
natural force into his own hands and disposes of it, and of himself:

[11] STh I 394; ThI I 363-364.
[12] STh I 395; ThI I 365.
[13] STh I 395; ThI I 365.

. . . the free decision tends to the end that man should dispose of himself as a whole before God, actively make himself into what he freely wishes to be. Thus the end to which the free decision is orientated is that everything which is in man (nature), hence the involuntary as well, should be the revelation and the expression of what man as person wishes to be; thus that the free decision should comprehend, transfigure, and transfuse the spontaneous act, so that its own reality too should no longer be purely natural but personal.[14]

Personal becoming is, therefore, identified with sanctity and perfection, and is just as humanly impossible,[15] a *horizon* of possibility man is incapable of reaching because he can never fully exhaust the potential of his nature. This can be put two ways, from the viewpoint of freedom and person, or from that of nature. And ". . . it makes no difference whether we say: ' The free principle is of itself too weak to achieve itself wholly in man's nature,' or ' The resistance of the material in which the decision tries to realize itself is too strong for the entire

[14] STh I 395-396; ThI I 365.

[15] " Hence we must distinguish two quite different dimensions of intensity in the case of the human act; one of these is the measure of the greater or lesser personal depth of an act, while the other measures the intensity and density of the act on a particular personal level. . . . There would now arise the question how this existential depth of an act can grow; whether, and how, man slowly gains the chance in the course of his natural and moral life to increase the radical existential depth of his actions; whether and how he manages to bring himself into play in *one* act and this with the *whole* reality of his spiritual and personal being right down to its deepest depths in one free decision, and what are the causes and conditions making it possible for him to do this. . . . There is evidently a development of man's capacity for an ever more total self-commitment by ever deeper personal acts. The impossibility of being able to commit oneself totally at every moment—the impossibility of a totally making-of-oneself in every moment what one wants to be—is, however, nothing more than what *is* called concupiscence in the strictly theological sense of the word (in contrast to the usual moral interpretation of this term). Hence growth in this possibility is nothing other than growth in overcoming concupiscence " (STh III 31-33; ThI III 20-22). ". . . [T]he Christian ought to *become* holy . . . he in some way or other becomes this slowly . . . he can become ever *more perfect* . . . he is capable of growing in holiness and love of God, and . . . he moves himself towards a definite goal in his religion and moral life, a goal which is not a simple question of a goal not attained or not yet attained, but a goal toward which he really moves by approaching nearer and nearer to it" (STh III 19-20; ThI III 10).

success of the intention.' " [16] In other words, ". . . one can either say, ' The personal decision does not wholly make its own the potentialities of its material,' or ' The free principle does not succeed in overcoming the resistance of its nature-material.' " [17]

Note that this inability to become fully is given in conscious experience. If we were not conscious of ourselves as always " more " than we can enact, express, and concretize, then the entire dynamic process would be unfree. But we are aware that free acts, *because* they are free, leave us changed by them: it is I who have done the changing.—I myself am changed. *Free ethical activity is as self-creative as is humanly possible.*

In the concrete man of the present order free personal decision and self-determination are not capable of perfectly and exhaustively determining the operative subject throughout the whole extent of his real being. The free act does indeed dispose of the whole subject, insofar as it is as free act an act of man's personal center, and so, by the root as it were, draws the whole subject in sympathy with it. And yet man's concrete being is not throughout its whole extent and according to all its powers and their actualization the pure expression and the unambiguous revelation of the personal active center which is its own master. In the course of his self-determination, the person undergoes the resistance of the nature given prior to freedom, and never wholly succeeds in making all that man is into the reality and the expression of all that he comprehends himself to be in the core of his person. There is much in man which always remains in concrete fact somehow impersonal; . . . man in this régime does not overcome even by his free decision the dualism between what he is as nature prior to his existential decision and what he becomes as person by this decision, not even in the measure in which it would absolutely speaking be conceivable for a finite spirit to overcome it. Man never becomes wholly absorbed either in good or in evil.[18]

To emphasize that Rahner means something really metaphysical here, we can follow his elaboration of that last sentence by contrasting man's inability fully to become personal

---

[16] STh I 396, n.; ThI I 366, n.
[17] *Loc. cit.*
[18] STh I 399-400; ThI I 368-369.

(due to his material nature) with angels' (used as a limit-concept) power to do so instanced as the capacity for repentance in men and angels. " Looked at metaphysically, repentance is only possible where man's immoral free decision has not the power so exhaustively to impress evil upon his being that no starting-point for a new decision remains over from which a fresh redisposition of the elements of the human person could ensue." [19] As for the angel, ". . . he is ' impenitent ' precisely because he was in a position exhaustively to shape his entire nature through his personal decision; hence too no remainder is left over in him, either psychologically or ontologically, which might have escaped this personal decision and from which the reshaping of the person could begin." [20] When there is no " remainder," no unenacted potentiality remaining, full becoming is then reached; nature has been taken up into person and disposed of in a free ethical decision. It could hardly be more clearly said that personal becoming makes an ontological difference, and is no mere accidental determination,[21] no merely psychological phenomenon. What a pure (non-incarnate) spirit accomplishes in one act, a human (incarnate) spirit needs a whole lifetime (and even a " purgatory " after this life) to accomplish.

Pure spirit is not, of course, an ideal to be striven for by man; if SW said anything at all it was that the *human* person becomes himself only in and through matter. Thus when Rahner says that ". . . it is the goal of all moral growth that man should increasingly bring the whole of himself into play

---

[19] STh I 397, n. 2; ThI I 367, n. 2.

[20] STh I 404, n. 1; ThI I 373, n. 1.

[21] " The history of man, his free action, and the absolute climax of his freedom are not to be considered as accidents attached to the unmodified substance of a nature conceived as one thing to be registered among others. It must be regarded as the self-realization [*Selbstvollzug*: self-enactment] of a being which only attains its own reality in such a process of freedom, which is therefore not to be regarded so much as a ' faculty ' which man ' has ' as the power of free disposal which one is, in order to be able to bring one's own imposed being, as itself, to its proper fulfilment " (STh IV 168; ThI IV 130-131. See also STh IV 165-171; ThI IV 128-132, esp. STh IV 169, n. 10; ThI IV 130, n. 10).

in a morally good decision . . . ," [22] he is not implying a possible spiritualism (or angelism). He is rather emphasizing that to be a person is to *become* a person, in time and history. Thus he ends this essay insisting that personal becoming is a free activity, issuing from my free, active personal center, not something that happens to me:

It has always been the case that man only learns slowly and arduously to know who he is and all that is in him.[23] When and where man is present to himself with the utmost clarity (and it is rationalistic, unhistorical superstition, not a postulate of a rational metaphysical anthropology, to suppose that he must be capable of this at any moment he chooses), he may not know why he finds himself to be like this; but he can notice the *fact* that he does not feel in order.[24]

We examined this essay in search of a metaphysics of personal becoming, and have found in it material to advance our inquiry. Besides the older distinction of spirit and matter, we now have that of person and nature. And we have also found the process of enactment of nature by person placed unequivocally on the ontological plane: man *ontologically* becomes a person through and in his free, ethical acts, deciding his very essence as a whole in his moral decisions. Rahner's approach to another philosophical-theological question has now more clearly emerged as a " personalist " approach. Rahner has obviously been content to let the *inter*personal remain implicit. At this time, despite statements in HW which admitted of interpretation in the direction of the necessity of interpersonal

---

[22] STh I 405; ThI I 373-374.

[23] " But right to the end of his history man will never be quite done with learning what in him is essence and what merely contingently factual model. The whole spiritual and cultural history of man testifies to this. For in this history he continually experiences new modes of the single process of the realization of his essence [*Wesensverwirklichung*: actualization of his essence], which he would never have been able to infer from his essence *a priori*. And in each new mode he learns anew by living out the difference between essence and its concrete historical realization, the synthesis of which he had held before to be more or less incapable of being dissolved " (STh I 327-328, n. 1; ThI I 301-302, n. 1).

[24] STh I 413; ThI I 381.

love in community for persons to reach fulfillment, he continues
to speak mostly in terms of an *intrapersonal* becoming, i. e., of
what goes on *within* the person, permitting but not making explicitations about how this " within " depends on what happens
between (inter) persons. This assessment applies also to the
essay on death and to the first essay on freedom, to be treated
in this section. Not until more than ten years from this time
(1941), in 1953, will we find him, writing on guilt (to be treated
in the fourth section of this study), explicitly dealing with the
interpersonal in a way that begins to be more satisfying.

2. *Death: Final Self-enacting Self-disposition.* Let us turn
now to the question of death. We shall find that a " personalism," emerging more clearly with each essay, is once again
Rahner's position: to be a person is to have the task of becoming a person.

To turn, incidentally, to Rahner's essay on death *after*
having studied his essays on purgatory (indulgences),[25] guilt,[26]
time,[27] and after the study of nature and person (concupiscence), as well as his less extensive treatments of resurrection
of the body, hell, and heaven [28]—to mention only the few that
come readily to mind—would be to become even more aware
of the admirable unity and consistency of his thought, flowing
from his fundamental principles (spirit, matter, becoming);
what he began to work out in SW and advanced in HW was
further advanced in being applied to the questions that gave
titles to the essays mentioned above (among others). In the
essay on death, man is again seen as the union of spirit and
matter, of person and nature, death being the culminating
act of personal becoming; purgatory does allow nature to
" catch up " with person, but time is the real possibility of becoming a person, and with one's time ended, one's free self-
enactment is ended, purgatory continuing only what was al-

[25] STh II 185-210; ThI II 175-201. See esp. STh II 206-207; ThI I 197-198.
[26] STh II 279-297; ThI II 265-281.
[27] STh III 169-188; ThI III 141-157.
[28] See STh II 219-220; ThI II 211.

ready decided. We can with profit dwell on Rahner's personalist way of viewing death. He does not neglect the natural view of death (*pace* Gaboriau[29]); but it has been emphasized enough, whereas a study of death as personal act has been neglected.

We begin by noting the continuing relevance of the distinction between person and nature.

Man is a union of nature and person. He is a being who possesses, on the one hand, antecedent to his own personal and free decision and independent of it, a specific kind of existence with definite laws proper to it and, consequently, a necessary mode of development; on the other hand, he disposes freely of himself and is, in the last analysis, what he himself, through the exercise of his liberty, wills himself to be. Death must consequently possess for him a personal and natural aspect.[30]

While admitting, of course, that death "happens to" man, who, as nature, dies as other living things die, Rahner focuses on the free and personal aspect of death.[31] For man as person, death has more meaning than the end and finish of his biological existence. It means the "finishing" of man in another sense, a sense completely consistent with Rahner's conception of *Person* as *Personwerdung* and *Persönlichung* (which we could translate as personal becoming and "personization," after the model of "hominization").

Death brings man, as a moral and spiritual person, a kind of finality and consummation which renders his decision for or against God, reached during the time of his bodily life, final and unalterable. This statement, however, does not totally exclude man's further development after death, nor does it presuppose a lifeless concept of man's future life with God. The doctrine of purgatory,[32] of the

---

[29] See F. Gaboriau, *Interview sur le mort avec Karl Rahner* (Paris: Lethielleux, 1967).

[30] ThT 15; ThD 13.

[31] ". . . [I]t is *man* who dies. In death something happens to him as a whole, something which, consequently, is of essential importance to his soul as well: his free, personal self-affirmation and self-realization is achieved in death definitively" (ThT 19; ThD 18).

[32] "That doctrine implies a further maturing of man, even after death, though in accord with his final decision during life, through temporal punishment for sin

coming resurrection of the body and the future consummation of the whole universe, in fact indicates a further development of man towards his ultimate perfection in every respect.[33]

Becoming is intrinsic to person right through and beyond death itself. The impression is of a dialectical struggle between man's spirituality and materiality, consistent with the tension described as concupiscence, a struggle [34] that has not even finished running its course until after death, although the direction of its course has been decided before death. Just as nature resisted person before death, so also even after death one's nature lags behind the project which the person has made of himself. Personal becoming as process, as becoming, is presented even as a consistent explanation of the *eschata*. For our purposes it suffices to note that ". . . death of its very nature is a personal self-fulfilment " [35] . . . and that ". . . the finality of the personal life-decision is an intrinsic constituent of death itself as a spiritual and personal act of man." [36]

Again we would have been able to predict that Rahner would take this position, since it follows from his premises of personal becoming through a person's free, ethical acts: to recognize a truly personal aspect in death is to find death a free, human act. Person becomes person through such acts; thus,

. . . death cannot merely be an occurrence which is passively undergone (though it is clearly that), and a biological event which man as a person faces powerlessly from the outside, but it must also be understood as an act that a man interiorly performs. Moreover, rightly understood, it must be death itself which is the act, and not simply an attitude the human being adopts towards death but which remains extrinsic to it. Just as man is both spirit and matter, liberty and necessity, person and nature, his death too must exhibit this real, ontological dialectic, so intrinsic and essential to him. . . . in death the soul achieves the consummation of its own

(i. e., the endurance of the repercussions of the world on the never perfectly right moral attitude of man " (ThT 24; ThD 24).

[33] ThT 26; ThD 26-27.
[34] See STh III 89-93; ThI III 72-75.
[35] ThT 29; ThD 30.
[36] *Loc. cit.*

personal self-affirmation, not merely by passively suffering something which supervenes biologically, but through its personal act. Death, therefore, as the end of man as a spiritual person, must be an active consummation from within brought about by the person himself, a maturing self-realization which embodies the result of what man has made of himself during life, the achievement of total self-possession, a real effectuation of self, the fullness of freely produced personal reality.[37]

Now because our search is for a metaphysics of personal becoming, and not for a theology of death, we can omit the specifically theological in this essay. But there is no reason to rest, as though finished, when once it becomes clear that Rahner's concept of person is inseparable from person-as-becoming. The *how* of our becoming is more important than the fact, a fact far clearer now than ever expressed in SW, and more developed than in HW, where only the essentials were provided. Rahner repeatedly states, and we have begun to see in how many ways, that the person is self-realization, self-actualization, self-attainment, self-appropriation, self-possession, self-affirmation, self-formation, self-fulfilment, self-completion, self-enactment, self-achievement, self-effectuation, self-decision, self-disposition, etc. We have already seen that the how of this self-enactment is self-transcendence. And Rahner repeatedly states that the *how* is through free, ethical acts, those eminently personal acts that constitute the enactment of man's nature. But death itself is here understood precisely as just such a person-enacting (personizing) act. Perhaps, in fact, death makes this aspect of personal becoming even more clear, since death is at once both a depersonization and personization.[38] But death has this significance as summing up a life only because death is present throughout the whole of that life, unless the person tries to

---

[37] ThT 29-30; ThD 30-31.

[38] "Death appears both as act and fate, as end and fulfilment, as willed and as suffered, as plenitude and emptiness. It seems to involve an empty, unsubstantial, uncanny character, a kind of depersonalization [*Entpersönlichung*: depersonization], loss of self, destruction, and at the same time the plenitude of a person's attainment of total self-possession, the independence and pure immanence that characterize personality " (ThT 38-39; ThD 41).

escape from his being-toward-death.[39] Rahner clearly understands death as much more than an unfortunate final disaster miserably undoing and depersonizing man, not the business of the last day but of every day: indeed death reveals the meaning of the everyday personal becoming of man.

Clearly it cannot be an act of man, if it is conceived as an isolated point at the end of life, but only if it is understood as an act of fulfilment (a concept which an ontology of the end of a spiritual being can fully justify), achieved through the act of the whole of life in such a manner that death is axiologically present all through human life. Man is enacting his death, as his own consummation, through the deed of his life, and in this way death is present in his actions, in each of his free acts, in which he freely disposes of his whole person.[40]

[39] See Rahner's article on Heidegger. See also STh III 89-93; ThI III 72-75: " Man can, of course (to use a Heideggerian phrase) try to run away from the ' ontological structure of his being,' from this ' being made for death ' which concerns the whole man. He can try to cover up this his death-situation by talk, by keeping himself busy, by immersing himself in daily routine, by taking flight into the anonymity of ' everyone; ' he can therefore also take the sting out of every Passion—by trying as much as possible to avoid it, by taking flight into amusements, into harmlessness, into bourgeois optimism, by the soporific of a hope for improvement (of an individual or social kind)—and he can cover up its character of the relentless approach of death and of a ' prolixitas mortis.' But when man makes a personal existential decision with regard to this death-reality of his human existence, then his decision can only consist of a ' yes ' to this reality. For only by saying yes to it, can a free person turn a necessary fate externally imposed on him into a free act of the person himself. . . . Asceticism, therefore, is nothing other than the personal, free grasping-of-his-own-accord of his necessary being-unto-death. . . . Passion expresses the necessity of death in man taken as nature, whereas asceticism expresses the freedom of death in man taken as person. . . . Dying—at least when it is accomplished in a personal way and by a yes given to the Christian revelation of life—is the most complete and definitive act of hoping faith, and this is the real meaning of Christian death."
[40] ThT 41; ThD 43-44. " Man's death, insofar as it is his own personal act, extends through his whole life. . . . any moral act of man is to be considered as a disposing over his entire person with regard to his interior destiny, and . . . such a disposition receives its final character only in death. . . ." (ThT 57-58; ThD 62-63). ". . . death, as a human action, is precisely the event which gathers up the whole personal act of a human life into one fulfilment " (ThT 63; ThD 69). " Death is an act. Certainly it is the extreme case of something undergone, the event in which what is obscure and beyond control disposes of man, ineluctably taking him from himself, in the ultimate depth of his existence. Yet at the same

Rahner's personalism transcends discussing death in a narrow traditional way. He follows and develops the *fil conducteur* of his entire anthropology, person as becoming. His essay on concupiscence showed this, and the same has appeared in his essay on death: the constant and unifying perspective is how the human person enacts that potential which he essentially is.

I admit to a certain dissatisfaction in prescinding from the theological aspects of death (as we did also from concupiscence). Without considering God as person, involved in the " good death," man's personness can come off looking pretty abstract. For Rahner personal becoming is clearly theonomous: but rather than enter into the kind of detail appropriate to elaborating the theological aspects of death, I remain on the philosophical level because Rahner provides plenty of concrete detail in other essays for those interested in pursuing the point. By remaining " philosophical " I mean considering the differences between the uses of freedom for good or evil taken as affecting man himself rather than his relations to God. Besides, from everything said about freedom so far, it is clear

time death is an act, and in fact the act of all acts, a free act. A man may be unconscious at the moment he is dying. Death may take him by surprise, if what we mean by death is the instant at the end, in which the death which we all die throughout our lives orientated towards this moment is manifested. But just because we die our death in this life, because we are permanently taking leave, permanently parting, looking towards the end, permanently disappointed, ceaselessly piercing through realities into their nothingness, continually narrowing the possibilities of free life through our actual decisions and actual life until we have exhausted life and driven it into the straits of death; because we are always experiencing what is unfathomable and are constantly reaching out beyond what can be stated, into what is incalculable and incomprehensible; and because it is only in this way that we exist in a truly human manner, we die throughout life, therefore, and what we call death is really the end of death, the death of death. Whether this death of death will be the second death or the killing of death and the victory of life, depends completely on us. Hence, because death is permanently present in the whole of human life, biologically and in the actual concrete experience of the individual person, death is also the act of human freedom " (ThT 76-77; ThD 84-85). ". . . whenever someone dies freely, the whole of his life is present " (ThT 97; ThD 109).

that Rahner's understanding of freedom must be our next concern; he makes nearly everything hinge on one's use of freedom. Before turning to his *first full* treatment of freedom, let us conclude the present study by examining briefly what he states about freedom here. " Good and bad freedom are not simply the same activation of the same liberty only in different directions and towards different objects. Just as freedom, as an intentional power, is specified by its object, so it is itself really specified by this object,[41] i. e., it is different in itself according to the different objects towards which it is directed. And it can be described through this difference, which is intrinsic to it. . . ." [42] One's death is not a morally neutral event,[43] but has the character of one's free acts and their objects. To reject a neutral death is to reject a neutral personal becoming, since death is the ultimate personizing act. It is thus inevitable that we must study freedom in general and ethics in particular, if we are to understand personal becoming, because free acts, precisely as self-enactments of the person *as* free, ontologically determine the very essence of the person.[44] It is therefore to freedom that we must next turn attention.

Needless to say, in conclusion, there is much more in this essay on death than is reflected in the above treatment. We

[41] " If we are reluctant to admit the possibility of innocently missing the final peak of life which, after all, in itself is obligation binding on every man, then we have to reject the idea that death can be a moral act of the merely natural order without relation to salvation or perdition " (ThT 85; ThD 95).

[42] ThT 97; ThD 109.

[43] " Everything depends on the object of one's freedom. Freedom, is this intramundane sense of the psychological and moral capacity to decide to act in this way or that, receives its meaning and value ultimately from the object for which and upon which one decides " (STh II 98, 108; ThI II 92, 101).

[44] ". . . [T]he ' act ' of a sub-personal being has essentially a more extrinsic relationship to the nature of this being than in the case of a being which is aware of itself and realizes itself in freedom. In this case, the being is entrusted to itself. Though it cannot use its freedom to ' destroy ' itself or eliminate itself, the free act still affects the nature in such a way that it is not merely the subject of the act, but becomes in a certain sense the act itself. Man for instance does not merely commit evil actions: he himself becomes evil by these actions. And vice versa, where a free spiritual being is willed and accepted, the self-realization as such is will and accepted, and not merely ' made possible ' and (eventually) foreseen " (STh IV 169, n. 10; ThI IV 130, n. 10).

have concentrated only on those points relevant to the question of personal becoming. It would be repetitive to dwell longer on the topic; the intrinsic relationship between death and becoming a person is clear enough for now (in his study of time, Rahner returns to some of these same basic points).

In summary, for Rahner, death can be seen from the viewpoints of nature and person. He aptly uses the term *Entpersönlichung*, depersonization, to speak of how death appears to nature, and contrasts it with death's meaning for person. Death as depersonization is loss of self, bondage, emptiness, complete dispossession of self, and a suffering of fate; death as personal becoming, as personization, is just the opposite, a self-appropriation, freedom, self-fulfilment, self-possession, and a self-disposing act.

3. *Freedom I.* Our approximately chronological order suggests that freedom would most appropriately be next; the logic of personal becoming also suggests this. So far we have (1) seen the basic constitutive principles of person identified (in SW) as spirit and matter, (2) identified becoming as the very essence of the relation between these constituents, not only for their own constitution (emanation) but also for the self-enactment of the constituted essence (innerworldly causality), (3) noted the importance of freedom and love (in HW), (4) found (concupiscence) how these principles derive momentum and face inertia as the person strives, throughout the history of a whole lifetime, to enact nature in his self-becoming, and (5) have just seen (death) how the dialectic of spirit and matter, person and nature, is a process of enactment (spirit enacts itself in matter, person enacts itself by enacting that spiritual-material nature) culminating in death seen as a free, personal act. Human self-enactment is free. As my free act has the value of its object, my life (my battle with concupiscence) and death share the value of my use of freedom. Thus we turn now to freedom.[45]

---

[45] Note that the concupiscence essay first appeared in 1941 and then again in 1954, that on death in 1949 and then in 1957, and the present essay on free-

Again note the focus: freedom is important because it is primarily through free activity that personal becoming is effected. Becoming is intrinsic to man not merely as it is for

dom dates from 1952 but appeared in the second volume of the STh in 1955. Rahner profited from the time between early and later appearance of some of his studies, reworking them, adding to them. While the study of freedom will be our next major stop along the route, other essays from the second and third volumes of STh, also from the same period, will be used as minor stops and will appear (as before) in footnotes, insofar as they relate to the matter being treated in the text.

I would like to offer a word of assurance to anyone resigned, perhaps unwillingly, to a purely arbitrary sequential treatment of Rahner's major essays, such as the order of their appearance in English. The order chosen here is not the strict order of composition or publication. There is a real, identifiable evolution in Rahner's concept of person. The foundations laid in SW and even in HW dealt with person almost exclusively in less than explicitly " personalist " categories; love as will-to-person (in HW) was a portent of future ideas. In the distinction (in the essay of concupiscence) between person and nature, added to the earlier one between spirit and matter, Rahner went beyond SW and HW while making this advancement a linear one flowing from the metaphysics of spirit becoming itself in matter; concupiscence became another way of talking about personal becoming. As we have just seen, death is also made more meaningful when seen from the viewpoint of personal becoming, Rahner's *fait primitif*.

Rahner did not really deal with the free act in depth, nor did he even scratch the surface of the most important factors of personization, until he studied love and the interpersonal; but the fact is that he *did* go on to do so, as we shall see, and fully consistently within the sweep of his dynamic of person as personization. Up to the time of the *first* essay of freedom, that is, in 1952, he was still working out metaphysical foundations, as though each time, in each essay, he set out to apply his metaphysics, as worked out in SW and HW, to a particular question (in theology, spirituality, etc.), and then realized that a little more " working out " was called for. Thus the " applications " became occasions for *developing* his ideas, and his essays consequently (and predictably) began to show an evolution. The consistency is evident and unquestioned, but the essays were more than mere explicitations of already worked-out concepts. Hints there are, and they help confirm the consistency, but in light of later essays the earlier omissions become all the more noticeable. If it can be said without contradiction, Rahner gave the impression of discussing person impersonally, at least until freedom, guilt, and love came in for explicit study.

As we turn to Rahner's essay on man's dignity and freedom, recall that we are trying to narrow the focus somewhat as we proceed to study Rahner's increasingly mature treatments of person. We have seen much on the basic nature of the human person, but for the most part in terms of the fundamental constitutive principles. We can expect gradually to narrow the focus down to the particular acts (flowing from that nature) which are most relevant to an explana-

any finite being, but *a fortiori* because man is free and can thus take even his basic nature into his own hands, can decide who and what he is and is to be. Thus to know man as person, as free, is to have to take this becoming into account, and to define man is thus to offer an open definition, i. e., one that remains open to all man can become in history.

A knowledge of essences which includes the concrete knowledge about the possibilities of nature (which in part are to be freely realized), must rely on a twofold method: (1) On a transcendental method. ... (2) The reflection on the historical experience man has of himself, without which the notion of man remains ' empty ' and without which this notion has no clearness and consequently no power in history. Such reflection is indispensable because only in this way can we recognize the metaphysical possibilities of man as a free being who, because he is free, cannot be adequately deduced from something else clearly given. Since this reflection, being itself a ' historical *becoming* ' process, is essentially unfinished, the understanding of the essence is permanently *in via* in spite of its a priori and transcendental metaphysical element. To give an adequate design of man (what he is and *ought to become*) by an a-priori-rationalistic reason is impossible. Man must always refer also to his history and thus even to his future in order to know what he is. ... Because man really knows ' concretely ' about himself in this historical experience only—an experience which is still in a state of *becoming*—there is no manifest knowledge of essence without tradition (of a natural kind and of the kind of saving history) and without a venturing, planning, devising, anticipation of the future. ...[46]

This free becoming is not some epiphenomenal or accidental addendum, but is the very construction of the human essence itself; the very capacity freely to construct the human essence is, in fact, an essential part of that essence. It is because man is personal and free that his essence is given to him as an open task, to be shaped in self-disposing, self-enacting deeds. Rahner

---

tion of person as becoming. We have already noted that concupiscence, death, purgatory, indulgences, hell, heaven, and many other " doctrines " have new clarity and sense from the viewpoint of Rahner's concept of person. The next two essays, both taken from STh II (i. e., on freedom, 1952, and on guilt, 1953) will advance us closer to a fuller grasp of this concept; from STh III only one essay (on time) will be treated.

[46] STh II 249-250; ThI II 236-237, my emphasis.

thus does not attempt to define man in the usual closed way, but rather in terms of the kind of acts that effect personal becoming. He offers the following terms [47] to characterize " man's personal nature ": (1) " man is *spirit;* " (2) " he is *freedom;* " (3) " he is an *individual;* " (4) " he is a *community-building* person; " [48] (5) " he is (qua human person) an *incarnate, mundane* person; " [49] (6) he is *characterized by* " *the supernatural existential.*" [50]

To put it somewhat differently, in terms of the human " existentials," Rahner continues:

With this essence and this dignity of man there is given a plurality of human existential dimensions (*Existentialien*): (a) He is a *corporeal-material* living being, in a biological community of life with its material surroundings, and with a care for its will to live. (b) He is a *spiritual-personal,* cultural being with a diversity of personal communities (marriage union, family, kinsfolk, a people, the State, the community of nations), and with a history. (c) He is a *religious, God-centered* being (by nature and grace), with a

---

[47] See STh II 251-253; ThI II 239-240.

[48] " Person is not the opposite of community; rather, both are correlative realities, i. e., qua person, man is intended for community with other persons (God and men), and there is community only where there are persons and where persons are protected; *he is a perfect person in the measure in which he opens himself in love and service for other persons* " (STh II 251-252; ThI II 293, my emphasis. Note how this recalls the high point of HW where openness is the necessary condition for establishing encounter, dialogue, and mutuality—and thus personal becoming— and where love is seen as will-to-person.

[49] Person as incarnate ". . . realizes himself in his ultimate core only in a spatio-temporal, pluralistic expansion, in concern for his bodily existence (economy) and within a community communicated in a tangible manner (marriage, parent-and-child relationship, the State, Incarnation, Church, sacraments, symbol, etc.). The personality of man, therefore, cannot be relegated to an absolutely internal realm. It requires a certain space for realizing itself. Such a space, although it is to a certain extent ' external ' to it (body, earth, economy, sign, symbol, State), is nevertheless essentially necessary and hence must be so constructed that it permits personal self-realization " (STh II 252; ThI II 239-240).

[50] " The supernatural existential . . . means: the person, as we have just outlined him, is called to direct communion with God in Christ, perennially and inescapably, whether he accepts the call in redemption and grace or whether he closes himself to it in guilt (by the guilt of original sin and of personal sin). . . . The supernatural existential is related to what we have called the personal nature of man, as gratuitous gift of God, as grace. In this way man exists in nature and ' supernature ' " (STh II 252-253; ThI II 240).

'Church,' in a history which either damns or saves. (d) He is a *Christ-centered* being, i. e., his being possesses an ontic and spiritual-personal capacity for communicating with Jesus Christ in whom God has forever made the countenance of man his own and has opened the reality of man, with an unsurpassable finality, in the direction of God; only thus was the real possibility of a direct communion of all men with God established with finality. Hence we can speak ultimately of God only by engaging, even in the midst of all this (in the midst of theology) in anthropology, and ultimately any information about anthropology, about the nature and dignity of man, can be given only when we engage in theology about God and from God.[51]

Rahner gives the above outlines, as though to show where freedom fits, and then immediately sets about studying various aspects of freedom. These outlines, which describe certain identifiable structures of the human person, really identify capacities for action. Man's freedom is conceived first as a capacity (an opening), which as such can be defined in the only way possible, viz., as open, and then as fulfilled, as given content; thus freedom is a capacity fulfilled by action terminating in an object; but this " definition " stops without going further. By being open, it is reflexive, a created participation in self-causation (power to become). Freedom is a possibility[52] as well as a self-achievement.[53] It is a possibility *for* self-achievement, for personal self-becoming. No more clearly could Rahner have manifested his central concern to be personal becoming; not only did his studies of concupiscence and death turn out to be approaches to person as becoming, but here again freedom is seen to be but another way to speak of this one main insight, viz., the temporal, relational, free nature of

---

[51] STh II 253; ThI II 240-241.

[52] Ultimately ". . . freedom is the possibility, through and beyond the finite, of taking up a position toward God himself. . . . And so freedom is possible only where there is a transcendental openness to the infinite God, that is to say in the spiritual person " (STh II 259; ThI II 246).

[53] " *Freedom is self-achievement* [Selbstvollzug: self-enactment] *of the person,* using a finite material, before the infinite God. . . . *Freedom . . . is the manner of the appropriation and realization of the person . . . it consists in being able to effect oneself once and for all into finality* " (STh II 260-262; ThI II 246-248, my emphasis. Freedom's own essential goal is ". . . the true *achievement of the person* " (STh II 262; ThI II 249, my emphasis).

person. Freedom is precisely the *power of becoming,* and its arena of action is ". . . in love and service for other persons." [54] Freedom has no meaning unless one understands what it is freedom *for,* and it is for the enactment of persons. "Freedom . . . is the manner of the appropriation and realization of the person." [55] One can, of course, do rather badly by his freedom, but freedom is not correctly conceived as the power to go against nature and law, but as the power to effect oneself, to enact oneself, in harmony with the very end and meaning of person, which is to love.[56] *The* commandment is: Thou shalt love!

If freedom does not consist in a power to go against oneself but in the power of personal becoming, then it becomes clear that "the moral law as such (in contrast to the forced compliance with it) is not a limitation of freedom, since it does after all presuppose freedom of its very nature and turns to it (since it is fulfilled only when it is obeyed freely), and since it orientates freedom to its own essential goal, viz., the true achievement of the person." [57] Thus freedom's own goal is achievement of person, and ethics is its logic; hence Rahner calls ethics ". . . the laws of the spiritual person . . . ," [58] thus bringing ethics also into the unifying perspective of his controlling insight and central theme.

There is, finally, a text that sums up well what has been said about both death and freedom; it also makes even clearer that both death and freedom are most meaningful when understood in terms of that theme:

But if it be true that all life points of itself constantly forward to death, that it is all the time a process of dying, then clearly death is merely a more obvious indication that there is present in the

[54] STh II 252; ThI II 239.

[55] STh II 261; ThI II 247.

[56] "Freedom, however, does not consist in always being able to do the opposite of what has been done up to now, but it consists in being able to effect oneself once and for all into finality" (STh I 262; ThI II 248). Being able to "effect oneself into finality" is an expression that readily rejoins the above concept of death, again showing the internal consistency of Rahner's personalist anthropology.

[57] STh II 262; ThI II 249.

[58] STh II 254; ThI II 241.

existence of every man a deeper region in which everyone is left to himself, a line of being pointing to himself alone. In death it just becomes unavoidably evident in all its clarity that everyone has to make something of himself, to do and to suffer something by himself alone. What region of being is it, then, which reveals itself in death, which issues in it as its ultimate conclusion, which gives itself its final mark and seal in it?

It must be something in which man has to do simply with himself as such, something which is strictly his own task, which he alone can fulfill and in which no one else can substitute for him. But this is the case only where *he himself is, in the strictest sense of the word, the task, where he is at once doer and deed, where doing and what is done are the same, both identical with himself. This is the case with man's liberty,* where with the whole force of his nature he gives ultimate meaning and character to his whole being, *where he forms his own existence* into what he wants to be. Here he is essentially alone. For the doing and what is done are inalienably his, they are as much his own as he is himself. For his action is the forming of his eternal physiognomy; it is himself in his eternal uniqueness. And hence only he himself can ever perform this act of eternal destiny. Everything that is done to a man, everything that happens to him, remains subject to the ultimate pronouncement of his liberty, in which he is still capable of understanding and accepting his lot (what is done to him, what is alloted to him); so everything that remains on this side of that ultimate personal verdict is not yet what finally counts in man. Only to a being that is not free is its ' lot ' really its destiny; for the free being his destiny lies in himself. . . . But when man with his whole being is called to a free decision about himself, he finds himself without intermediary before his God. . . . it is a case of that supremely personal actualization of the individual's being.[59]

In his study of guilt,[60] Rahner not only shows the foregoing analyses to be correct, but also advances another step forward toward a truly (overdue) *interpersonal* concept of person and becoming. In fact, the virtue of that essay, to which we can now turn, is not so much its analysis of guilt (man's materiality and temporal existence sufficiently ground the possibility of conversion) but its different (and difficult) approach to the phenomenon of personal interdependence.

[59] STh III 315-316; ThI III 264-265, my emphasis.
[60] STh II 279-297; ThI II 265-281.

IV

APPLICATIONS AND DEVELOPMENT:
THE MIDDLE PERIOD

1. *Guilt: The Emerging Interpersonal.* The present essay is
for our purposes a study of person as *social* becoming (personal
becoming as *inter*personal becoming). Until we study Rahner's
essays on love, this is his most important contribution to an
interpersonal theory of free, ethical self-enactment. It is among
his more philosophically challenging essays (along with the
Quaestio Disputata on hominization and the similar study of
the unity of spirit and matter) .[1]

It is important, and easy by now, I hope, to recognize that
to know that personal becoming is Rahner's central doctrine
is to unify and make understandable his multitudinous essays.
That this is basically a philosophical position,[2] its roots going

[1] STh VI 185-215; ThI VI 153-177.

[2] The following is a good summary of that position, emphasizing Rahner's commitment to a doctrine of person. " Man is that strange being who attains self-
consciousness only by being conscious of something other than himself, who
deals with himself by occupying himself with something else (even if this be
merely the perception or thought of himself), who catches sight of himself only
by perceiving an object. Man always requires some material distinct from himself
which will act as the Archimedean point, so to speak, from which alone he can
attain himself. He must be in-the-world in order to be capable of being personal;
he must diffuse himself in order to concentrate himself on himself; he must ' go
out ' (as the German mystics used to say) in order to be able to enter into himself and into the very core of his person. Thus we may quite rightly say that
in the case of man, who is a creature and essentially in-the-world and who is at
home with himself only by being-with-others, the act of freedom springing from
the core of his person, where man is ultimately concerned with himself and his
relationship to God (both indissolubly bound up with one another), is necessarily
achieved in a material which, although different from the real spiritual core
of the person, is nevertheless the prerequired object on which the act of freedom
is exercised. Man's relationship to himself, and his action on himself and before
God, is inevitably mediate, i. e., by means of objects " (STh II 284; ThI II 269-
270). In other words, personization is self-personization, but it is not for that
reason possible in isolation: it is self-personization through and in and with the

119

back to SW, is also evident; it is also, of course, theological.[3] There is one long text containing Rahner's profound formulations of the interpersonal. There is no way round it; nothing will do but to work it out. Therefore I will first quote it, then analyze it. (Because of its length I'm dropping the text, the longest quoted in this study, into a note,[4] to save space.)

world, the world of things (objects) and especially the world of other persons. (Though this "especially" may not be obvious in the text, it will be soon.) Rahner goes on to present ". . . an ontological conception of man's nature . . ." (STh II 286; ThI II 272).

[3] "Indeed, the culminating point of the process of becoming a person [*Personwerdung*: personal becoming, personization], which takes place through the grace of a most direct relationship to God, signifies the highest form of communion of persons who have become in this way most personal in the one eternal kingdom of God—the highest form of the eternal communion of all saints. 'Individual and community' . . . are two sides of the one reality of achieved and redeemed persons which can only increase or decrease together and to the same degree" (STh II 129; ThI II 122).

[4] "Man is a being constructed, as it were, from the interior towards the outside. He has, on the one hand, a spiritual-personal nucleus giving him an 'intentional' transcendental relation to 'Being as such and in its totality,' and hence to God, and rendering him capable of hearing the word of God as such. Man's transcendent orientation and consequent freedom and openness towards all being allow him to maintain a selective, deciding, consenting or denying attitude towards individual things (and the merely represented totality of being and hence God in this sense), since he always transcends everything limited and desires the whole, Being as such, God. On the other hand, man always has to achieve [*vollziehen*: enact] himself as a person in an 'intermediary reality' (*in einem Mittleren*), formed by the union of his animated corporeality and embodied spirituality together with their concrete, material and propositional objectifications, and by the external world of equally real persons and things as well as by the objectifications produced there by 'external' actions. This 'intermediary reality'—which alone provides man with the means of cognitive access to himself, free control over himself, and a conscious, free attitude towards God—is at the same time different and unseparated from the 'seminal' (*ursprünglich*) human person. There is no permanently fixed boundary-line between these two spheres of man which are continually undergoing osmosis into one another; man constantly transforms himself into the objectifications of his body, thoughts, and actions-in-the-world; he deposits himself into them without being absorbed by them (like brute-animals) and without having to deliver himself to them completely; and when he objectifies himself in this way in the world, he is constantly referred back again to himself and to God. These objectifications are 'he himself' and yet not he himself; he is in the Other and becomes the Other, but never in such a way that he can be in the Other as he is in his own self. For he is never contained totally in the

Since part of the difficulty of this text comes from its terminology, I suggest a distinction, consistent with (though not

Other which expresses him and shows him to himself and to others. And the
Other is also never completely only his expression, since the intermediary material itself includes structures alien to the person to which the person cannot refuse to submit himself up to a certain point and in varying degrees, if he is
to be at all able to express himself in the Other by forming himself into it and
so fulfil himself in this intermediary reality. Only by passing out of the depth
of his being into the world can man enter into the depth of the person where
he stands before God; this is roughly what the medieval mystic would already
have said. Thus we may say that we must distinguish between [1] the 'seminal'
person (*ursprünglicher Person*), understood as transcendent spirit and as freedom
before God; [2] the world-like and piecemeal 'intermediary reality' (*Mittleren*)
in which the person, searching for himself, must achieve himself; and [3] the
'achieved' person (*endgültigen Person*) who has freely fulfilled himself via his
intermediary reality. By the fact that the seminal person achieves himself in the
intermediary 'world' of his animated body and external surroundings, this constitutive sign (i. e., the intermediary reality of the person) becomes relatively independent; it may even remain when the act of the seminal person no longer persists.
The connection between the act of the seminal person as such and its constitutive
sign in the intermediary 'world' of the person is fluid, both as regards their
interdependence and as regards the expressive capacity of the constitutive sign.
The intermediary 'world' of the person is at the same time the medium of the
constitutive sign and the medium of influences exerted on the person by the
'Other.' Realities different from the person, the surrounding world, Nature,
heredity, other persons, and so on, reflect themselves into this intermediary
reality and create in this way an a priori basis for the possibilities of personal
self-achievement in the sphere of the constitutive expression of the person; for
personal self-achievement requires such an expression in the same medium
as the 'Other.' In this way (and only in this way) the 'outer world' influences
the person himself; it naturally does so in the many different ways in which the
intermediary sphere of personal exercise of freedom can be determined: by physical
influences, psycho-somatic influences of speech, and so on. Insofar as the seminal
person *and* the Other find fulfilment in identically the same realm of the intermediary 'world' of the person, there is 'interpenetration' in this medium between Action and Passion, between what is done and what is imposed, one's own
and the Other; one's own is covered up by the Other and the Other becomes the
property of the person; thus, the person posits the constitutive sign as the 'other
part' of himself—while, conversely, the surrounding world, originally strange to
the person, finds fulfilment by forming itself into the very medium belonging to
the person as sphere of his self-fulfilment.

"The person finds certain pre-determined structures in its nucleus, psycho-
somatic medium, and surrounding world which precede freedom and its formative
control over the person. . . . the analysis of the nature and necessity of these
structures is the task of theology, metaphysical anthropology, ethics, and all the
other anthropological sciences . . ." (STh II 286-289; ThI II 272-274).

explicit in) Rahner's ideas: Where Rahner speaks of the Other,
read " otherness," and then distinguish *two* othernesses (as
Rahner does, without saying so), which I call *first otherness*
and *second otherness*. Now (and Marcel can help us here)
first otherness is my own body, the material co-constituent of
my being (along with spirit) ; my body—as neither something
I merely have (as I have my pen, coat, or bicycle) and could
dispose of without radically changing who or what I am, nor
" something " I identically am (as is my " I " or personal center
of consciousness and freedom)—is actually the ambiguous mid-
point between being and having. As such my body is genuinely
the first otherness of my spirit and mediates my consciousness
and freedom into the world; my first otherness is the medium
of being able to be in a world at all. " World " then, though
also " otherness," is *second* otherness, not given except as mediated through *first* otherness. But " world " must be understood
correctly, as I have emphasized in calling attention to Rahner's
evolving concept of the *inter*personal; i. e., world means primarily the *other person,* and secondarily the impersonal world
of things. Man's becoming depends radically on both othernesses; his personal becoming occurs, in its first, unfree emanation of spirit " into " matter, as first otherness, necessary because human spirit is finite. His personal becoming occurs in
its second, *free* stage in and through second otherness, i. e.,
other persons, and things. (We can omit the interesting and
important truth that one's appropriation of one's body, from
birth on, as conscious and free, is itself mediated primarily
through other persons, so that, even first otherness depends
on personal second otherness.) Both are radically necessary
for human becoming, which thus shows itself to be *inter*personal
becoming, the radical necessity of community for becoming a
person.

Rahner neglects to distinguish these two othernesses, speaking merely of *the* other. Thus at one moment his " intermediary
reality " is his own body (" his animated corporeality ") and
at the next moment, without his signaling the shift, it is the
other person and the world (" the external world of equally real

persons and things ") ; and then he turns right around and
resumes speaking of " *this* intermediary reality," when he should
maintain the clarity of two othernesses. May I suggest a
second reading of the text with this distinction in mind: at
first you will be trying to decide which of the two othernesses
is meant by this or that description Rahner offers; but then,
I trust, remaining obscurities aside, some new insight will
emerge into Rahner's concept of the meaning of finite spirit's
radical dependence on otherness as two othernesses for becoming, with primacy to the second, because free. Only then
will his concept of person as becoming become a metaphysics
of personization as interpersonal becoming.

This point clear, a few more points must be made. Once into
the realm of second otherness (or the interpersonal and "inner-
worldly," as SW put it), we must distinguish three concepts
but only two beings. The three concepts are (1) the (potential) person as an original source of possibilities for becoming, (2) the same person as "achieved," i.e., as having
enacted these possibilities through, with, and in (3) others
(persons and things). Only two beings (persons) are meant,
not three; one same individual is called original or "seminal"
and then, after interaction with the "intermediary reality,"
becomes an "achieved" person.[5] Despite the neutral (and
therefore almost neuter) ring of the term "intermediary reality"
(perhaps intermediate or medium says it better), primarily
another person is meant. Buber would speak here of the "between," and Rahner too speaks of a *Zwischen*.[6]

We are not to think of this intermediate, therefore, as some-

---

[5] ". . . [T]he 'seminal person' is a *continuing* dimension of the one person,
fulfilled in the 'achieved person' via the 'intermediary reality of the person'"
(Trans. note, ThI II 272).

[6] See STh III 314; ThI III 264. The point in this passage is that in a perfect
community of love there is no third something which forms the medium for the
two persons in their personizations, but rather they mediate one another. As
with Buber, the between of communion is constituted by the self-transcending
acts of the two persons and is not distinct from them. See my article, "Person
and Community. Buber's Category of the Between," *Philosophy Today*, 17 (1973)
62-83.

thing to which we relate across a chasm of non-being; no false
bridge is needed. Man is already always in the world by being
sensible. "There is no fixed boundary-line between these two
spheres of man which are continually undergoing osmosis into
one another; man constantly transforms himself into the objectifications of his body, thoughts, and actions-in-the-world."

The best way to explain what Rahner means by the constitution of the intermediate, the "Other," would be to review his
explanation of sensibility in SW. Suffice it to say that the
other is absolutely necessary, not only for the minimal act of
sensation, but for everything which depends on sensation, including personal becoming; there never was any doubt about
this, nor is Rahner merely restating that familiar thesis: he
is saying that personal becoming depends on a *personal* other,
and, even more important to this theological focus, that the
ultimate becoming, even though this is through God, as ultimate person, must also occur in and through becoming in the
world. Thus whatever difficulty remains in the text comes from
Rahner's terminology, not from the ideas. While he is adapting
the thesis of SW, i. e., man's need to turn to phantasms, his need
for being and acting in and with the world in order to be and
act at all, he is also saying the "the world" means not only the
impersonal world of things but mainly the personal world. Furthermore, it is not just an "already out there" world but the
world as "formed by the union of his animated corporeality
and embodied spirituality together with their concrete, material, and propositional objectifications, and by the external
world of equally real persons and things as well as by the objectifications produced there by 'external' actions."

The intermediary reality is the union or combination of my
action and that of the persons and things of the world. There
is something from the "inside" (of the knower) and something
from the "outside," and it is only the union which is "world."
In other words, the world is partly "constituted" by the person interacting with it, not in the sense that anything becomes
different in the things themselves, but in the sense that those

" things " become the particular objects sensed, known, and loved by this person partly because of how and what he contributes to the concrete acts of sensing, knowing, and loving. The senses are already always making a difference to knowledge (and consequently to love) because the content of human cognition and appetition depends on them. " Only by passing out of the depth of his being *into the world,* can man enter into the depth of the person where he stands before God." [7] Let us admit that Rahner is only *beginning* to make explicit his primacy of second otherness as *personal* world; I would never claim that he has, in this essay, fully arrived at his final position. It still seems wordless, not dialogal.

Now there is a further possible misunderstanding of the intermediate sphere of reality because of the possibility of persons being " intermediates " for one another. We should expect that persons fulfil and achieve themselves only in other persons; thus two persons would be, in Rahner's terms, all three: both would be seminal *and* achieved *and* intermediaries-for-the-other. Thus there is no problem in his saying: " insofar as the seminal person and the Other find fulfilment in identically the same realm of the intermediary ' world ' of the person there is ' interpenetration ' in this medium. . . ." This means more than that two persons unite in some third object.[8] To " find fulfilment " in the " world of the person " is for two persons to interpenetrate one another, as persons, i. e., as freely opening to one another. The rest of the paragraph refers to Rahner's metaphysics of sensation: the self loses itself, in its senses, to the other (the sensed object), while that other becomes part of the self, etc. But it must not be missed that Rahner is striving

[7] See the essay on the unity of love of God and love of neighbor (STh VI 227-298; ThI VI 231-249), to be treated later. Rahner is consistent in opposing any mysticism that attempts to bypass the world; see his VP.

[8] " Thus we have the third kind of community we must distinguish, the *community of love.* It is founded upon a kind of mutual sharing of one's personal being, which is carried by love over into the other and intermingles with his. Here the basis of community is no longer a third term in which men meet one another: in love of person for person they meet one another in themselves " (STh III 314; ThI III 264).

(the language reflects it) to make this model work also on the level of person and of the free interaction of persons fulfilling and achieving (personizing) themselves in one another as necessary " media " or " mediations." He is thus attempting to apply to the realm of will and love the principles worked out (in SW) in the context of intellect and cognition. To apply a model from one realm to another realm causes difficulty and confusion: at one moment the medium seems to be the interaction of the senses and the world; at another it seems to be interaction with another person. The point, of course, is that we meet persons in the world and can, to a limited extent, deal with persons as with any being in the world. Rahner simply leaves to us the task of recognizing where the realm of freedom enters to transform our understanding of " medium " into " person." In other words, Rahner is again talking about personal becoming. He is affirming that becoming a person demands a " medium," an " intermediary reality," an " intermediate," basing his " deduction " of man's sociality on the metaphysics of turning to phantasms.

Now since our purpose in studying this essay is fulfilled when we have gleaned Rahner's ideas on person, we omit its many other aspects. We have noted Rahner's increasing emphasis on the social nature of becoming and have indicated the metaphysical basis he provides for man's dependence on other. His is admittedly, even here, not fully a " personalist " doctrine of interpersonness; it is based on an *almost* impersonal metaphysics of cognition (the " almost " cautions us not to think of SW alone but to remember how love is placed at the very heart of knowledge in HW); his special focus is on the facts of sensation as a composite act of the senser and the sensed. He has nevertheless advanced his concept of personal becoming, while leaving until another time a more personal treatment of the interpersonal.[9]

---

[9] This is the place to mention a few other texts concerned with man's reference to others, with his need for others in order to become himself.

"(A) Man is to be conceived of as spirit, and as a bodily spirit: both together, so that he is body in order to be spirit, and only is a spiritual person as such (in the

There is one final point in this essay. It concerns the ontological meaning of the fulfilment and achievement of person.
As noted, Rahner's concept of personal becoming is ontological,
not merely psychological, not merely on the epiphenomenal or
accidental level; the free self-disposition culminating in death
goes to the very core and center of person as such. In this

concrete) by incorporation. ' Corporeality ' is understood in the first place as spatio-
temporal determination. Thus man has a world, i. e., he is a here and now in the
one continuum of space and time and is himself a spirit who has a space-time. He is
not a personal spirit first ' and then ' also an entity with a body. But bodiliness
is the necessary mode in which alone he can reach the achievement of his spiritual being.

" (B) The personal spirit is a spirit referred to others. An absolutely lonely spirit
is a contradiction in itself and—so far as it is possible at all—is Hell. If (A)
is correct, then what (B) means is that the bodily spirit which is man exists by
necessity of nature (also) in relation to a Thou, which is itself present in its own
spatio-temporal world as such. It is not only as an isolated person but also as
isolated *man* that an individual man is incapable of perfection—or is Hell. Where
there is man, there is necessarily—not only in fact—*human* community, i. e., bodily
personal community, personally spatio-temporal community " (STh I 313; ThI
I 287).

" Being a free, personal spirit, he is never merely a function of society, and
yet, being a corporeal being, he never has an individuality which is absolutely unrelated to society. He is always at home with himself, but he can never see
himself except through the objectivations of his spirit: in the corporeal word,
in the objectivated thought of his science and philosophy, in his artistic work. He
is unique and irreplaceable, but can only find himself when he forgets himself
in the love of another to whom he turns " (STh IV 474; ThI IV 383). Note
how this last phrase echoes *conversio ad phantasmata*, the " turn to phantasms: "
human knowledge is a turn to phantasms, human love, a " turn to other persons."

". . . [M]an is precisely in this way open, one who does not possess within himself what he essentially needs in order to be himself " (STh III 42; ThI III 31).

" Man is placed in an ineradicable dualism of two basic lines of self-fulfilment;
he is a being who is thrust out of himself into the world and the human community, and he is a being who turns back upon himself. This double bent, to
take possession of himself and what is not himself, in knowledge and love, constitutes his essential nature. The going out of himself and entering into himself
condition each other. If he did not go out into the world, to the Other as ' thou '
and (so far as one can still call this a going out) to God, he would find nothing on
entering into himself but the hellish emptiness and empty isolation of the damned.
And if he only went out of himself, then he would indeed be alienated from himself, lost, scattered piecemeal. Gathering and scattering, entry into oneself and
going out of oneself belong to each other essentially " (SG 477-478; see also 480;
MG III 110-111; see also 114).

essay the term nucleus is used and means the same thing. He speaks, in the context of conversion, of " a fundamental transformation of the whole nucleus of the person." It is clear this means a re-orientation of the person's *freedom*. Free acts, therefore, reach to the very " nucleus " of the person, from which they issue. It means no merely accidental becoming, but a determination deciding the very who (and, in part, the what, i. e., that " part " of nature that is habits or " second " nature) of the person in his ontological essence. Without such a position, Rahner's concept of personal becoming would lack truly metaphysical significance. Person becomes essentially in his free acts, especially in his free, *ethical* acts.[10] Thus again: *The person's ethical self-enactment (self-disposition) is his ontological self-enactment.* Thus, consistent with his understanding of death as present through the whole of a life, Rahner recognizes that one's ethical self-disposition ordinarily does not come about through a dramatic conversion, but through the gradual taking a position that results from many daily self-enactments; one constructs one's total attitude by the many acts of ordinary life:

[10] " Is man ontologically and ethically really constructed in so loose and pluralistic a fashion in the carrying out of his existence, that one ' piece ' of the man could be quite sound and another quite corrupt, and that then in the final result the whole would have to share the lot of the corrupt part? It will surely be more correct (in spite of all the various species of virtues and vices) to conceive of man, where he disposes of himself as a whole before God in freedom, as really stamping the whole of his being through and through (which does not necessarily mean that he succeeds in this ' wholly ' at every moment) and that ways of behavior which contradict *this* decision in freedom do not possess that deep-rooted source in the innermost core of the person which is a prerequisite for an action which is also subjectively gravely culpable, even though such a personally peripheral way of behavior may be *objectively* of great and even the greatest gravity. . . . The real fundamental decision of a person has rather the tendency to integrate into itself the life of the person in its entirety. . . . The essential difference is also without any doubt founded upon the essentially different personal depth from which the particular act as related to the core of the person proceeds and, if maintained in its process from the person, molds the person. If this is correct, then the same *essential* difference (not merely a difference of degree!) must in the nature of things subsist *also* between *good* acts. There are ' light ' and ' grave ' good deeds " (STh III 430-431 and nn. 2 and 4; ThI III 365-366 and nn. 15 and 17).

... there can be (according to the quite usual teaching of theology) a ' virtual,' implicit repentance, i. e., one in which the person does not directly fix his gaze upon his past action and renounce it as such, but without any such reflection on his past (because he does not think of it or does not explicitly recognize it any longer as sinful) he freely takes up an attitude toward moral good of such a kind that even without any express reflection his earlier attitude is in its essential core given up and rejected. How much of the growth in moral maturity and wisdom of years does take place in this form.[11]

2. *Time: Materializing eternity.* From STh III, devoted to theology of the spiritual life, we will only pause briefly over one essay, "The Comfort of Time." It is " in time " that man becomes. This fact has many levels of meaning and interpretation. Although man's free self-disposition is rooted in a spiritual principle, it takes place in time, and thus personal becoming is temporal. This is a familiar notion, worked out in SW, repeated in the essays on concupiscence, death, freedom, and guilt. Here Rahner does not advance his basic doctrine significantly, but shows another side of becoming, i. e., its ontological link with the maturation of years.

The older we become, the surer we are that we truly are. It is perfectly true that one thing cannot be taken away from us, . . . viz., what we were and hence are. It is becoming and not what has become which passes away. What perishes is not the secret extract of life but the process of its preparation. When this process, which we normally call our life, has come to an end, then the perfect has arrived and this is ourselves as we have become in freedom.[12]

We experience, with time and maturation, that a personality is truly something laboriously constructed, and not just in a psychological sense. An old saw says something about every man over fifty being responsible for his face, and we all recognize some truth in this. But how much truer is it to say this of the deep core of the person, unseen and so much harder to know.

[11] STh III 434-435; ThI III 369.
[12] STh III 173; ThI III 144-145.

When we take any cross-section from a person's life and compare it with another, years earlier or later, we recognize how unpredictable is the person, how impossible to say who and what he will become.

So long as this eternal element in us is still in the process of becoming, it remains an open question as to what it will be: either something freely given over to God in his grace or something refused to God and thus condemned to its own closed finiteness. This decision can take place at any moment in time, it can even change (as long as we still have room for freedom in the finite). But then such a decision (once it has really been taken) is on every occasion concerned with disposing the whole person, no matter how much the material of the life in which it is exercised may change. Such a decision does not only determine the disposition of the whole person (since it determines its eternal destiny as a whole and not merely a part of our existence, merely 'implicating' everything else); it also acts as the result of the always present totality of the person and thus out of the latter's previous life, because only the whole person can master the whole. It risks the life which has gone before; it works with the gains of its previous life. It may do this in a more or less intensive manner, i. e., it may win a greater or lesser amount of the personal reality which is still possibility into the 'essence' of life preserved in the (apparent) past, but it cannot act other than as the act of the one (as such) who had lived this life up till now in 'this' particular way. . . . The intensity, the existential depth, the freely acquired personal characteristic, all of which have developed in one's life up till then, all enter as intrinsic elements into the new act of decision and put their stamp on it. In every moment of the free, personal achievement of existence, the past becomes an inner, essential principle of the present and its acts. . . . the present 'disposition' necessarily contains the whole previous life (at least this), because one cannot turn the clock back; one's past is conserved in the present of the person out of which arises every act by which a person really decides about himself as a whole in freedom.[13]

Note the continuity with Rahner's conception of freedom, the person's power to enact himself in the direction of the values around which his whole life revolves. "Time" is another way of saying that the human person, because finite and therefore material, *becomes*. Time is a comfort because we *need* time

---

[13] STh III 175-176; ThI III 145-147.

in order to become ourselves, and we are *given* time to do so. Even what seems to be an instant reorientation or conversion really must be understood as a summing up of a whole life-*time*. But it is not necessary to think of a " lot of time." Actually, very little " material " is required as a basis for that self-disposition which effects one's eternal destiny, and the same material can be used differently and thus serve for a person's fulfilment as well as his vitiation. But the main point is that when time has run its course, personal becoming is essentially complete (whether in good or evil), with purgatory and heaven or hell being the " catching-up " of nature with person. Again note that to speak of time as running and as having run its course is to speak of death as present throughout all of a life, of death as the " polishing " or finishing point of a life; it is also to speak of freedom as the power to stamp a life with a character. As Rahner puts it, " if we are saved, then the person we have become is the full realization of the one we were able to be; there is nothing left over. In the end, the law according to which we began—if it is fulfilled at all—is fulfilled completely." [14] To the objection that no one could possibly fulfil in his lifetime all his possibilities, he answers by agreeing, but assigns these " factual " possibilities to a different realm; he is concerned with *ethical* fulfilment and in this realm there is not the same infinite range of possibilities, but more a simple question of Yes or No, not one of degree.[15]

---

[14] STh III 179; ThI III 150.

[15] " . . .[O]ne must not overrate the significance of the difference in external situation for the proper achievement of man's existence. For otherwise it would be a strange arrangement of life by God, if in most cases of this free spiritual creature—which after all is called to realize its being freely—this realization did not come to its proper fulfilment. It is not necessary here to attempt to prove philosophically that there can be no spiritual creatures who, without any fault of their own, do not reach their proper perfection. . . . May we in a sense ' postulate ' that God leads everyone in such a way that each one finds his complete perfection if he finds perfect happiness at all? . . . no one escapes the necessity (now or later) of really having to catch up with himself by hard effort, so that eternal life may really be the full result of time. If we remember that ultimately good and evil are distinguished not as ' more ' and ' less ' but as ' yes ' and ' no '—even though the formally evil is a deficit in an existent—then it is not really so difficult to ensure that every life in the long run grows into the whole fulness of reality

This said, Rahner carries through to the point that this "final completion" is a full and perfect completion: "Purgatory can be conceived absolutely as the integration of all the manifold dimensions of man into the one basic decision of man (which no longer changes after death)." [16] Now to speak of "the one basic decision" recalls what we noted, under the heading of freedom, about the value certain acts possess because of the depth of self involved in them. Free ethical acts were identified as those enacting man to his very core. Rahner again affirms this doctrine in the present context, but puts it in terms of "mortal and venial." [17]

which is implanted in it. Thus, there only remains the question whether it fulfils itself in an absolute yes or absolute no to God. Hence, only these two possibilities and not merely shadowy forms of life are possible where the end has arrived in its complete finality. One may catch up with oneself more slowly or more quickly, more actively or more passively; but to remain forever 'behind oneself' is a merely abstract possibility which does not seem to belong to the world and history of the personal spirit. . . . Anyone who thinks differently seems to us to be thinking too much in terms of the experiences of the material world. In the world of the quantitative there certainly is more and less, and in it there cannot be anything which could not just as well be more, since in this world (as long as it keeps its proper form) perfection is impossible. But where there is spirit and freedom, there is final completion" (STh III 182-183; ThI III 152-153).

[16] "The payment of a punishment of this kind [purgatory] could in this case be conceived only as a maturing process of the person, through which, though gradually, all the powers of the human being become slowly integrated into the basic decision of the free person. . . . The profundity of the 'option fondamentale' which has been made during life can no longer grow in the life beyond. But this, in its turn, does not exclude the possibility of conceiving man as still really maturing in the purgatory condition of 'Purgatory.' We are not, at any rate, in any way compelled by the dogma of the Church to think of 'Purgatory' as a purely passive endurance of vindictive punishments, which, when they have been 'paid for' in this sense, release man in exactly the same condition in which he commenced this state of purification. For not every 'change' or 'process of maturing' must necessarily be already what is theologically described as growth in grace, increase of merit, advance in the degree of glory. Such a change of condition in the degree of maturity can just as well be conceived as an integration of the whole stratified human reality into that free decision and grace which, having been made and won in this life, is in itself definitive" (STh II 206-207; ThI II 197-198).

[17] "[T]he basic decisions about the relationship towards God (and thus also about its measure) are not really built up of those factors which are present in

What we find, therefore, in this essay on time, is a concept of person that is totally consistent with Rahner's basic principles. Personal becoming is the free disposition of self; a disposing of self can go, precisely because it is free, in either of two directions, and the person one becomes, the ontological reality of who and what one is, is in one's own hands. No one, not even God, can so love another as to make that other become a person despite himself, passively, receptively: personization is self-personization. In our loving others we leave them free; it is their response which is their own loving self-personization.[18] No one's love for another creates that other a person but rather provides the possibilities for the other's self-enactment. And time is the necessary " accompaniment " to finite spirits, i. e., to spirits who are in matter, and there-

the case of venial sin and of the corresponding existentially morally good, 'slight' acts. It is in the latter rather than in the former basic decisions as such (insofar as these are the result of a whole life) that the 'more or less' is at home. . . . It is an obvious fact that every mortal sin as such, regarded in itself, tries to integrate the whole of life into a no to God and hence is in itself the most terrible thing a man can do. It is also clear that, as a consequence, every such action certainly does not come up to the possibilities of spiritual, personal (supernatural) self-actualization which the person could have achieved had he not sinned. . . . However much 'experience' may seem to contradict it, there is nothing in the world which could be so indispensable for one's own self-realization that it could justify and give meaning to opposition to the holy will of God. Everything which signifies a fulfilment for man can be found on the way to God, even though this way may seem to lead only into the desolate and empty wastes of the kind of renunciation which makes man miserable. . . . Even sin, therefore, is always a real piece of existential realization, of real self-fulfilment, a part of the way towards the real goal (however much the imagination balks at this). One should indeed say that the deeper and the more radical sin is, the more the sinner involves and achieves his own person in this, and the more he must realize (even though in a radically false direction) the possibility of his existence. . . . For in everything one has done in the past, one really did only one thing after all (even though it became part of a synthesis together with the many other things one did, a synthesis which characterizes it even in its fulfilment), viz., one tried to attain oneself completely. . . . Eternity does not, properly speaking, come after time but rather is the fulfilment of time " (STh III 183-188; ThI III 153-157).

[18] ". . .[A] direct love for a man cannot penetrate efficaciously and creatively to that point where the man is in reality and properly 'himself.' All direct love does not reach as far as the real self, to the 'soul' in the sense of the capacity to make a personal choice for salvation " (STh III 322; ThI III 271).

fore cannot dispose of themselves fully in one time-less act, as
do pure spirits. Time is a "comfort," therefore, because it
seems good to man that he is unable to constitute himself completely evil in one act (and that he cannot constitute himself
good in one act is accepted as the necessary other side of the
coin); and it seems good that there is something about purgatory
which can be thought to resemble time, thus allowing the last
maturation of the person.

3. *Symbol: Materializing Meaning, Embodying Spirit.*[19] To
study Rahner's essay on symbol, as well as the later essay on
the identity of spirit and matter and the *quaestio disputata* on
hominization, is to feel oneself returning to the problematic of
SW, i. e., to the constitution of man's basic, "starting" essence
in its self-perfecting actions; all have strong philosophical content. Thus, were we following a thematic rather than a chronological order, these three (symbol, spirit and matter, and
hominization) would have been discussed with SW and HW.
But this would have meant mixing philosophy with theology,
at least to the extent that Rahner used theological as well as
philosophical sources in those essays,[20] and meant spanning almost twenty-five years, thereby obscuring the evolution of his
Personbegriff. Instead, note both consistency and development: symbol (because human, not subhuman or superhu-
man) is a phenomenon of self-becoming, personization. This

[19] A strict chronological order would suggest VP, NG, MG, and DEC before
STh IV. VP and MG, however, are better considered supplementary to more
detailed treatments elsewhere in Rahner's writings. NG's chapters on the individual and on ethics belong with the study of the individual in DEC, the former
complementing the latter (and later) treatments. Rather than moving to the
properly ethical realm so soon, we would do better to spend more time with the
foundations of ethics. This means first of all trying to establish man's nature
still more clearly (e. g., the essay on symbol), and then trying to advance our
understanding of the free act (e. g., the essays on leisure and power). In studying
these essays from STh IV, we always have one question in mind, viz., their
relevance for person in his task of becoming.

[20] The essay on symbol is called "The Theology of Symbol;" that on spirit and
matter is subtitled "A Christian Understanding;" the subtitle of *Hominization*
is "The Evolutionary Origin of Man as a Theological Problem."

next textual unit [21] represents nothing really new or startling; it is simply an attempt to use the notion of symbol in an ontological way. Rahner shows that the underlying idea is Thomist:

[21] "All beings are by their nature symbolic, because they necessarily ' express' themselves in order to attain their own nature. . . . Our task will be to look for the highest and most primordial manner in which one reality can represent another—considering the matter primarily from the formal ontological point of view. And we call this supreme and primal representation, in which one reality renders another present (primarily ' for itself' and only secondarily for others), a symbol: the representation which allows the other ' to be there.' . . . A plurality in an original and an originally superior unity can only be understood as follows: the ' one' develops, the plural stems from an original ' one,' in a relationship of origin and consequence; the original unity, which also forms the unity which unites the plural, maintains itself while resolving itself and ' dis-closing' itself into a plurality in order to find itself precisely there. . . . Being *as* such, and hence *as* one (*ens* as *unum*), for the fulfilment of its being and its unity, emerges into a plurality. . . . But this means that each being, as a unity, possesses a plurality— implying perfection—formed by the special derivativeness of the plural from the original unity: the plural is in agreement with its source in a way which corresponds to its origin, and hence is ' expression' of its origin by an agreement which it owes to its origin. Since this holds for being in general, we may say that each being forms, in its own way, more or less perfectly according to its degree of being, something distinct from itself and yet one with itself, ' for' its own fulfilment. . . . every being as such possesses a plurality as intrinsic element of its significant unity; this plurality constitutes itself, by virtue of its origin from an original unity, as the way to fulfil the unity . . . being is of itself symbolic, because it must realize itself through a plurality in unity. . . . The self-constitutive act whereby a being constitutes itself as a plurality which leads to its fulfilment . . . is however the condition of possibility of possession of self in knowledge and love . . . a being ' comes to itself' in its expression, in the derivative agreement of the differentiated which is preserved as the perfection of the unity. For realization as plurality and as possession of self cannot be disparate elements simply juxtaposed in a being, since possession of self (in knowledge and love) is not just an element, but *the* content of that which we call being (and hence self-realization). And it comes to itself in the measure in which it realizes itself by constituting a plurality. But this means that each being—inasmuch as it is, has, and realizes being—is itself primarily ' symbolic.' It expresses itself and possesses itself by doing so. It gives itself away from itself into the ' other,' and there finds itself in knowledge and love, because it is by constituting the inward ' other' that it comes to . . . its self-fulfilment, which is the presupposition or the act of being present to itself in knowledge and love. . . . a being, to attain fulfilment, constitutes the differentiation which is retained in the unity. . . . A being comes to itself by means of ' expression,' insofar as it comes to itself at all. The expression, i. e., the ' symbol' . . . is the way of knowledge of self, possession of self, in general " (STh IV 278-285; ThI IV 224-230).

. . . the manifest, visible ' figure ' on the one hand (*eidos* and *morphe* together), and the ' essence ' which gives rise to the figure on the other hand, make up together the full sense of one concept. For how does the figure-forming essence of a being (material, to start with) constitute and perfect itself? It does so by really projecting its visible figure outside itself as its—symbol, its appearance, which allows it to be there, which brings it out to existence in the world: and in doing so, it retains it—' possessing itself in the other.' The essence is there for itself and for others precisely through its appearance. . . . But apart from the concept of formal causality, there are other concepts of Thomist ontology which belong to the sphere of the self-realization which is a self-proclamation and hence—in the broadest but original sense—constitutive of a symbol. Here the concept of ' resultance ' should be noted. St. Thomas does not merely think of a finite being as a reality simply complete, constituted by God in its essence and faculties. He does not merely see it as a passive and static reality, which then sets a number of accidental acts, of an immanent or transient nature, which emanate indeed from the substance by efficient causality and to this extent ' determine ' it, but leave it untouched in its inner nature. He also recognizes an inner self-realization of the total essence itself . . . prior to its accidental ' second ' acts: a self-realization which objectively and conceptually, according to St. Thomas, cannot be simply reduced to formal and material causality . . . and can still less be subsumed under the categories of the ordinary (second) ' activity.' Thus St. Thomas recognizes, e.g., a ' resultance,' an ' out-flowing ' of the faculties from the substance. Thus for him the essence as a whole builds itself up—for the faculties belong to the totality of the essence, in spite of their being accidents; the substantial kernel emanates into its faculties and only thus attains its own possibilities; it finds itself—since it must be spiritual and so on by projecting from itself the ' otherness ' of its faculties.[22]

Now this is just the doctrine of SW in other words—resultance and out-flowing refer, of course, to emanation—as becomes clear when Rahner applies the notion of symbol to man's " body." Thus we see that " the bodily reality of man, and so his acts in the dimensions of space and time, history and society, are conceived of as symbolic realities embodying his person and his primordial decisions; " [23] " the human body . . . is the

[22] STh IV 286-289; ThI IV 231-233.
[23] STh IV 300; ThI IV 242-243.

natural symbol of man;"[24] ". . . the body can and must be considered as the symbol, i. e., as the symbolic reality of man. . . ."[25]

Essential to finitude is relation to otherness, both in being (creation, origin from otherness) and in becoming: if a being could fulfill its needs in and of itself there would be no way to understand why it had not already done so; becoming is always through otherness: "The symbol strictly speaking (symbolic reality) is the self-realization of a being in the other, which is constitutive of its essence. Where there is such a self-realization in the other—as the necessary mode of the fulfilment of its own essence—we have a symbol of the being in question."[26] Thus ". . . the body is the symbol of the soul, inasmuch as it is formed as the self-realization of the soul, though it is not adequately this . . . the soul renders itself present and makes its 'appearance' in the body which is distinct from it."[27]

Personal becoming, the necessarily interpersonal expression of finite being, is clearly the central working concept for Rahner's whole anthropology. Symbol means spirit's act outside itself toward others in order to enact its own reality. Rahner sees the symbols of the heart, the sacraments, and the Church itself as lending themselves to this developed notion of symbol, as clarified in its light. For our purposes the basic notion of person becoming through incarnate action is the main point to be grasped. If this notion is clearer for some when expressed in terms of symbol, then pausing over this essay was useful. It is not a necessary constituent of Rahner's philosophical concept of person, but another approach and expression.

We now have Rahner's sketch of the broad sweep of human life as a whole, unfolding in time, within the dialectic of spirit and matter, person and nature, culminating in death, whose final decision effects heaven or hell, purgatory being the last fulfilment of nature catching up with person, all this through

[24] STh IV 301; ThI IV 243.
[25] STh IV 305; ThI IV 246.
[26] STh IV 290; ThI IV 234.
[27] STh IV 306; ThI IV 247.

free ethical acts in general and love for others in particular, and everything flowing from the metaphysical principles of spirit, matter, and becoming as worked out in his philosophical works. Rahner continues working more and more on the "fine points," the details that fill out this broad sweep from birth to death. Obviously the main focus is still on the free act, with personal becoming accomplished through the most excellent of free acts, love,[28] which Rahner at least stated in HW and studied in detail in STh V and VI. Becoming is, however, not restricted to love; person is enacted by every use of freedom. Therefore the full range of free acts, particularly the ethical, because a person enacts himself as a whole through them, must be studied. Since freedom is itself only understood in terms of freedom *for*, not just freedom *from*, we face the problems of work and leisure, of freedom as task, of the proper use of power, of the range of man's self-creation (man as experiment, as changing his nature, as the new man, with the new morality, all in later volumes). But where philosophically can we locate these and questions of theology, religion, grace, Christ, the supernatural existential, etc.? I must deal with them as Rahner does, under the aegis of the anonymous Christian, proposing to each person certain explanations and interpretations of his experience.*

[28] Love has yet to receive Rahner's attention in a separate essay; and later both freedom and love receive new treatment in second essays (thus my Freedom I and II, Love I and II).

* Editor's Note—As stated in the Preface, three sections have been omitted: (A) "Work and Leisure: Uses of Time, Uses of Freedom," (B) "Power: the A Priori of Freedom in Particular and of Enactment in General," and (C) "Salvation History, Personization History." For the interested reader, the following references indicate the relevant texts interpreted by the author in these sections.

A. STh IV 469; ThI IV 379. STh IV 475-478; ThI IV 383-387. STh IV 476-477; ThI IV 384-385. STh IV 478-479; ThI IV 386-387. STh IV 482; ThI IV 389.

B. STh IV 495; ThI IV 399. STh IV 501; ThI IV 403. STh IV 487-488; ThI IV 393. STh IV 489-490; ThI IV 394-395. STh IV 491; ThI IV 395-396. STh IV 491-492; ThI IV 396. STh IV 502, 503, 505; ThI IV 404, 405, 406.

C. STh V 115; ThI V 97. STh V 116-117; ThI V 98-99. STh V 122-124; ThI V 103-105. STh V 238-241; ThI V 209-212. STh V 503; ThI V 446-447.

4. *Love I: There is one commandment: Thou shalt love!* The more specific intention of this essay is to compare the " commandment " of love with the other commandments. It will be enough to take the two concepts of love and commandment and see how they relate to one another: for Rahner love is the personizing act *par excellence,* and the commandment to love is the commandment to become a person.

After stating that ". . . every moral value is ultimately a personal value . . . ," [29] Rahner relates love to *person* right from the start of this essay, calling it the only value-response proper to person.[30] He then proceeds to relate it to *person as becoming*:

. . . as long as we regard the virtues only statically in their ' nature,' they do in fact implicitly contain each other, always presupposing that we see their full nature [*volles Wesen*] in its adequate realization [*Wesensvollzug*]. But precisely this realization of nature has its own history—it ' *becomes* '—and is not always fully given; a virtue realizes itself only gradually and thereby, it is true, realizes also love. Morality is the free personal acceptance of one's own pre-established nature, confidently coming to grips with one's own dynamic reality in all its united though multiple dimensions and precisely coming to grips also with that nature which *realizes itself only when it turns lovingly to another person* and when it accepts its own nature as the nature of the mystery of love. This acceptance does however, have its history; it is not present all at once (as in the case of the angels), but *is temporal and becomes.* This means, however, that something already ' is ' at a particular moment in time and can already be described in its nature; it means that there already is ' something realized ' which nevertheless comes to its proper completion only in the completed whole of which it is but an element. We must not overlook the mystery of the temporal moment in the history of a temporal being . . . man's existential acceptance of his own nature has a history; man always discovers new dimensions of his own personal nature (and in the same way and at the same time necessarily discovers such different dimensions of the personal reality of others). [Each moral becoming is] . . . a temporal moment in a movement tending towards

---

[29] STh V 495; ThI V 440.

[30] " The value-response due to the person, however, is simply love and nothing else, since every other evaluation lowers the value of the person " (*ibid.*).

the total acceptance of the whole personal being of man; this ' already ' acquired individual virtue becomes perfect only once it is really integrated into the totality of the acceptance of one's own nature, i. e., love.[31]

Rahner identifies the historical becoming of the person with self-enactment of his nature as that of a loving person. This is by no means the first time that love has been placed fully at the center of personal becoming. When freedom was discussed, love was seen to be the optimum use of that freedom, already identified as the domain of those acts which most profoundly came from and returned to the innermost core or heart of the person. Free acts, it was said then, tended to integrate the entire person as a whole in a certain value-direction. Now *love* is seen to be *the full self-enactment of the person*:

. . . love is not the end of the integration of these partial moments of man's self-realization: rather, *love is this self-realization itself as such and as a whole,* without this wholeness being merely the sumtotal of moments. . . . *In love, the person realizes himself completely,* and by love, everything which had already happened previously in the spiritual history of the person's gradual self-discovery is accomplished and integrated in this one act . . . *it is the sole complete self-realization of the one person in its very unity. . . .*[32]

Rahner here affirms the basic notion of person as an evolving potential. Love, as referring to person *as a whole,* is the index of person. One becomes a person in love, learns who and what he is in love,[33] realizes (enacts) himself completely in love. But love itself is also subject to becoming, and thus *the development of love in the person indicates the very becoming of that person.* Rahner consequently identifies the history of one's loving with the history of one's personal becoming. Love itself, therefore, is a potential to be enacted.[34] Here we see

---

[31] STh V 496-498; ThI V 441-442: some emphasis added.

[32] STh V 498-499; ThI V 443; my emphasis.

[33] " . . . The one person . . . himself . . . learns who and what he is (as a whole person) when he loves " (STh V 499; ThI V 443).

[34] " Love may already be present and yet may still have the task of realizing itself. The temporal nature of man necessitates not only a gradual temporal approach to love in successive stages, but necessitates also the kind of historical nature of love itself to be in successive stages. Love may already be present—it

more clearly than ever just how central to Rahner's entire anthropology is the concept of becoming, of a potentiality to be enacted in time, linked with the equally basic concept of dynamism toward the full becoming, or enactment, of that potentiality. The following text is one of the best for stating this concept and relating it to the becoming of the person in and through love:

. . . the full nature of any virtue even as such exists only once it has fulfilled and lost itself in love. The concept of the ' fulfilled nature ' of a virtue is certainly somewhat obscure and vague. Yet, if we do not wish to do harm to the fitting description of *reality as it really is in its becoming,* then we must be careful not to face this concept with the dilemma that a being is or is not, and that there is no third possibility. An embryo is also already a human being; human nature is already ' present ' in the three-day old embryo; a beginning has been made which is irrevocably the beginning of a human being, and is this and nothing else. Yet man is nevertheless a being having eyes and capable of singing, a being which loves, and it cannot be said that these possibilities have nothing to do with the nature of man. The nature of the embryo is intelligible—even though it is a reality by itself—only in and in view of what it is yet to become. Potency is not only prior to act but is an active potency only in its active intentness towards act, and this dynamism of the full development of nature is something without which potency itself cannot be understood. This dynamism itself, however, can be grasped only from the point of view of full act and the full realization of the nature. Hence, *the notion of a full realization of nature* (which must not be understood in a quantitative and additive sense) *is a necessary one.* Hence it can also be said that it is possible to find human self-realization in a stage in which it is not yet fully present (although the real movement towards full self-realization has already begun, and we therefore find ourselves already in the moral sphere), and then we are dealing with man's individual virtues which are not the same as love. *This human self-realization can also be viewed as full self-realization* (even though still continuing historically) *which indeed ' engages ' man completely, and then we have love.*[35]

may, in other words, already be man's ' commitment in freedom ' in the very core of the person—and yet the integration of all the dimensions and capacities of man, his love of God with his whole heart and might, may still be a task not yet completed by this man ' (STh V 499; ThI V 443-444).

[35] STh V 499-500; ThI V 444: my emphasis. " It is an internally connected history

Furthermore, Rahner's apparent digression concerning Aquinas's view that love must come at the beginning of personization serves to *emphasize* the nature of person as *becoming*.[36] Rahner partly criticizes Aquinas's view precisely because it does not allow for temporal historical development in personal commitment (love). In Rahner's view, a person's first real ". . . taking possession of himself by his freedom . . ."[37] does occur comparatively early in his history, but it is preceded by ". . . a groping ' preliminary practice ' for the real total self-realization, a ' training period ' in which man already has certain moral experiences which are a necessary presupposition for his realizing sufficient matter to make it seriously possible to speak of a real self-commitment."[38] Such a conception of love as the *beginning* obviously implies that love must develop, since love is also the *end*. Thus the basic and initial decision to love, no matter how weak and " formal " (the form later to be filled by the content of historical acts of love) it is at the beginning,

. . . by the very nature of personal reality . . . characterizes rather that beginning of man's spiritual history which, as a genuine source, continues to govern the development of this historical life of the spirit into the individual virtues. This fundamental decision of love alone gives these virtues their whole, otherwise impossible,

of a realization of nature, not overlooking the fact, of course, that in a spiritual history the earlier phase remains ' preserved ' and actualizes itself ever anew with regard to the object corresponding to it " (STh V 502; ThI V 446).

[36] " It seems to us that Thomas Aquinas placed that total ' commitment ' which we call ' love ' at the very *beginning* of human self-realization. His reason for this seems to be that he cannot conceive a spiritual movement of freedom except in virtue of an original orientation to the goal as such, which original choice towards the goal is simply the love (or the refusal) of the absolute Good and Being which supports the whole movement of the Spirit. This probably explains the noticeable lack of interest in St. Thomas for a more exact psychological description of the various stages of the process of justification. This would also explain the presupposition on which his whole theology of justification is based, viz., that the acceptance of justification is exercised by virtue of the grace of justification and so is fundamentally a momentary event which itself does not admit of a temporal duration " (STh V 503-504; Th IV 447-448).

[37] STh V 505; ThI V 448.

[38] STh V 506; ThI V 449.

deep-rootedness in the core of the spiritual person and thus helps them to perfect their own essential nature, a perfection aimed at by them of their own, already given, nature. . . . man—in his free realization of himself as a person—can realize and accept these individual values in temporal succession and can already recognize and affirm their particular nature without having already realized himself completely in the one love. This does not dispute but rather includes the fact that these individual virtues themselves attain the fullness of their nature in love." [39]

From the foregoing it is clear that love itself (as habit, virtue) is subject to becoming, to development in each one's personal history. Love sums up the other virtues and is their index; love's role in the summing-up or focusing of the person is proper only to love and is "non-transferable," so to speak. "There is only one 'virtue' which asks man for himself—really himself wholly and completely—and this is the virtue of love and it alone; all other virtues only 'participate' in this nature of the one love; insofar as they are destined, even though out of their own nature itself, to be more than just themselves." [40]

For Rahner one of the basic differences between love and the other virtues is love's nature as an "*infinite becoming*," a quality worth noting especially in light of love's being the chief act of person and of the person's becoming; not only is person, as personization, a becoming without limits, but love, which is person in act as most properly person—and is very will-to-person—is also a measureless becoming.

For love cannot be performed or negotiated. It is never simply present but is always on the way to itself. Whereas the other virtues, as it were, transcend themselves, love is always present only in its transcendence into its own nature. . . . love itself is of its very nature measureless. It must be love with all one's might, with all one's heart and spirit. As long as we are pilgrims here below, we never 'have' *this love*. For who can honestly say that he loves God and his neighbor with *all* his heart? Moralists make subtle distinctions about this in order to bring out the fact that one can love even now, in a determined moment of one's still temporally

---

[39] STh V 506-507; ThI V 450.
[40] STh V 508; ThI V 451.

unfolding existence, just as the Gospel demands it: with all one's heart. But whatever may be said about these distinctions, ultimately this whole ethical system trying so desperately to be absolutely objective cannot avoid admitting that if someone were to refuse point blank any willingness and any attempt to love God more than he does now, then in such a case there would no longer be any love at all. Moralists usually express this admission by saying that the striving after perfection is a duty imposed under pain of grave sin on every man and not just on certain categories of people, even though the manner of realizing this obligation (e. g., by fully determined means, such as the Evangelical Counsels, or by other forms of radical renunciation) does not simply thereby fall under this duty itself. Yet what else is this obligation to strive after perfection but the duty of a greater love than one actually possesses? What else is it but an admission that one only achieves the love one ought to have by admitting that one has not yet attained that love to which one is obliged? This unique characteristic of love is not destroyed or ' dulled ' by admitting with the moralists that one also has a duty for the future which one has actually to admit now; but precisely as a duty for later on this commandment of greater love is always valid but not ' for always,' i. e., for every moment. For the readiness of really becoming freely involved in a development and a dynamism towards a later condition is surely something quite different from someone admitting today that he must pay his tailor bill tomorrow, which today he is still able to leave quite unpaid. He must start out *today* on the adventure of a love which not until tomorrow will be what it should be tomorrow because, and if, he has really opened himself to it *today* in an inner readiness which he could refuse, in which latter case love would not become tomorrow what it *ought to become* then, because it was not today what it ought to have been today. Love today is, therefore, what it should be today only if it acknowledges today that it is something of which more will be demanded tomorrow. It is true love even for today only to the extent in which *it reaches out to become more* than it is today, only if it is really on the way and forgets what it is now, reaching out for what lies ahead of it.[41]

Love, as a becoming without finite measure, has a horizon on which man can set no limits; and human becoming shares this characteristic.

In the above quotation, Rahner introduces the notion of

---

[41] STh V 508-509; ThI V 451-452; some emphasis added.

obligation and with it the notion of commandment. Perhaps love is presented as commandment only so that men will take it seriously. Everyone who has studied the notions of love and the person, in no matter what academic discipline, can easily get indigestion from all the rhapsodizing about these two over-worked subjects. Love talk seems prone to a rich diet of the choicest words. And it always seems so far removed from the real world; one occasionally, in reaction to this, is inclined to think of Sartre's negative presentation as a refreshing breath of honesty in the midst of so much moralizing and idealizing. I believe that part of what is felt as indigestion can be described as an impatience and embarassment with oneself and society for failing to incarnate and implement those words of ardor about love and person. Banal as it sounds, part of the truth is that to read and write about love and person on the one hand and then to cut corners in real, everyday life, is obviously either not to take the matter seriously, in which case it seems only words from the first, or indeed to take it quite seriously, as something truly personal, and then to feel the disharmony be-tween one's words and works; and it certainly then seems a lot easier to change one's words, or at least to make light of them, play them down, or otherwise try to make one's conduct less self-condemning. Perhaps, then, to call love a *command-ment* is to try to get love taken more seriously, to lift it from the warm and sticky world of romantic and sentimental " love," and place it, perhaps a bit coldly, in the world of law. No mat-ter what the reason, Rahner's treatment of love here in this essay is such that he avoids the usual alienating " love " lan-guage quite successfully while at the same time keeping the requisite force in his expressions. For Rahner, love as a com-mandment is practically the same as becoming a person as a commandment, i. e., the task of every man to enact (realize, actualize) himself. Thus he says: " One may speak of *a com-mandment of love* as long as one does not forget that this law does not command man to do something or other but *simply commands him to fulfill himself,* and charges man with himself,

i. e., himself as the possibility of love. . . ." [42] It is because he sees love in this light that he is so strong in his statements about the unique unifying role of love in enacting man as a person, in his deepest center and core of himself:

> . . . *love* itself does not represent some assignable performance which could be accurately determined; rather, it *is that which every man becomes in the irreplaceable, characteristic way of his own unique realization of nature,* something which is known only when it has been accomplished. . . . This one heart which man has to engage—the innermost center of his person (and on this basis also everything else found in the individual)—is something unique: what it contains within its uniqueness, what is engaged and given gratuitously in this love, is known only once it has been done, when the person has really caught up with himself and hence begins to know what is in him and *who* he is in the concrete. By this love, therefore, man embarks on the adventure of his own reality, all of which is at first veiled from him. He cannot comprehend and evaluate from the very start what is actually demanded of him. *He* is demanded; he himself is staked in the concreteness of his heart and of his life lying still before him as an unknown future and re-vealing—once it has been accomplished and only then—what is this heart which had to wager and expand itself during this life.[43]

Thus love seems to be a commandment and a commission because personal becoming, the adventure of self-enactment in and with others, is a commandment and a commission, just as personal becoming becomes a commandment because love is a commandment. And because it is of its very nature an open becoming, and thus as such an unknown which stretches forward into the future, toward its horizon, becoming a person is truly an adventure into the measureless, just as is ". . . love which consists in venturing into the boundless. . . ." [44]

This notion of " venturing into the boundless " cannot fail to recall Rahner's familiar notion of the essence of spirit as openness. Love, as will-to-person, must remain as fully open as that which it wills, of course; and since person, as a measure-

---

[42] STh V 514; ThI V 456; my emphasis.
[43] STh V 510; ThI V 452-453; my emphasis.
[44] STh V 512; ThI V 455.

less becoming, is the willed fruition of love, so must love itself be a measureless openness, an openness and readiness placing no *a priori* limits on itself. This is the meaning of love's openness to that " more " that ". . . will be demanded tomorrow." [45]

Of itself, all love is ready in its immeasurable nature to accept all love offered by the other, and to perfect itself in this acceptance. Consequently, morality and the fulfilment of the law always consist in one's readiness to allow oneself to be loved by God in the full measure and with all the demands on one's own love that is determined by God's love, and to enter into the experience of the radical and profound nature of this love which comes out to meet us. To this extent, all love of God is a readiness for the supernatural community of life, while this in its turn means nothing else than the most radical intimacy of God's love for us in which his most absolute divinity is communicated to us. . . . The basic meaning of the Christian ethos is not that we must respect objective material norms which God has imposed on reality. For all these material norms become real norms only once they become the expression of the very structure of the person. . . . The only ultimate structure of the person which expresses it perfectly is the person's basic capacity for love, and this capacity is boundless. Hence, man too is boundless; every sin is ultimately merely the refusal to trust in this boundlessness; sin is the less love which, because it refuses to wish to become greater love, is no longer love at all.[46]

In this essay Rahner has clearly affirmed the relationship between love and person and especially between love as a *becoming* and person as a *becoming;* i. e., he has affirmed his thesis of person as becoming and of personal becoming through love. There is more here than a routine coupling of the two notions of love and person. It would be a mistake to write off Rahner's understanding as just another " personalist " view which turns out to be as gratuitously denied as affirmed. We must place his statements against the background of his philosophical principles as presented earlier and locate his ideas within the context of the contemporary focus on freedom as the essential note of the person. If nature is essence seen as a source of acts,

[45] STh V 509; ThI V 452.
[46] STh V 512-514; ThI V 455-456.

then to be a person is to be a source and product, a cause and
an effect, of love, *the* free act par excellence. Thus if activity
(*operatio*) is nature itself seen in its own second act, then love
is person as seen in act. Love as a habit (*virtus*) and love as
act *mean* person: person is at once the "nature" (essence,
source) whence issue these acts of love and the essence constituted by these acts of love. This saying is not so paradoxical
as it may seem, not more paradoxical nor difficult than the
question how a habit can be both a source of actions and the
result or product of those actions. This "paradox" is itself
but another emphasis on becoming. The virtue of love, as
habit, does not constitute a new power not there before; habits
are specifically *human* phenomena, proper to free beings who
are also *potential* beings. God, as perfect and without potentiality, has no habits. Man, as a finite, incarnate spirit,
"creates" his nature because he "creates" his "second" nature. Man is not who and what he is because of one or another
isolated act, but because of the attitude and set he gives his
life, the stamp of virtue or vice he puts upon and into it, i. e.,
because of the habits he freely acquires, in his own self-appropriation, in time. Man, as incarnate, enacts himself in time
precisely through the self-enactment occurring in acquisition of
habits. The notion of self-construction does not contradict tradition. Love is not only act but virtue (habit), i. e., a person's
self-enactment takes a definite direction.

V

BECOMING II, FREEDOM II, LOVE II:
THE LATER ESSAYS

Despite there being a STh XII, the last significant statement on our topic, except for one essay in STh X, treated in the concluding summary, occurs in STh VI. Since it has been my method to interpret each essay for its maximum light, noting later essays only for their advances and developments, it becomes possible to say that after the second essay on love, in STh VI, no major change occurs in the basic doctrine begun forty years ago with SW.

The three headings of this final section, becoming, freedom, and love, refer to four chief sources. Becoming signifies the essay on hominization, in the series *Quaestiones Disputatae*, and the essay on the unity of spirit and matter, in STh VI; other minor essays provide supplementary material and derive from STh V[1], STh VI again, STh VIII, IX, and X. The chief source for the discussion of freedom and love is STh VI, with supplementary material from STh X. In addition, the LThK and SM, as well as Rahner and Vorgrimler's KThW, provide brief treatments of matters we have treated more at length. This itinerary reveals my judgment that with STh VI we have, substantially, Rahner's mature positions on the essential facts of his concept of person. STh XI, on the history of the practice of confession, is not useful here. STh VII, IX and X, therefore, contribute refinements and applications rather than new positions. STh VII consists of short articles on the spiritual life.

There is another way of organizing this same material, recalling the idea of first and second otherness. Thus under first otherness would fall becoming as treated under hominization,

[1] Recall that the English translation began to split the German into two, beginning with STh VII. STh VII thus became ThI VII and VIII; STh VIII became ThI IX and X; etc.

the essay on spirit and matter,[2] and the essay on evolution.[3] The rest of the treatment of becoming, e. g., the essay on " experiment man "[4] and that on the "new man,"[5] plus those (major) essays on freedom and love, would then come under second otherness. Thus, under first otherness we examine the kind of becoming that is more relevant to man as material, as incarnate, than to man as spirit. Man as spirit, on the other hand, is more the concern in the concept of second otherness. Despite possible confusion, we might say that under hominization Rahner is more interested in man's " body," while in the latter (second otherness), he is more interested in man's spirit (even though hominization is the question of the origin of man's soul in the evolutionary context). I am tempted to call the former hominization and the latter personization (except that the person is the whole) because second otherness is primarily the result of freedom.

1. *Becoming II*. The question of hominization, though broader than that of evolution, is largely the problem of how man, through evolution, came to have the " starting essence " with which he now finds himself. There is, predictably, a certain review of and overlap with SW; but this essay, coming some thirty years later, offers new points worth integrating into that consistent position.

In *Hominisation*[6] we face the difficulty that the problem called hominization, as it turns out in Rahner's treatment, is to explain how spirit can come from matter, the difficulty

[2] STh VI 185-214; ThI VI 153-177.

[3] STh V 183-221; ThI V 157-192.

[4] STh VIII 260-285; ThI IX 205-224.

[5] STh V 159-179; ThI V 125-153.

[6] *Hominisation* is the transliterated German title as well as the English (i. e., British-English) way of spelling what in American-English would take a " z," thus hominization. There are three articles concerned with *Hominisation* and the essay on the unity of spirit and matter. J. Donceel, " Teilhard de Chardin and the Body-Soul Relation," *Thought*, 40 (1965), 371-389; J. Donceel, " Causality and Evolution: A Survey of Some Neo-scholastic Theories," *The New Scholasticism*, 39 (1965), 295-315; H. Falk, " Can Spirit Come from Matter? " *International Philosophical Quarterly*, 7 (1967), 541-555.

arising because earlier (in SW) we were explaining how matter emanated from spirit. Now so flagrant a conflict, more than mildly irritating, provokes one to resist letting the author have it both ways. Are we supposed to presume a deeper unity? Are we totally to discount the temporal? Are we supposed not to question whether we should speak of spirit before matter or matter before spirit? To draw some useful insight from this difficulty, one that advances our understanding of his doctrine of person, we should be open to suggestions from his perspective as well as to new ways of speaking of spirit, matter, and becoming.

To say, e. g., that matter is what we know first, evidenced by the idea of *im*materiality, which for many is the sole admissible (and, significantly, negative) meaning allowed for the concept of spirituality, is to imply at least a logical priority of the material over the spiritual (immaterial). We might call such a perspective empirical, materialist, objective, in contrast with one which begins with the subject and claims that what is first and better known is spirit; this second perspective could be called rationalist, idealist, subjective. That man admits of both viewpoints as possible perspectives on himself suggests his dual, composite nature, his hylomorphic unity.

Rahner's is clearly the latter perspective. In PH he says: " What ' spiritual ' means is an immediate non-empirical datum of human knowledge, though it needs, of course, to be articulated and interpreted by reflection. It is only on the basis of that knowledge that it is possible to determine the actual metaphysical meaning of ' material.' It is an unmetaphysical and ultimately materialistic prejudice common among scientists to suppose that men primarily deal with matter and know precisely what matter is, and then subsequently and laboriously and very problematically have to ' discover ' spirit in addition, and can never properly know whether what it signifies cannot after all be reduced to matter in the end." [7] Rahner's frank dualism is, of course, Aristotelian and Thomist, not Platonic or

[7] PH 44; HE 47.

Cartesian: unwilling to be either an idealist or an empiricist, in any monist sense, he refuses to reduce matter to spirit or spirit to matter, all the while attributing primacy to spirit.[8]

Rahner therefore clearly holds for a logical priority of spirit over matter, as well as a priority of nature, or ontological priority. In a sense this smacks of the " Gordian knot " approach to the problem of the meaning of spirit. To anyone wanting to reach a genuine metaphysics of person, the problem always gets back to the meaning of spirit. Once the buck is passed to spirit, it has to stop. Traditionally—or, let us say, before Descartes and the turn to the subject—especially in the Aristotelian-Thomist tradition, sensible reality was interpreted both as the first known and as a material thing; that the *res sensibilis* could as well be one's incarnate self or another incarnate spirit, went practically unnoticed. Thus the problem of knowing the meaning of spirit was acute because derivative. Rahner's Thomism, via Rousselot and Maréchal, very Kantian, Fichtean, and Hegelian, and thus very much from the viewpoint of substance as subject, reverses the problem, finding it easy to say what spirit is and practically impossible to say what matter is. Whereas spirit was formerly defined in terms of matter (as the *im*material), now matter is defined in terms of spirit.[9] Thus Rahner says: ". . . spirit is a reality that can only be understood by direct acquaintance . . . It is only possible to say what matter actually is by contrast with spirit so known." [10] This introspective appeal is completely consistent

---

[8] This primacy is shown, in one way, by attributing spirituality analogously to God: " We only term God ' spirit' because the spirituality that we experience rightly seems to us to be what is higher in the world, and because it includes in its very essence a transcendental conscious relationship to the fundamental original ground of all that exists, which we call God, and consequently, through this limitlessness of its orientation, it positively and intrinsically does not include the negativity of what *is* absolutely and in every respect merely finite " (PH 47; HE 51).

[9] E. g., PH 48; HE 52: ". . . it is not at all so directly evident what ' matter ' is . . . ' spirit ' is already posited and its nature experienced by asking a question about it. . . . matter is, namely—what is closed to a dynamic orientation above and beyond itself towards being in general."

[10] PH 49; HE 53. Matter is called " ' solidified ' spirit . . ." (PH 51-52; HE 57).

with Rahner's transcendental approach which, as we have seen before and will see again, explains being in terms of knowing.

Now we have already noted, in SW, that "finite spirit . . . is spirit in the world . . . ,"[11] and that "matter, therefore, is the outward expression and self-revealing of personal spirit, in the finite realm."[12] Thus, the three key concepts remain spirit, matter, and becoming, the last being the most problematic because it names the relation between the other two, a " definitive" relation in the full sense of the term. And because a study of Rahner's concept of person is a study of (at least) his concept of finite spirit's becoming (through and in) matter, and because his treatment of these concepts is more detailed and direct here than in SW, we can see the importance of PH.

There is one last methodological point that must be faced before we enter into the line of reasoning proper. The ground of Rahner's general theory of causing and becoming, the point on which he has been criticized by anti-transcendentalists, is his method of arguing " subjectively," i. e., from knowing about knowing, experienced interiorly by a subject, to knowing about being. As he says, ". . . for human beings the ontologically first and fundamental case or paradigm of a being and of its fundamental properties is found in the being himself who knows and acts."[13] Disallow argument from this ground, and the whole development of cause and becoming is also disallowed and declared vain. Rahner's point is at least, of course, that being, acting, causing, and becoming are nowhere more accessible to man than in himself, in his own conscious experience as being, causing, changing, becoming.[14] In addition, the *paradigm* for being is the knowing subject, spirit as self-presence (becoming such in and through self-absence), not the so-called " real "

<hr/>

[11] PH 54; HE 59.

[12] PH 54; HE 60-61.

[13] PH 70; HE 81.

[14] A position which is, *prima facie*, not very Thomist is also held by J. de Finance, in *Existence et liberté* (Paris: Vitte, 1955); de Finance is, of course, another Thomist who has not closed himself to contemporary thought but has developed his Thomism in the light of and in dialogue with that thought.

things in the "already out there real world." Thus Rahner
is unequivocal: ". . . if the genuine concept of becoming is
to be attained, it must be attained in the operation of cognition
itself." [15] It is not idle to warn the reader that granting Rahner
this methodological point is crucial, since his argument about
becoming as self-transcendence will follow directly from that
event (i. e., self-transcendence) as worked out in his metaphysics of knowledge.[16]

This point made, we turn to the argument proper, insofar, as
always, as it is relevant to his concept of person. The basic
general question is how beings can become more,[17] can transcend their present selves.[18] The more specific question in PH
is the origin of the soul within an evolutionary framework.
After considering and dismissing the traditional theories of
change in terms of eduction from the potency of matter (*educ-
tio e potentia materiae*) and *concursus,* Rahner tailors a con-

---

[15] PH 71; HE 82. Despite the mention of cognition alone Rahner does not
intend this *sensu negante* but *sensu aiente*; i. e., willing, freedom, and love just
as clearly affirm being and manifest becoming as does knowing, perhaps even more.
His general treatment of freedom and love shows this. The following quotation,
though concerned with the supernatural existential, is a further indication of this
truth: ". . . the concept of *potentia obedientialis* must not be confined, as it too
often is, to man's *knowledge*. If, according to Scripture, God is love and not
'thought of thought,' no understanding of man and of the absolute fulfilment
of his being (by grace) can succeed, unless man is considered as freedom and
love, which again may not be considered just a by-product of the act of knowledge" (STh IV 235-236; ThI IV 186-187).

[16] This is not the place to critique Rahner's general methodology. Suffice it to
say that although transcendental anthropology as a turn to the subject seems
to be altogether sound and greatly to be preferred to the naive realism of an
older empiricism, nevertheless, as an absolute starting point for knowledge of being
and becoming, it must be "corrected" by a return to the *inter*subjective; in so
saying I once again affirm my judgment that Levinas's primacy of the ethical
over the metaphysical illuminates a basic methodical need in Rahner, and in
Aristotle, Aquinas, and in Hegel and Heidegger, for that matter.

[17] On becoming *more,* as contrasted with merely becoming different, see PH 62-
64; HE 71-73.

[18] Rahner's expressions are ". . . transcend themselves . . . ," ". . . active
change and becoming of finite beings . . . ," ". . . an active transcending of their
own natures, whereby an existent itself by its own activity . . . actively moves
beyond and above itself" (PH 61; HE 69).

cept to the situation and then asks whether such a concept is
valid or merely a smokescreen to cover our lack of a valid concept.[19] Now since the reason why we need a concept at all is
to understand change as an increase in being, which is itself
understood as possible only to God, the concept or theory Rahner constructs is offered as a statement of how God can be
at once the transcendent Ground of all becoming and still
allow the agent real causality (*contra* occasionalism). Here
Rahner feels he has something new to suggest, thanks to his
method of transcendental deduction already mentioned. And
what, in fact, do we find in this something new? Once again,
now with more force and detail than before—and not to our
surprise, since we have so often in this study reaffirmed it as
Rahner's basic thesis of his anthropology, philosophical and
theological—we find offered anew the concept of personal becoming. Thus he says: ". . . becoming is to be conceived as
the becoming and operation of a being which fulfils itself and
so reaches its own accomplishment," [20] and this paradigm of
becoming, the enactment of person, is to be the validation
of the general doctrine of becoming. In other words, out of
the experience of personal self-enactment through self-transcendence is to be derived a theory of all cases of becoming. More
precisely, by doing a transcendental deduction on human self-
transcendence, i. e., by learning what must be the a priori situation of man in his becoming (the transcendental a priori conditions for the very possibility of human becoming), Rahner
can then name the conditions of all becoming.

It is at this point that one who has understood SW simply
coasts through the explanation Rahner then offers, and one who
has not, begins to gnash his teeth. Since we have already been
down that road, we need not do so again. Suffice it to say
that basing himself on his metaphysics of knowledge, specifically here on the openness of spirit dynamically transcending finite
objects as it moves toward the horizon of being as such, Rahner

[19] PH 61-70; HE 69-81.
[20] PH 71; HE 82.

claims to validate, in the experience of this transcendence of
the finite by the finite toward the infinite, a concept of the
infinite's supporting the finite, without interference, obtrusion,
or special *ad hoc* intervention, non-objectively (the horizon is
not an object but is known only as the condition of the knowledge of what *is* known as an object).[21] In the experience of
knowing (objective knowledge, i. e., knowledge of objects),
Rahner identifies four [22] characteristics of the non-objectively
known horizon: the horizon is essential, immanent, superior,
and in a causal relation to the dynamic tendency of the agent
toward that horizon. Now these same characteristics were
those Rahner built into his theory tailored to the needs of explaining hominization as the origin of the soul in an evolutionary framework. But because that question is not our precise concern, and because the explanation comes from SW in
the first place, we omit the intricacies of the ensuing discussion. What remains relevant in PH can be detached, now that
we have understood the context adequately.[23]

Rahner, in identifying the four aspects mentioned above,
has added to the concepts of *Vorgriff* and finite spirit, and thereby to the content of his concept of person. In his present application this is an affirmation of the possibility of becoming
in and through dependence upon God as the absolute supporting ground of being. "Becoming involves," he says,
". . . that the agent advances beyond and above itself from
its own lower plane to a higher, in a self-transcendent movement." [24] Further, " the agent's rising beyond and above itself
in action and becoming takes place because the absolute Being
is the cause and ground of this self-movement. . . . it is . . . true
self-transcendence." [25] Thus he can conclude that ". . . there
belongs to the essence of a spiritual being an ever-open onto-

---

[21] PH 71-74; HE 82-87.

[22] *Ibid.*

[23] It is very tempting to dwell at length on these pages of *Hominisation*, but
digression here would be a luxury.

[24] PH 75; HE 88.

[25] *Ibid.*

logical transcendence towards being in general, and so a rising above and beyond self." [26] To be a person is to be spirit and to be spirit is to have the task of self-enactment through self-transcendence.

Rahner goes on to speak of the evolutionary development of matter towards spirit and the creation of the soul, applying his general theory of becoming, i.e., becoming as supported by the ground of absolute Being, which explains how the "more" can come from the "less." We can conclude treatment of this essay by saying that we have here more than an a fortiori argument supporting the thesis that personal becoming is Rahner's key concept: we have a metaphysically and methodologically consistent explanation of the *possibility* of becoming (a becoming previously, and often, seen to be *necessary*), and an explanation, in the precise terms required, of the interrelations of spirit and matter. Finally, we have once again implicitly, and to that extent disappointingly (though, in Rahner's defense, the context was not entirely appropriate), the opening for the affirmation that personal becoming is essentially interpersonal becoming since the self-enactment requires self-transcendence toward some other than oneself. That conclusion, however, takes us into second otherness, whereas PH explicitly concerned only first otherness; thus Rahner did not develop his principles in a manner befitting that further application. Nevertheless, since the dynamic transcendence toward the unobjective horizon of being always takes place in the presence of some "object," [27] and since it is not inconceivable but rather probable that the nature of that object," as the *content* of that "object," should not be totally irrelevant to the *formality* or structure of that dynamism, then it seems quite appropriate that more self-enactment should occur when self-transcendence takes place toward another person; in this way will that "articulation and interpretation" of experience which Rahner admits to be necessary,[28] lead to right conclusions about the nature of spirit, person, and becoming. This conclusion

[26] PH 76; HE 90.   [27] PH 89; HE 107.   [28] PH 44; HE 47.

is not facile, and it must again be suggested that an already interpersonal or dialogal starting point would be more concrete, realistic, and fruitful.[29]

After PH the essay on the unity of spirit and matter, in STh VI, adds little new. Its comparative brevity contributes clarity by omitting even the abbreviated transcendental deduction of PH, itself an abbreviation of SW. It would therefore be repetitive to conduct a full study of that essay; in fact even to cite a few (of the many possible) quotations about becoming as self-transcendence, etc., especially when Rahner admits that whole sections of the essay are merely taken over from PH,[30] seems unnecessary. The same can be said of the essay on evolution in STh V. Although it antedates PH, and thus also, of course, the essay on spirit and matter in STh VI, and gives essentially the same basic doctrine on spirit and matter as appeared in those later efforts, yet, because of its better and more detailed development of that doctrine, PH must be the preferred source. And as with the essay on spirit and matter, that on evolution offers many quotations such as to fill footnotes to overflowing. In other words, both the 1962 article on evolution and 1963 essay on spirit and matter basically are repetitions of PH with applications, deletions, and simplifications; one could therefore read them as supplementary.

2. *Freedom II.* We can be brief in treating Rahner's essay on freedom because, as the second treated, only part will be new; and even that new part will receive its adequate consideration only when we take up (next) the essay on love, since freedom is the capacity to love. As was true before, freedom, because it is understood as rooted in man as spirit, and thus as transcendence of finite particulars toward the unlimited horizon of being,[31] can be easily misunderstood merely as the ca-

---

[29] We are again reminded of Metz's attempts at "personalizing" HW, attempts judged vain by E. Simons in *Philosophie der Offenbarung* (Stuttgart: Kohlhammer, 1966); see 93 ff.

[30] See STh VI 556; ThI VI 401.

[31] See STh VI 216-217; ThI VI 179.

pacity to choose from among those finite goods.[32] In this new essay on freedom, especially in the sections entitled " Freedom as Total and Finalizing Self-Mastery of the Subject "[33] and " Freedom Regarded as a Dialogic Capacity of Love," [34] Rahner again confirms that his central concept is that of person to be actualized in transcendence. Now when person is defined in terms of spirit, and spirit is defined as capacity for being, and then being is distinguished, in terms of spirit, as true and good, spirit is then itself further distinguished as capacity for the true and the good, or intellect and will. Rahner's " personist " understanding of this tradition, consonant with the modern " turn to the subject," [35] is to place the essence of freedom not in its effect on objects but in its effect on the subject. Thus if becoming a person is self-actualization in and through self-transcendence, then freedom is the power or ability (*Vermögen*) for this self-actualizing self-transcendence: ". . . freedom is . . . the capacity to make oneself once and for all, the capacity which of its nature is directed towards the freely willed finality of the subject as such." [36] And as we shall see in the final part of this section, while Rahner here, under the heading of *freedom*, brings to completion (especially as freedom to love) his doctrine on person as becoming in self-actualization (or self-enactment), in the next, under the heading of *love*, he brings to completion his doctrine of person as becoming in self-transcendence, naming human interpersonal love as the metaphysically necessary condition for personal becoming; he thus brings his one and whole doctrine to fulness, uniting all its parts.

But before we turn to that final point, let us examine in more detail Rahner's understanding of freedom, first as the ability or power of self-enactment into that fulness which is the whole person, and second as the power or capacity to love, this latter point being a hint of and a bridge to the full essay

[32] See STh VI 220-221; ThI VI 182-183.
[33] STh VI 221-225; ThI VI 183-186.
[34] STh VI 225-229; ThI VI 186-190.
[35] In P. Eicher's terms, " die anthropologische Wende."

on love. Rahner clearly states that ". . . by his freedom man
can determine and dispose himself as a whole. . . ."[37] The
becoming occurring through free action is neither primarily
some change in the world of objects and things, no matter
how significant, nor merely a "moral" or "juridical" event,
in the sense of accidental, or imputed to the subject, as we
have seen before, but the very *becoming whole* of that subject,
the very becoming who he is, becoming wholly good or evil in
his being (insofar as his finitude, as understood in terms of
the study of concupiscence, so allows): ". . . man by his free
decision really *is* good or evil in the very ground of his being
itself. . . ."[38]

Using a new expression, reminiscent of, but more trenchant
than, the distinction between "freedom from" and "freedom
for," Rahner speaks now of "freedom of *being*," a phrase which
can only mean *freedom to become*: "freedom is first of all
'freedom of being.' "[39] This he understands as ". . . a transcendental mark of human existence itself . . . ,"[40] not ". . . merely
an external event happening to man . . . ,"[41] and thus a true
self-enactment: the *potential* person *becomes* an *actual* person,
an enacted person; "Freedom . . . is the *self*-exercise [*Selbst-
vollzug*: self-enactment] of the man . . . , this freedom in which
man is capable of achieving himself. . . ."[42]

[36] STh VI 221; ThI VI 184.

[37] STh VI 222; ThI VI 184.

[38] *Ibid.* In my judgment, this primacy of the ethical, at least in the sense that
a free, ethical act makes an ontological or metaphysical difference, i. e., a difference to and in the being who a man is, can be understood as a primacy of
the ethical over the metaphysical, in more than Fichte's sense, i. e., in the sense
Levinas gives to the ethical as the absolutely original encounter, "beyond being,"
in the face to face encounter of another human person, before thought and freedom. In the following essay on love Rahner emphatically places himself metaphysically at the point where Levinas begins phenomenologically, thus implicitly
transcending whatever dependence on Western objective philosophy, from Aristotle
and Aquinas through Kant, Hegel, and Heidegger, he displayed for the thirty years
until these two incomparably important essays on freedom and love.

[39] *Ibid. Seinsfreiheit* is the term Rahner uses.

[40] *Ibid.*

[41] STh VI 223-224; ThI VI 185.

[42] STh V 508-509; ThI V 451-452, some emphasis added. Thus emerges the
possibility of joining Rahner, whose metaphysical anthropology is at once the

But how does this self-enactment take place? Is it a solitary, acosmic event? So often Rahner's early terminology and his explanation in terms of the self and its horizon of being have allowed an impersonal interpretation, as we noted when mentioning Metz's five notes to HW2, notes which Metz knew were fully justified both by the facts and by Rahner's evolution. What Rahner had left implicit, except for hints here and there,[43] before 1965, finally and fully become explicit in his affirmation not only that self-transcendence is the absolute condition for self-enactment, as in first otherness, but also that this self-transcendence must be necessarily towards another human person in I-Thou interpersonal love, to use Buber's terms. This affirmation, banal, perhaps, from someone else, has greater significance when Rahner finally is able to identify with it, because it comes not from the *de facto* but from his *de jure* transcendental metaphysics of person as finite spirit becoming through first and, most important, *second* otherness. Rahner does not merely gratuitously assert, remaining vulnerable to an equally gratuitous denial, but thoroughly grounds this doctrine in his transcendental method, thus manifesting perfect continuity and consistency with that method and his starting point. In the present essay on freedom, first given as a lecture in November, 1964, Rahner signaled ideas he would develop and publish more fully first in early 1965. After examining his works through the years ending with the publication of STh XII in 1975, we can safely say that, with the essay on love in STh VI, Rahner reached his mature and definitive position on person as becoming. Let us turn now to that essay rather than delay over the formulations in the essay on freedom, preferring to place in notes any " note-worthy " parallel texts.

3. *Love II*. The bridge to the present essay from that on freedom is, as was said, that freedom, fully understood, is freedom

most profound and implicitly the most contemporary metaphysics of person, with Levinas, whose phenomenology is the most profoundly interpersonal and implicitly the most metaphyical phenomenology.

[43] See STh VI 556-557; ThI VI 401.

to love,[44] i.e., the ability or power to become through loving. As free, love issues from and reaches to the essential core of the loving person [45] bringing self to fulness.[46] But is this freedom to love going to turn out to be the philosophically classical "love" of being, in the sense of a Platonic reverence for the universal idea or form, a Hegelian Absolute, or Heideggerian Being, or the theologically classical love of God? Yes and no. Rahner brings transcendental anthropology fully into the contemporary world, reversing the traditional reduction of love of neighbor to love of God, by a thorough understanding of love of God as radical love of one's fellow *human* being.[47] This doctrine must not be understood as a philosophical sell-out of transcendence to immanence or as a simplistic option of the many over the one; Rahner's transcendental method, if one has understood SW and the necessity of *conversio,* is, in fact, a satisfying experience of transcendence given in immanence and the one in the many. Nor may it be understood as a theological sell-out to secularization, to atheistic Christianity, or to any death-of-God theology and its denial of transcendence, the supernatural, or grace; Rahner's specifically theological concepts of the supernatural existential, the anonymous Christian, the experience of grace, etc. (and they too ultimately receive their full understanding only in terms of Rahner's philosophy [48]) are always the simultaneity of transcendence and immanence, of multiplicity in unity. Rahner is contemporary in his thoroughly existential affirmation [49] of the primacy of multi-

[44] " Freedom is always self-realization [*Selbstvollzug*] . . . the capacity of love. . . . the basic act of man into which absolutely he can synthesize his whole nature and life . . ." (STh VI 225; ThI VI 187).

[45] Freedom's source and goal is ". . . the innermost center of the person . . ." (STh VI 226; ThI VI 188).

[46] " The only ultimate structure of the person which manages to express it completely is the basic capacity of love . . ." (STh VI 227; ThI VI 188).

[47] " Human freedom . . . is always freedom . . . *vis-à-vis* some intramundane Thou . . ." (STh VI 228; ThI VI 189). " The *transcendental* opening out . . . requires an intramundane Thou [*Du*]. The original relationship to God is— love of neighbor " (STh VI 228-229; ThI VI 189; Rahner's emphasis).

[48] See W. Shepherd, *Man's Condition* (New York: Herder and Herder, 1969).

[49] Rahner cites with approval Kierkegaard and Blondel when speaking of ". . . the

plicity over unity, of freedom and love over the reductiveness of knowing, of individual person over universal idea. Granted that this was a latter-day explicitation, it was implicit in the basic metaphysical doctrine of a finite spirit radically dependent on otherness, both first (natural and pre-free) and second (personal and free). Rahner is *metaphysically* affirming that subjectivity requires intersubjectivity in order even to be subjectivity: ". . . freedom is really subjectivity and . . . subjectivity is in itself and in its self-presence a more original reality than individually existing objects. . . ."[50] This freedom, understood as a self-disposing by the subject towards finality, is necessarily mediated by . . . intersubjectivity. . . ."[51] Thus, just as subjectivity is being found at " full strength," more than in objects or in the *Umwelt,* so also freedom and its agent, subjectivity, are at full strength only in intersubjectivity.

Thus, empowered by a presumed and presupposed phenomenology of love,[52] and emboldened by a theology of love which he interprets to say not " merely " that salvation is in loving rather than in knowing but that ". . . the love of God and the love of neighbor are one and the same thing . . . ,"[53] Rahner moves to a transcendental metaphysics of love, i.e.,

concept of subjectivity in Kierkegaard, the notion of ' *action* ' in Blondel . . ." as showing that ". . . there is such a basic act of freedom which embraces and shapes the whole of existence " (STh VI 224; ThI VI 186; repeated in STh VI 245; ThI VI 203).

[50] STh VI 231; ThI VI 191.

[51] STh VI 233; ThI VI 193; though " intersubjectivity " here is translating the relatively less forceful *Mitwelt,* it should be clear that this latter term has more explicit in it than we are allowed to say may have been in Heidegger's *Mitwelt,* at least in *Sein und Zeit* (see pp. 118, 125, 129, and 300; in English, pp. 153-155, 162-163, 166-168 and 346). This text of Rahner's also includes the impersonal world, or *Umwelt,* and by not quoting it I mean only to emphasize his use of *Mitwelt.*

[52] Rahner frequently in this essay on love says, somewhat apologetically, that he cannot offer such a phenomenology, all the while admitting its necessity. It is in Levinas that the beginnings of such a phenomenology can be found, although D. von Hildebrand's *Metaphysik der Gemeinschaft* (Regensburg: Habbel, 1930, 1955, 2nd ed.) and S. Strasser's *Das Gemüt* (Utrecht and Freiburg: 1956) precede some of it.

[53] STh VI 280; ThI VI 233.

a metaphysics yielded by the transcendental method.[54] Rahner
is not actually offering here a wholly new metaphysics derived
from a wholly new starting point, viz., the intersubjective encounter (instead of the "encounter" with objects and "ob-
servation" of causality and change in the world of objects).
Rather he simply refers us to the metaphysics of horizon, gen-
eralizing to "whole" spirit what occurs in "part" of spirit
(i. e., in intellect), and then deducing for or applying to will,
freedom, and love, the same doctrine of "transcendence in
immanence," or transcendence beyond the ground only in the
presence of the ground (love of God, the divine person, in this
case, being given only in the actual present act of love of
neighbor, the human person, just as knowledge of being was
given only in knowing objects).[55] Once again we are aware
of SW as the basis of all of Rahner's metaphysical anthropology, both philosophical and theological, because of the consistent application of his transcendental method.

Let us now complete treatment of this essay, fittingly by
quoting his own words, some with comment, some without. In
the sections of the essay entitled "Love of neighbor as the
basic activity of man"[56] and "Love of neighbor as man's
manifestation of his wholeness and essence"[57] interpersonal
love is identified with the depth and breadth of personal becoming, not only reaching to the deepest center of a person
but also integrating more of the potential for personhood, in
the widest reaches of human existence, into free personal becoming. Under the first heading, basing himself on the primacy
of the ethical and rooting this in freedom as self-disposability

---

[54] See STh VI 284-285; ThI VI 237-238: "Love as a reflected and explicit
mode of action and as an unconceptualized transcendental horizon of action."

[55] "The transcendental horizon is . . . the subjective possibility [and thus the
ground!] for the individual object to show itself at all . . . ; the transcendental
horizon is that which is itself given only in the encounter with the object of
a concretely historical experience . . ." (STh VI 284; ThI VI 237). These two
are "moments" or constituents of *one* experience; the very experience itself requires *both*, and this *absolutely*. Neither is given without the other.

[56] STh VI 286-289; ThI VI 239-241.

[57] STh VI 289-292; ThI VI 241-244.

(recalling the first essay on freedom), Rahner states: " love of neighbor . . . is . . . the basis and sum total of the moral as such." [58] He goes on to articulate this by explaining that

> . . . the true and proper surrounding of man is his personal environment of persons in the world through which man finds and fulfils himself (by knowledge and will) and—gets away from himself. . . . the world of things is of significance only as a factor for man and for his neighbor. This follows first of all from the a priori structure [worked out in SW]. . . . the world of things can be a possible object for man's concern only as a moment of the world of persons. [59]

We have come a long way from the " impersonal personalism " of HW (and, a fortiori, of SW) in this affirmation of the primacy of the personal; and yet Rahner insists that it was all implicit there (thus confirming the interpretation this study presents). This can only mean, if Rahner's transcendental method be taken seriously and consistently, that while *subjectivity* (i. e., person as spirit, as intellect and will, will meaning freedom, especially freedom to love, to be and to become through loving) *is the paradigm for being,* [60] *intersubjectivity is the paradigm for becoming.* In terms of first and second otherness, Rahner here is affirming, on a metaphysical basis and level, the radical necessity for second otherness, the other person, for human becoming. In fact, as has been said before, first otherness is mediated through second otherness. [61] " Materially . . . the a posteriori object is the necessary mediation of the knowing subject to itself *and so . . . the human personal Thou is the mediation, the ' being-within-oneself,' of the subject.*" [62] In other words, that necessity of phantasms established in SW, for all its traditional abstraction, is here claimed to mean the necessity of the personal other for the very coming-

---

[58] STh VI 286-287; ThI VI 239-240.

[59] STh VI 287; ThI VI 240.

[60] This point has been made in conection with discussion of that method itself.

[61] Confirmation of this metaphysical thesis comes from phenomenology; for one example see the work by W. Ver Eecke based on the studies of hospitalism by René Spitz.

[62] STh VI 228; ThI VI 240-241; my emphasis.

to-himself of the person.[63] Rahner offers a supporting " argument " by referring to the dependence of knowledge on love;
of course the primacy of love over knowledge was affirmed already in HW when the very intelligibility of the existence of
contingent beings was shown to require an act of will whereby
the unnecessary is freely posited in being. Rahner merely applies these ideas again:

> . . . the free self-disposal . . . is precisely the loving communication
> with the human Thou as such. . . . since knowledge . . . attains
> its proper and full nature only in the act of freedom . . . it has
> a fully human significance only once it is integrated into freedom,
> i. e., into the loving communication with the Thou. The act of
> personal love for another human being is therefore the all-embracing
> basic act of man which gives meaning, direction, and measure to
> everything else.[64]

Lest one miss the meaning of this affirmation, note again
that Rahner is operating on the level of being, of metaphysics,
not phenomenology.[65] Thus: ". . . the essential a priori openness to the other human being . . ." [66] as belonging ". . . as such
to the a priori and most basic constitution of man . . . is an
essential inner moment of his (knowing and willing) transcendentality." [67] There is no mitigating this radical dependence on
second otherness for personal becoming: ". . . the whole incalculable mystery of man is contained and exercised in this
act of love of neighbor. . . . [For a person] love . . . is the whole
of himself in which alone he possesses himself completely, meets
himself completely. . . ." [68] This metaphysical dependence re-

---

[63] "*As person*" probably should be added, in order to allow for that minimal
consciousness and elemental choosing on the animal, potentially human, level,
conceived in terms of those unfortunate cases, such as hospitalism, of human
deprivation.

[64] STh VI 288; ThI VI 241.

[65] Phenomenology, i. e., in the admittedly narrow sense of description of what
appears. Phenomenology in the sense of an uncovering of the very structure of
being through its presence to consciousness turns out to be another transcendental
method.

[66] *Ibid.*

[67] *Ibid.*

[68] STh VI 289; ThI VI 242.

fers not only to the " whether " of personal becoming but also to the " how much " : ". . . . by love of the Thou . . . man really experiences in it who he is . . . ; . . . the totality of reality . . . opens itself only if man opens himself radically in the act of love and entrusts himself to this totality." [69] Finally:

. . . in the act of love for another, and in it alone and primarily, the original unity of what is human and what is the totality of man's experience is collected together and achieved . . .[:] the love for the other concrete Thou . . . is man himself *in his total achievement* [*Vollzug*]. . . . this love is really the fulfilment [*Vollzug*] of the total and hence also spiritually transcendental nature of man. . . .[70]

4. *Summary and Conclusion: Interpersonal Experience.* By way of summarizing the whole and concluding this study of Rahner's concept of person as becoming, let us look at an essay from STh X. But before turning to that essay on experience of otherness as God and of otherness as another human person,[71] let us take a few moments to recognize several essays of supplementary significance between STh VI and XII.[72]

[69] STh VI 290; ThI VI 242.

[70] STh VI 290; ThI VI 243; *Vollzug* is, of course, enactment or actualization, the familiar and favorite term for that " drawing " (*ziehen*) to fullness (*voll*) which reminds us that personhood is a potential to be actualized, brought into act (en-acted).

[71] See " *Selbsterfahrung und Gotteserfahrung,*" STh X 133-144. The theological use of the term and concept of person in trinitarian discussions need not occupy us here. That the term has a history and difficulties is interesting and instructive, but not necessarily a philosophical justification for those usages. See Rahner's *The Trinity* (New York: Herder and Herder, 1970; trans. by J. Donceel) esp. 103-115, " The Problem of the Concept of Person." The entry " Person " in the KthW, by Rahner and H. Vorgrimler (Freiburg: Herder Bücherei, 1961) 282-285 is also good; in English as *Concise Theological Dictionary* (American title drops the " Concise "), trans. by R. Strachan and ed. C. Ernst (London: Burns and Oates, 1965) 351-354. In general, of course, this brief work, as well as SM (often working from and bettering the LThK) is very useful for briefer summaries of Rahner's main ideas previously treated more fully in the essays we have studied.

[72] STh VII and VIII, as noted above, were each published in two English volumes. STh VII, as noted before, concerns the spiritual life; STh VIII, IX, X, and XII return to dogmatic theology; STh XI contains Rahner's early works

There are three essays in STh VII which reexamine themes treated previously. The short essay " On Christian Dying," [73] without adding anything new, restates simply the essential idea of freedom as power of final becoming. The essay, " Why and How Can We Venerate the Saints? " [74] reemphasizes man as essentially intersubjective, as becoming through others, becoming good or evil, holy or not, especially through personal love as the basic human act; and the unity of love of God and love of neighbor is reaffirmed. The essay, " On the Evangelical Counsels," [75] underlines the universality of the task of becoming (call to perfection), again in terms of personal love " even " as criterion of becoming through the counsels (vows).

In STh VIII five essays deserve mention. The essay " One Mediator and Many Mediations," [76] emphasizes man's inter-communicative existence as the basis of mutual mediation of all men on every level of becoming and offers a sort of " socialism " of grace, merit, and indulgences. The essay on " The Experiment with Man: Theological Observations of Man's Self-Manipulation," [77] and " The Problem of Genetic Manipulation," [78] both serve to apply the ideas of becoming and freedom to contemporary issues, again to show that free becoming is man's task and responsibility. The short and unlikely essay, "A Brief Theological Study on Indulgence," [79] serves to support a point of this study in viewing indulgences as a mode of becoming. And the essay, " Immanent and Transcendent Consummation of the World," [80] once again affirms that all self-fulfilment requires others.

on the history of the sacrament of penance. Uniform in appearance with the twelve (to date) volumes of the STh is a *Register* (Index) to STh I-X compiled by K. Neufeld and R. Bleistein.

[73] STh VII 273-280; ThI VII 285-293.
[74] STh VII 283-303; ThI VIII 3-23.
[75] STh VII 404-434; ThI VIII 133-167.
[76] STh VIII 218-235; ThI IX 169-184.
[77] STh VIII 260-285; ThI IX 205-224.
[78] STh VIII 286-321; ThI IX 225-252.
[79] STh VIII 472-487; ThI X 150-165.
[80] STh VIII 593-609; ThI X 273-289.

In STh IX we find more on man's dependence on others for self-enactment and on love as self-transcendence,[81] as well as a brief treatment once more of the theme of death,[82] and a further emphasis on freedom and becoming.[83] In STh X there is still another essay on death,[84] and again free becoming is central; there is published (in German for the first time) an old philosophical essay on truth,[85] dating from 1938 (published in Portuguese) and translated into English in 1964.

It is the essay on self-experience and God-experience,[86] however, that can serve as the focal point of these later volumes of STh, volumes whose essays add nothing substantially new to the culminating essays of STh VI. In this essay Rahner illustrates both his form and matter, his structure and content, his method and conclusions. The primacy of the subject, as source of paradigms, as *very* paradigm, plus the transcendental method as a way of reaching the nature of that subject (nature understood as the conditions of possibility of that subject's experience), produce not only a model of approach to other anthropological questions, philosophical and theological because transcendental, but also produce experientially self-verifiable conclusions. The most important conclusion is Rahner's latter-day explicitation of this same primacy of the subject as actually a primacy of the *inter*subjective, i. e., of *person* (since this word must be understood as an essentially relational concept: person in community—though, of course, so also should subject, at least in the ordinary sense of there being no " subject " without an " object ") .[87] We have already seen becoming as evolution, whether only as explicitation (something it seems a user of transcendental method can always claim) or as ac-

---

[81] STh IX 242-256; ThI XI 230-244.

[82] STh IX 323-335; ThI XI 309-321.

[83] STh IX 519-540; ThI XII 181-201.

[84] STh X 181-199; ThI XIII 169-186.

[85] STh X 21-40; ThI XIII 13-31.

[86] STh X 133-144; ThI XIII 122-132.

[87] Discussion remains possible on whether this is a latter-day conclusion or a latter-day explication of an already (and from the beginning) implicitly and transcendentally necessary structure.

tually something new added in later years. Now in this essay
we find, as it were, a theoretically more remote basis, both in
method and in content (revealed by that method), of Rahner's
ideas on person as becoming. Experience in general precedes
the distinction into knowledge and freedom (intellect and will,
as the two "powers" of spirit); thus a transcendental theory
of experience—one thinks of Merleau-Ponty and late Sartre
who speak of lived experience (le vécu) instead of consciousness—underlies one of knowing (and thus of the key concepts
of spirit, matter, and becoming, as in SW, HW, and PH, to
mention only a few sources and to think now only of first otherness) and one of loving (and thus of this spirit-in-matter in its
second becoming, through second otherness, in freedom and
love, as in HW and in the essays of freedom and those on love
of God and love of neighbor). In other words, Rahner is here
claiming that prior to the articulation of man's structure and
content through conscious, reflective, explicit use of transcendental method, there is already a unity of experience of self
(*Selbsterfahrung*: self-experience) and experience of God (*Gotteserfahrung*: God-experience [88]) which is the condition of possibility, as source and ground, of all that can be worked out
in terms of knowledge and freedom (love) .[89]

[88] In a strictly philosophical attitude one would, of course, have to insist that
this God-experience "really" is a life-experience (*Lebenserfahrung*) or a being-
experience (*Seinserfahrung*), i. e., an experience of being as the infinite horizon
enabling us to experience finite beings, including ourselves (*Selbsterfahrung*)
as finite; naming this "God" would seem to be an act outstripping strict philosophical bounds. Yet we must also recognize Rahner's claim in numerous essays
which, since not directly relevant to our theme and our philosophical treatment,
have not been cited, that philosophy must eventually become theology when it
reaches fulfilment since (as is clear in his ideas on grace, the supernatural
existential, and the anonymous Christian) the concrete, contemporary philosopher
also lives, experiences, knows, and loves within an already and always graced
horizon.

[89] Thus this essay's main point is already contained in Rahner's ideas of the
supernatural existential and the anonymous Christian: the very horizon of experience itself has been changed by the historical event of Christ, so that it
is now impossible to experience anything as a pre-Christian did. See STh X 134;
ThI XIII 123: "The transcendental directedness of man to the unencompassable,
ineffable mystery, which is the condition of the possibility of knowledge and free-

Let us turn to the text itself. The first point is that self-experience is the condition for God-experience, and *vice versa*.[90] There is the familiar notion, of course, that in transcending toward the infinite horizon of being finite objects are experienced (then known) as finite.[91] I want to emphasize the *vice versa*, the *und umgekehrt*. These two, self-experience and God-experience, *mutually* condition one another; they are given, actually in one complex, multi-faceted activity.[92] But even more I want to call attention to two questions: How does experience of my life or of my own being (*Lebens-* or *Seinserfahrung*) "become" experience of God (*Gotteserfahrung*)?; and : Is there another experience which makes possible *both* self-experience and God-experience? These two questions have one answer, the answer this study has emphasized, and called second otherness. It is the point of the most valid criticism of Rahner (yet one which he can escape), the point of the doctrine of unity of love of God and love of neighbor.

The constant refrain of this study (that the concept of person is central to Rahner's transcendental anthropology, both philosophical and theological, and that this concept is one of person as becoming, becoming first as spirit becomes itself in world or matter, and second as this constituted "starting" essence of materialized-spirit-spiritualized-matter now freely relates to a world primarily constituted by others like myself) has emphasized second otherness, the arena of freedom and love,

dom and thus of very life as a subject, has the meaning of an actual, even though unthematic [implicit] God-experience."

[90] See STh X 136; ThI XIII 125: "... the original *God*-experience is the condition of possibility and constitutive element of self-experience ..."; "... without God-experience no self-experience is possible ..."; "... self-experience is the condition for God-experience because a reference [relation] to being as such and thus to God can be given only where (precisely in the *Vorgriff* toward being as such) the subject himself is given in distinction from his act and its object."

[91] See STh X 137; ThI XIII 126: "Man's transcendentality toward absolute being, in knowledge and freedom ... is also the condition for the possibility that the subject experience himself strictly *as* such and in *this* sense has already and always 'objectified' himself."

[92] Thus Rahner speaks of the *unity* (not the identity, or *Selbigkeit*) of experience of self and experience of God; see STh X 135-136; ThI XIII 124-125.

of at least the ethical, as the most important condition for personal becoming, because it is free. Rahner has already claimed the unity of love of God and love of neighbor. Now he claims the unity of experience of self and experience of neighbor. The point not to be missed is that it is not experience of things, of objects, which conditions the experience of self, of being a self, of becoming a self, of becoming a person, but another person.

" Man comes to himself only in encounter with other men, with the other person who presents himself historically to his experience in knowledge and freedom, with the other person who is not a thing but a man." [93] Rahner admits that in the abstract one might try to conceive of this self-becoming as happening through an " object." But " object " here, in itself, is, he wants to emphasize, a neutral term which gets involuntarily or instinctively thought of as a thing.[94] " But in actuality it's quite otherwise," he says.[95]

Man's other, i. e., the being with whom man is [acts, lives, knows, loves],[96] is not just any object with which he can bring into act his experience of himself. The true, living, concrete life-experience, which is identical with concrete self-experience has, relative to its ' objects,' a structure in which not all beings stand with equal right on the same plane; this life-experience is, despite the predominance today of the thing-oriented sciences, sciences which also include man as one such thing in their range of objects, an experience of a world of persons, a world in which things are elements in the encounter with and because of persons, not the other way around. In the knowledge and freedom of the concrete, active living of life, the I is always related to a you, just as originally with the you as with the I, always experiencing himself only inso-

---

[93] STh X 138; ThI XIII 127.

[94] STh X 138; ThI XIII 127: Rahner seems almost autobiographical in this " wir " and in the phrase " in einer alten philosophischen Gewohnheit." Note that the translation is mistaken in making *unwillkürlich* mean " not without reason," for it means " instinctively," " involuntarily "; i. e., it's something to be *resisted*.

[95] STh X 138; ThI XIII 127.

[96] This long way of translating *Mitmensch* seems necessary because the standard " fellow creature " or " fellowman " doesn't sufficiently call attention to the neutrality Rahner wants the term to have in this context. *Welt*, on the other hand, usually can be divided into *Umwelt* (things) and *Mitwelt* (persons).

far as distinguishing himself from and identifying himself with
the other person in the encounter. The original objectivity of self-
experience happens necessarily in the subjectivity of the encounter
with other persons in dialogue, in trusting and loving encounter.
One experiences oneself not in experiencing *things* but in experiencing *persons*.[97]

What has Rahner essentially said? Now he has a unity of
three experiences: experience of self, of another person (finite,
human), and of God (of being—or Being—and then, inter-
pretatively, or as " articulated," God—infinite, divine person).
These three experiences are three relations, or experiences of
the subject or self as living three relations: to himself, to his
fellow human person, and to God.[98] Rahner already said that
self-experience occurred in unity with God-experience.[99] Now
he says that " self-experience happens in unity with experience
of others." [100] In 1965 he had already, and forcefully, affirmed
the unity of love of God and love of neighbor, and on the basis
of the same methodological paradigm that allowed his thesis of
self-transcendence in PH, essential to a true concept of person
as becoming, viz., the transcendental method of horizon in the
activity of intellect (cognition) and will (freedom, love). In
other words, just as God (as Being—or ground of being [in
this example, being as knowable—the true]) is co-known non-
objectively in every act of knowing objects, and just as God
(as the infinite good or value) is co-loved implicitly in every
act of choosing finite goods, so Rahner here is, as it were,
getting these two acts down to their ground as the *basic experience of relation to otherness*. And what does he say? He
says what has been his constant, if sometimes none too trans-
parently presented, thesis, right from the start: one becomes
oneself through others, the thesis of this study, Rahner's doctrine of personal becoming. One becomes a knower both

[97] STh X 138-139; ThI XIII 127. Rahner's emphasis.

[98] STh X 139-140; ThI XIII 128.

[99] God is here conceived, again, at least as that ground of being supporting cognition of all objects as objects, as intellect moves toward it as horizon, and supporting love of freedom toward all finite goods as not the whole of goodness to
which will opens.

[100] STh X 139; ThI XIII 128.

through the other who is God (the non-objectively co-known supporting horizon) and through the other who or which is the objectively known. One becomes a lover, in like manner, through the other, as when, in loving the concrete other, the source and support of all being and goodness is co-loved.

Now it may be said that if we reduce experience to knowing and loving, then all we do is use one word to include two, as when spirit includes intellect and will (as its emanations and specifications relative to being's transcendentality as truth and goodness and *vice versa*). Rahner is, however, attempting here, in this essay of 1971,[101] to show a radical, metaphysical dependence of person on person for becoming. This is more than saying the radical, metaphysical dependence of finite, created being on God as infinite creator, source of being; that applies as well to things and does not speak to or about persons; thus even *my* knowing *things,* and even knowing them *as* finite and thus as requiring an *in*finite horizon as measure, etc., is not of itself an experience of myself, a *Selbsterfahrung,* and therefore not really a God-experience; hence the woefully inadequate nature of " proofs " for God's existence based on such " experience." Thus also the necessity of experience of the *personal* other (" *der* " *Andere* instead of " *das* " *Andere*).

That this reading of Rahner is so can be shown clearly. To use our terms first and second otherness, e. g., it has already been said that second otherness is even the medium to full first otherness; in other words, the other person is even the mediation of my own body; the way I appropriate my incarnate self is in and through relation to you. Now Rahner could not assent to this unless he held a primacy of the other, and a primacy of person-experience (person-knowledge, person-love) over thing-experience, and he does.[102] My own experience of my own embodiment presupposes my encounter with your em-

---

[101] In 1969 and 1970, and even earlier, he had already been using and working in terms of experience; see " *Gotteserfahrung heute,*" 161-176 in STh IX; ThI XI 149-165.

[102] This thesis, increasingly common among psychologists, thus has a metaphysical as well as phenomenological basis, as, e. g., in Buber, Kwant, Strasser, A. Brunner, and Levinas.

bodiment, the embodiment of another person.[103] Furthermore (and this is extremely significant for our thesis that Rahner's concept is one of personal becoming, i. e., that one becomes a person through community, through other persons), Rahner denies full reality to a " person " (or better, an individual) who is not in relation: " he who hasn't found his neighbor is truly not present to himself; he is not a concrete subject, capable of self-identity, but at most an abstract philosophical subject, a man who has lost himeslf." [104] Abstract, untrue, lost, without identity—these mean without relation, a purely " philosophical " (rational, logical) conception. The individual finds himself and becomes a person through finding his neighbor, through relation, in which he is also now true, concrete, a living person, not a dead abstraction.[105]

So there is self-encounter or self-experience (self-identity, self-knowledge, self-appropriation) only when one encounters another person, in the experience of distance and relation.[106] Now how and where does God-experience fit in? Is it cause or effect of experience of another, itself the cause or at least condition of self-experience? [107] Rahner speaks of these three as three aspects of one experience, as three aspects which mutually or reciprocally condition one another.[108] But is there no priority, even of time, if not of logic? Rahner clearly comes down strongly on the side of love of the finite human person as the most essential of the three. In essence he says that only in loving another *person* can I and do I open up to the breadth of horizon that is God, and only this openness is a true and deep enough enactment of my freedom to touch the innermost core of my personhood and thus account for personal becoming.

[103] STh X 139; ThI XIII 127.

[104] STh X 139; ThI XIII 128. This is the contemporary distinction between individual and person, individual being the abstract entity conceived as without relations, person being the concrete entity conceived with all its relations.

[105] Note the opening words of the quotation above: " The true, living, concrete, etc."

[106] STh X 138; ThI XIII 127.

[107] And when we now read self-experience, let us also understand self-identity, self-knowledge, self-appropriation, freedom, etc., i. e., personal becoming.

[108] STh X 139; ThI XIII 128.

Sometimes Rahner seems to be saying that experiencing God is the goal, end, or purpose of experiencing self and others, and then God-experience seems to mean not just the background or supporting condition of experience (love, knowledge) of self and others—which is the usual way God as horizon "operates" in Rahner's treatment, e. g., in the concepts of genuine becoming as becoming more, not just becoming different (self-transcendence), as in PH, or in the concept of objective knowledge (but less so in the concept of love of God and love of neighbor) —but now *reaching* God, so that knowing and loving others become means to this end.[109] Any language, of course, of means and ends must be guarded so that person, whether human or divine, be preserved from any reduction to pure means.

Sometimes, on the other hand, Rahner seems to be saying that love of neighbor is everything, the fulness of the law, man's whole destiny, that in loving one's neighbor or not one finds or loses oneself and thus is saved or not, and that in loving one's neighbor one has already found God, even if only implicitly.[110]

What we must say, then, can be put in the old and familiar terms of *in se* and *quoad nos,* or ontological priority and logical priority. In other words, in terms of what must be absolutely first, prior, more basic, etc., experience (knowledge, love) of God is Rahner's meaning. Yet this ontologically prior and already always given experience of God is itself by no means logically prior, but only subsequently the product of articula-

---

[109] This is the way we could read his statement (in STh IX 166; ThI XI 154): "This God-experience must not be conceived of as though it were *one* particular experience *alongside* others. . . . God-experience constitutes rather . . . the ultimate. depth and radical essence of every spiritual-personal experience (of love, fidelity, hope, etc.) and is thus precisely at the origin of the one totality of experience in which the spiritual person appropriates [takes possession of] himself and becomes responsible for himself" (Rahner's emphasis).

[110] Thus STh X 140; ThI XIII 128-129: ". . . love of neighbor is the fulness of the law and . . . in it the destiny of man as a whole is decided. . . man finds or loses himself in his neighbor; . . . man has already found God . . . only if he has truly reached out to his neighbor and in that other reached himself, in an act of unconditional love."

tion and interpretation in history, a history of self and God
in unity.   And these reversing (mutual, reciprocal) priorities
are the very reason why a transcendental method is needed and
why it can succeed. As Rahner says,

> . . . the relatedness of the subject, in every act, with the same
> transcendental necessity, applies both to God and neighbor as it
> applies to the subject himself, if God and the other person . . . are
> not [to be merely] particular regional occurrences within the general
> area of experience, but actualities given with transcendental neces-
> sity, realities which open up and support experience as a whole.[111]

As Rahner often said, on the strength of the transcendental
method, beginning with SW, God, as support or ground of
being, is given to man as the very condition of the possibility
of man's experience at all and as such. God is just as immediately given as what He grounds, in human cognition and freedom,
but He is not given objectively but non-objectively, as the
condition for what *is* given objectively. What Rahner has lat-
terly emphasized is that the nature or content of this " object "
is not a neutral question; the *Mitmensch*—the " with " of
man—is not arbitrarily either of things or persons, but must
be first and foremost personal, or man's self-enactment is
aborted and his openness inadequate: only in another human
person, encountered in dialogue, in love, can self-transcendence
occur and can my freedom be engaged.

Thus while, in the absolute order, experience (love, knowledge) of God is the transcendental a priori condition for the
very possibility of experience (love, knowledge) of self and
experience (love, knowledge) of another, in the temporal order,
the order of discovery, of time and of history, experience (love,
knowledge) of another human person is the transcendental a
priori condition for the very possibility of experience (love,
knowledge) of self and of experience (love, knowledge) of God.

ANDREW TALLON

Marquette University
Milwaukee, Wisconsin

[111] STh X 140; ThI XIII 129.

BIBLIOGRAPHY

1939

1. ALLERS, Rudolf. Review of *Geist in Welt*, 1st edition, in *The New Scholasticism* 13, 377-381.

2. VAN STEENBERGHEN, Fernand. Review of *Geist in Welt*, 1st edition, in *Revue néoscolastique de philosophie* [now *Revue philosophique de Louvain*] 42, 606-608.

3. VON BALTHASAR, Hans Urs. Review of *Geist in Welt*, 1st edition, in *Zeitschrift für katholische Theologie* 63, 372, 375-379.

4. ZELLER, H., S.J. Review of *Geist in Welt*, 1st edition, in *Gregorianum* 20, 471-474.

1940

5. FABRO, Cornelio, C.P. Review of *Geist in Welt*, 1st edition, in *Divus Thomas* 43, 168-171.

6. DE VRIES, Joseph, S.J. Review of *Geist in Welt*, 1st edition, in *Scholastik* [now *Theologie und Philosophie*] 15, 404-409.

1091

7. COLLINS, James. "The German Neoscholastic Approach to Heidegger." *The Modern Schoolman* 21, 143-152.

1948

8. ROBBERS, H. *Wijsbegeerte en Openbaring*. Utrecht: Het Spectrum.

1949

9. FRIES, Heinrich. *Die katholische Religionsphilosophie der Gegenwart*, Heidelberg: F. H. Kerle.

10. TRÜTSCH, J. *Ss. Trinitatis inhabitatio apud theologos recentiores.* Trento (see pp. 107-116.).

1950

11. QUINN, Edward. "Hearers of the Word: Discussion of *Hörer des Wortes.*" *The Downside Review* 68, 146-157.

1951

12. VON BALTHASAR, Hans Urs. *Karl Barth. Darstellung und Deutung seiner Theologie*. Köln (2nd ed., 1962: see pp. 303-312; 4th ed. Einsiedeln, 1976.)

13. DIRKS, Walter. "Wie erkenne ich, was Gott von mir will? Zur Berechtigung einer 'Situationsethik.'" *Frankfurter Heft* 6, 229-244. (Reprinted as paperback: Frankfurt, 1978: Fischer Taschenbücher 8106.) (See also No. 22.)

1952

14. KENNY, John Peter, S.J. "The Problem of Concupiscence: A Recent Theory of Professor Karl Rahner I." *Australasian Catholic Record* 29, 209-304. (See also Nos. 17 and 41.)

15. NINK, Casper, S.J. *Ontologie*. Freiburg. Passim.

1953

16. HUFNAGEL, A. "Der Intuitionsbegriff des Thomas von Aquin." *Theologische Quartalschrift* 133, 427-436.

17. KENNY, John Peter, S.J. "The Problem of Concupiscence: A Recent Theory of Professor Karl Rahner II." *Australasian Catholic Record* 30, 23-32. (See also Nos. 14 and 41.)

18. KENNY, John Peter, S.J. "Reflections on Human Nature and the Supernatural." *Theological Studies* 14, 280-287.

19. MALEVEZ, Léopold, S.J. "La gratuité du surnaturel." *Nouvelle Revue Théologique* 75, 561-586 and 673-689.

1954

20. ROEGELE, O.B. "Deutscher Theologe von Weltruf." *Rheinischer Merkur* 9 (No. 31), 6.

1955

21. VON BALTHASAR, Hans Urs. "Grösse und Last der Theologie heute. Einige grundsätzliche Gedanken zu zwei Aufsatzbänden Karl Rahners." *Wort und Wahrheit* 10, 531-533.

22. DIRKS, Walter. "How Can I Know What God Wants of Me?" Cross Currents 5, 76-92 (translation of No. 13 by Sally Cunneen).

23. DONCEEL, Joseph, S.J. *Philosophical Psychology.* New York: Sheed & Ward. (See also Nos. 50 and 246.)

1956

24. GIBELLINI, R. "La generazione come mezzo di trasmissione del peccato originale nel Decreto Tridenttino 'De peccato originali.'" *Studia Patavina* 3, 389-420.

25. METZ, Johann Baptist. "Karl Rahner—Rückgang durch sein Arbeitsfeld." *Korrespondenzblatt des Canisianum* (Innsbruck) 90 (1956-1957) 57-62.

26. QUINN, Edward. "Renewal of Theology." *The Downside Review* 74, 289-301.

27. SWEENEY, J. F. "Recent Developments in Dogmatic Theology." *Theological Studies* 17, 368-413.

1957

28. BRUNNER, August, S.J. "Die Erkenntnis des Willens Gottes nach den Geistlichen Übungen des hl. Ignatius von Loyola." *Geist und Leben* 30, 199-212.

29. DONCEEL, Joseph, S.J. "A Thomistic Misapprenhension?" *Thought* 32, 189-198.

1958

30. CORETH, Emerich, S.J. "Metaphysik als Aufgabe," in Coreth, E., ed., *Aufgaben der Philosophie.* Innsbruck: Felizian Rauch Verlag. (See pp. 13-95.)

31. LOBKOWICZ, Nikolaus. "Zu Karl Rahners *Geist in Welt.*" *Philosophisches Jahrbuch* 67 (1958-1959), 406-410.

1959

32. CIRNE-LIMA, Carlos. *Der personale Glaube.* Eine erkenntnismeta-

physiche Studie. Innsbruck: Felizian Rauch Verlag. (See also No. 159.)

33. BRUGGER, Walter, S.J. *De Anima Humana.* Pullach: Berchmanskolleg.

34. ERNST, Cornelius, O.P. "A Theology of Death." *The Clergy Review* 44, 588-602.

35. HAARSMA, F. "Beschouwingen van Dr. Karl Rahner S.J. over natuur en genade." *Nederlands katholieke stemmen* 55, 115-122.

36. HAIBLE, E. "Die Einwohnung der drei göttlischen Personen im Christen nach den Ergebnissen der neueren Theologie." *Theologische Quartalschrift* 139, 1-27, esp. 7-9.

37. VOLKEN, L. "Um die theologische Bedeutung der Privatoffenbarung." *Freiburger Zeitschrift für Philosophie und Theologie* 6, 431-439.

1960

38. DE LETTER, P., S.J. "Divine Quasi-formal Causality." *The Irish Theological Quarterly* 27, 221-228.

39. HABBEL, Irmingard. *Die Sachverhaltsproblematik in der Phänomenologie und bei Thomas von Aquin.* Regensburg: Verlag Josef Habbel.

40. HUBER, N. Die Berufung des Menschen zur Gnade nach der Theologie der Gegenwart. Ein Betrag zur theologischen Anthropologie. (Dissertation in theology, Tübingen.)

41. KENNY, John Peter, S.J., "Problem of Concupiscence." *Theology Digest* 8, 163-166. (Condensation of Nos. 14 and 17.)

42. LAUBACH, J. "Karl Rahner," in L. Reinisch (ed.): *Theologen unserer Zeit.* Munchen. (See also No. 116.) (Relevant pp. are 222-244.)

43. NICOLAS, J.-H. "Une théologie interrogative." *Freiburger Zeitschrift für Philosophie und Theologie* 7, 428-433.

44. STAMPA, L. "Zur Theologie des Todes." *Freiburger Zeitschrift für Philosophie und Theologie* 7, 56-63.

45. "The Rahner Brothers." *Blackfriars* 41, 170-172.

1961

46. BURRELL, David B., C.S.C. "Many Masses and One Sacrifice. A Study of the Thought of Karl Rahner." *Yearbook of Liturgical Studies* 2, 103-117.

47. CONGAR, Yves, O.P. "Inspiration des écritures canoniques et apostolicité de l'église." *Revue des Sciences philosophiques et théologiques* 45, 32-42. (See also No. 69.)

48. CONGAR, Yves, O.P. *Sacerdoce et laicat devant leurs tâches d'évangelisation.* Paris: Editions du Cerf. (Relevant pp. are 329-356.)

49. CORETH, Emerich, S.J. *Metaphysik.* Eine methodisch-systematische Grundlegung. Innsbruck: Felizian Rauch Verlag. (See also No. 272.)

50. DONCEEL, Joseph, S.J. *Philosophical Psychology.* New York: Sheed & Ward, 2nd edition. (See also Nos. 23 and 246.)

51. KÜHN, U. *Natur und Gnade.* Untersuchungen zur deutschen katholischen Theologie der Gegenwart. Berlin.

52. McCOOL, Gerald A., S.J. "Recent Trends in German Scholasticism: Brunner and Lotz." *International Philosophical Quarterly* 1, 668-682.

53. McCOOL, Gerald A., S.J. "The Philosophy of the Human Person in Karl Rahner's Theology." *Theological Studies* 22, 537-562.

54. MEYER, Hans. *Thomas von Aquin.* Sein System und seine geistesgeschichtliche Stellung. Paderborn: Verlag Ferdinand Schöningh, 2nd edition.

55. MILLER, Barry, S.M. *The Range of Intellect.* London: Geoffrey Chapman.

1962

56. ALONSO-SCHÖKEL, Luis, S.J. "Motivos sapienciales y de alianza en Gn 2-3." *Biblica* 43, 295-316. (See also No. 154.)

57. BLAJOT, J. "Noticia de Karl Rahner, S.J." *Hechos y dichos*, 5ff.

58. BRÄNDLE, M. "Warum is die Bibel heilig?" *Orientierung* 26, 153-160.

59. Diederich, H. "Zur Diagnose der Häresie. Notizien zu *Häresien der Zeit.*" *Franziskanische Studien* 44, 287-301.

60. DONCEEL, Joseph, S.J. *Natural Theology.* New York: Sheed & Ward.

61. HÜBNER, S. "Kirchenbusse und Exkommunikation bei Cyprian." *Zeitschrift für katholische Theologie* 84, 49-84.

62. McCOOL, Gerald A., S.J. "The Primacy of Intuition." *Thought* 37, 57-73.

63. METZ, Johann Baptist. *Christliche Anthropozentrik.* Über die Denkform des Thomas von Aquin. München: Kösel-Verlag. (See also No. 295.)

64. MURRAY, C. "Basic Principles of Mariology: Karl Rahner and Duns Scotus." *Australasian Catholic Record* 39, 68-74.

65. STOECKLE, B. *Gratia supponit naturam.* Geschichte und Analyse eines theologischen Axioms unter bes. Berücksichtigung seines patristischen Ursprungs, seiner Formulierung in der Hochscholastik und seiner zentralen Position in der Theologie des 19. Jahrhunderts. Rome. (See esp. pp. 200-207, 251-256.)

66. VORGRIMLER, Herbert. *Karl Rahner, Denker over God en wereld.* Tielt: Lannoo. (Translation of No. 89 by Maurice Bogaers.)

67. WALDENFELS, H. ". . . *omnes vult salvos fieri* . . ." (1 Tim, 2, 4). *De sententia P. Caroli Rahner, S.J. circa voluntatem salvificam Dei universalem.* Tokyo: Shingaku Kenkyu, No. 12.

1963

68. BLAJOT, J. "El seglar y la teología según Karl Rahner: *Apostolado Laical* 1, 5-12.

69. CONGAR, Yves, O.P. "Inspiration and the Apostolicity of the Church." *Theology Digest* 11, 187-191. (Condensation of No. 47.)

70. DE LETTER, P., S.J. " 'Pure' or 'Quasi'-formal Causality." *International Theological Quarterly* 30, 36-47.

71. DE LETTER, P. S.J. "The Theology of God's Self-Gift." *Theological Studies* 24, 402-422.

72. DEMSKE, James M., S.J. *Sein, Mensch, und Tod:* das Todesproblem bei Martin Heidegger. Freiburg: Karl Alber Verlag.

73. GERKEN, John D., S.J. *Toward a Theology of the Layman.* New York: Herder and Herder.

74. HILL, William J., O.P. "Uncreated Grace: A Critique of Karl Rahner." *The Thomist* 27, 333-356.

75. JORDAN, P. "Council on the Right Road." Interview with Karl Rahner. *Catholic Messenger* 82, 1ff.

76. LANGEMEYER, Bernhard, O.F.M. *Die dialogische Personalismus in der evangelischen und katholischen Theologie der Gegenwart.* Paderborn: Verlag Bonifacius-Druckerei.

77. LEGRAND, F. "Une conception moderne du salut des infidèles qui fait obstacle à l'élan apostolique d'après P. K. Rahner. Des missionaires expriment leur inquiétude." *Le Christ au monde* 8, 457-465; replies 586-587. In English: "A Modern Conception of the Salvation of Infidels Which Hampers Apostolic Zeal According to Fr. Karl Rahner." *Christ to the World* 8, 421-428; replies 543-544. (See also No. 000.)

78. LOHFINK, Norbert, S.J. "Genesis 2f. als 'geschichtliche Ätiologie.' Gedanken zu einen neuen hermeneutischen Begriff." *Scholastik* 38, 321-334. (See also No. 179.)

79. MACQUARRIE, John. "Theologians of Our Time: Karl Rahner, S.J." *Expository Times* 74, 194-197. Also in *Studies in Christian Existentialism* (Montreal: McGill University Press/London: SCM Press/Philadelphia: Westminster Press, 1966), Chapter 14. Also in A.W. and E. Hastings (eds.) *Theologians of Our Time* (Edinburgh: T. & T. Clark, 1966), 132-142.

80. MACQUARRIE, John. *Twentieth Century Religious Thought.* The Frontiers of Philosophy and Theology. 1900-1960. London: SCM Press. (See also No. 455.)

81. MASCALL, E. L. "Grace and Nature in East and West." *Church Quarterly Review* 164, 332-347.

82. RICHARD, R. "Rahner's Theory of Doctrinal Development." *Proceedings of the Catholic Theological Society of America* 18, 157-180.

83. RÖPER, Anita. *Die anonymen Christen.* Mainz: Mathias-Grünewald Verlag. (See also No. 231.)

84. VAN ROO, William A., S.J. "Reflections on Karl Rahner's *Kirche und Sakramente.*" *Gregorianum* 44, 465-500.

85. SCHALK, A. "Beyond the Council. Fr. Rahner's Views." *U.S. Catholic* 29, 14. (See also No. 86.) See also *The Way* 19, 16-21 and 25-30.

86. SPADAFORA, F. "Reply to 'Beyond the Council. Fr. Rahner's Views.'" *U.S. Catholic* 29, 14-15. (See also No. 85 and No. 144.)

87. STOECKLE, B. "Erbsündige Begierlichkeit. Weitere Erwägungen zu einer theologischen und anthropologischen Gestalt." *Münchener theologische Zeitung* 14, 225-242, esp. 225-231.

88. TRETHOWAN, Illtyd. "The Union of Grace. A Suggestion." *The Downside Review* 81, 317-327.

89. VORGRIMLER, Herbert. *Karl Rahner.* Leben, Denken, Werke. Freiburg: Herder.

90. WALLACE, William, O.P. "Existential Ethics: A Thomistic Appraisal." *The Thomist* 27, 493-515.

91. "Karl Rahner on the Nature of the Church." *Tablet* 217, 1102-1103.

92. "Don't Make Dioceses too Small." *Tablet* 217, 1392.

93. "Guardini Retires, Karl Rahner Gets Post." *Catholic Messenger* 81. 1.

94. "Televising the Mass." *America* 109, 619-620.

1964

95. VAN ACKERN, Gerald, S.J. "Ad multos annos." *Theology Digest* 12, 145.

96. ARTOLA, A. M. "Judicios críticos en torno a la 'Inspiración biblica' de P. Rahner." *Lumen* 13, 385-403.

97. AUER, Johann. "Das Werk Karl Rahners." *Theologische Revue* 60, 145-156.

98. BAKER, Kenneth, S.J. "Rahner: The Transcendental Method." *Continuum* 2, 51-59.

99. BOMMER, J. *La confession—contrainte ou libération?* Paris: Editions Fleurus (trans. from German).

100. BURTON, K. "Why Blame It on Us Women? Women and the Church." *Sign* 43. 49.

101. DEJAIFVE, G., S.J. Review of *Gott in Welt* in *Nouvelle revue théologique* 86, 757-759 (see No. 123).

102. CORETH, Emerich, S.J. "Identität und Differenz." In No. 123, 158-187.

103. EBERT, Hermann. " 'Die Stunde der Transzendenz,' Das Gottesbild unserer Zeit." *Hochland* 56, 193-209. (See also No. 104.)

104. EBERT, Hermann. "The Hour of Transcendence: Origin of Man's Soul." *Philosophy Today* 8, 71-83. (Trans. of No. 103 by Caroline E. Schuetzinger.)

105. FERRETTI, Giovanni. "La filosofia della religione come antropologia in un'opera di Karl Rahner." *Rivista di filosofia neo-scolastica* 56, 96-106.

106. FIORITO, M. A., S.J. "En homenaje a Karl Rahner." *Ciencia y fe* 20, 151-161.

107. FLICK, M. "Problemi teologici sull 'ominazione.' " *Gregorianum* 44, 62-70.

108. GRANFIELD, P. "T.V. or Not T.V.: Fr. K. Rahner's Arguments against Televising the Mass." *American Ecclesiastical Review* 150, 440-442.

109. GREEN, J. "The Mass Prepared For, Thanked For." *Emmanuel* 70, 508-509.

110. HASTINGS, Adrian. "The Sacramentality of the Church." *Eastern Churches Quarterly* 16, 219-225.

111. HENKEY, Charles. "Episcopacy and Primacy." *Proceedings of the Catholic Theological Society of America* 19, 187-209.

112. KERN, Walter, S.J. "Einheit-in-Mannigfaltigkeit: Fragmentarische Überlegungen zur Metaphysik des Geistes." In No. 123, 207-239, Vol. I.

113. KÜNZLE, P. "Sakramente und Ursakramente." *Freiburger Zeitschrift für Philosophie und Theologie* 10, 428-444.

114. LAJE, E. L. "Es el papado sacramento? Reflexiones a propósito de una pregunta de Karl Rahner." *Ciencia y fe* 20, 465-468.

115. LAJE, E. L. "Karl Rahner y la institución de los sacramentos." *Stromata* 21, 19-21.

116. LAUBACH, J. "Karl Rahner." 188-201 in L. Reinisch, editor, *Theologians of Our Time*. Notre Dame: Notre Dame University Press. (See also No. 42.)

117. LAUER, P. "The Paschal Character of Christian Death." *Liturgy* 33, 87-90.

118. LEGRAND, F. "A Modern Conception of the Salvation of Infidels Which Hampers Apostolic Zeal According to Fr. Karl Rahner: Replies." *Christ to the World* 9, 84-86, 166-168, 272, 365-366. (See also No. 77.)

119. McBRIAN, J. "Incarnation and Eschatology." *Cord* 14, 211-216.

120. McCOOL, Gerald A., S.J. "Philosophical Pluralism and an Evolving Thomism." *Continuum* 2, 3-16.

121. McGOWAN, J. "Modes of Concelebration and Their Relative Value: Rahner's 'Many Masses and the One Sacrifice.'" *North American Liturgical Week* 25, 101-112.

122. MERTON, Thomas, O.C.S.O. "The Monk in the Diaspora." *Blackfriars* 45, 290-302.

123. MERTON, Thomas, O.C.S.O. "The Monk in the Diaspora." *Commonweal* 79, 741-745.

124. METZ, Johann Baptist; Walter Kern, Adolf Darlap, and Herbert Vorgrimler, editors. *Gott in Welt. Festgabe für Karl Rahner zum 60. Geburtstag*. Freiburg: Herder, 2 volumes. (See also Nos. 181, 182, 256, and 351.)

125. METZ, Johann Baptist. "Widmung und Wurdigung. Karl Rahner, dem Sechzigjährigen." In No. 123, 5*-13*.

126. METZ, Johann Baptist. "Freiheit als philosophisch-theologisches Grenzproblem." 287-314 in No. 123, Vol I. (See also No. 000.)

127. METZ, Johann Baptist. *Christelijke mensbetrokkenheid*. Over de denkvorm van Thomas van Aquin. (Dutch translation of No. 63 by A. F. Wyers.) Hilversum: Paul Brand.

128. MUCK, Otto, S.J. *Die transzendentale Methode in der scholastischen Philosophie der Gegenwart*. Innsbruck: Felizian Rauch Verlag. (See also No. 296.)

129. MÜLLER, Max. *Existentialphilosophie in geistigen Leben der Gegenwart*. Heidelberg: F. H. Kerle.

130. MUSCHALEK, Georg and Franz Mayr, S.J. "Das Schriftum Karl Rahners." In No. 123, 900-904.

131. MUSCHALEK, Georg and Franz Mayr, S.J. *Karl Rahner: Verzeichnis sämlicher Schriften, 1924-1964.* Freiburg: Herder Verlag. (Offprint from No. 123; exists in two forms, one with the Tabula Gratulatoria, one without.)

132. NIEL, Henri. "Tradition et modernité en théologie (K. Rahner & B. Lonergan)." *Critique* 20, 239-259. (See also No. 226.)

133. O'BRIEN, John A. "An Interview with Karl Rahner." *U.S. Catholic* 30, 6-8.

134. O'ROURKE, T. "To Prepare a Dwelling: On Poverty." *Round Table of Franciscan Research* 29, 121-126.

135. OTT, Heinrich. "Existentiale Interpretation und anonyme Christlichkeit." In Erich Dinkler, editor, *Zeit und Geschichte.* Festgabe für Rudoff Bultmann. Tübingen: J. C. B. Mohr. Pp. 367-379.

136. PANNENBERG, Wolfhart. *Gründzuge der Christologie.* Gütersloh: G. Mohn. Passim.

137. PONTIFEX, M. "On a Book by Karl Rahner" (*Theological Investigations,* Vol. II). *The Downside Review* 82, 303-311.

138. PRENDERGAST, R. J., S.J. "The Supernatural Existential, Human Generation, and Original Sin." *The Downside Review* 82, 1-24.

139. PUNTEL, L. B., S.J. "Zum Denken Karl Rahners. Bemerkungen zur Festgabe *Gott in Welt.*" *Zeitschrift für katholische Theologie* 86, 304-320.

140. RIAZA, Fernando, S.J. "Los sesenta años del P. Karl Rahner." *Razón y fe* 170, 261-268.

141. RIENSENHUBER, Klaus, S.J. "Der 'anonyme Christ' nach Karl Rahner." *Zeitschrift für katholische Theologie* 86, 286-303. (See also Nos. 190 and 230.

142. VAN ROO, William A., S.J. "The Church and the Sacraments." *Proceedings of the Catholic Theology Society of America* 19, 161-171.

143. RÖPER, Anita. *Sind Christen Heiden?* Die anonymen Christen. Kevelaer. (See also No. 231.)

144. SCHINELLER, J. Peter, S.J. "Karl Rahner's *Hörer des Wortes:* A Summary." *The Philosopher* (Student Publication of Shrub Oak Philosophate of 11, 1-14. Fordham University.)

145. SHERLOCK, T. "Poverty." *Nuntius* 46, 103-114.

146. SPADAFORA, F. "Reply to 'Beyond the Council: Fr. Rahner's Views.'" *U.S. Catholic* 30. (See also No. 86.)

147. STROTMANN, D. T. "Primauté et céphalisation. A propos d'une étude du P. K. Rahner." *Irenikon* 37, 187-197.

148. TOPEL, L. "Rahner and McKenzie on the Social Theory of Inspiration." *Scripture* 16, 33-44.

149. YAGÜE, Joaquin, O.R.S.A. "Karl Rahner y la metafísica tomista del conocimiento." *Augustinus* 9, 193-204.

150. "Big Diocese, Small Diocese. Views of Fr. K. Rahner." *America* 110, 560.

151. "Non-Christians and Their Religion. Views of Danielou and Rahner." *Clergy Monthly Supplement* 7, 168-172.

152. "Profile: Karl Rahner, S.J." *Catholic Book Merchandiser* 7, 24-26.

1965

153. ABESAMIS, Carlos H. "Some Reflections on Karl Rahner." *Philippine Studies* 13, 492-494.

154. ALONSO-SCHÖKEL, Luis, S.J. "Sapiential and Covenant Themes in Genesis 2-3." *Theology Digest* 13, 3-10. (Condensation of No. 56.)

155. BAKER, Kenneth, S.J. *A Synopsis of the Transcendental Philosophy of Emerich Coreth and Karl Rahner.* Spokane: Gonzaga University Press.

156. BIANCHI, Eugene, S.J. "Karl Rahner in New York." *America* 112, 860-863. (Interview.)

157. BOYD, A. "Rahner—Metz—Schillebeeckx: A Futuristic Encounter." *Homilectic and Pastoral Review* 66 (1965-1966), 942-949.

158. BROOKE, O. "Natural Religion and the Supernatural Existential." *The Downside Review* 83, 201-212.

159. CIRNE-LIMA, Carlos. *Personal Faith.* New York: Herder and Herder. (Translation of No. 32 by G. Richard Dimler, S.J.)

160. CURIC, J. "Rahnerova sluzba crkvi." *Bogoslovska Smotra* 35, 92-102.

161. DHAVAMONY, Mariasusai. *Subjectivity and Knowledge in the Philosophy of Saint Thomas Aquinas.* Rome: Gregorian University Press.

162. DONCEEL, Joseph, S.J. "Teilhard de Chardin and the Body-Soul Relation." *Thought* 40, 371-389.

163. DONCEEL, Joseph, S.J. "Causality and Evolution: A Survey of Some Neoscholastic Theories." *The New Scholasticism* 39, 295-315.

164. DULLES, Avery, S.J. "The Ignatian Experience as Reflected in the Spiritual Thought of Karl Rahner." *Philippine Studies* 13, 471-494.

165. ELDERS, L. "Die Taufe der Weltreligionen. Bemerkungen zu einer Theorie Karl Rahners." *Theologie und Glaube* 55, 124-131.

166. ERNST, Cornelius, O.P. "Some Themes in the Theology of Karl Rahner." *The Irish Theological Quarterly* 32, 251-257.

167. GARCÍA DONCEL, Manuel. "Dios en el mundo. Homenaje a Karl Rahner." *Selecciones de Libros* 3/4, 90-186.

168. GONZÁLEZ, A. Enrique. "La persona y sus proyecciones axiológicas en Karl Rahner." *Franciscanum* 7, 149-201, 321-390.

169. GOUHIER, A. "De la création en théologie. Essai sur une hypothèse de Karl Rahner." *Contacts. Revue française de l'orthodoxie* 17, 302-326.

170. GRANFIELD, P. "An Interview: Karl Rahner, Theologian at Work." *American Ecclesiastical Review* 152, 217-230.

171. HÖFER, Liselotte. *Pour une pastorale oecuménique.* Lyon: Editions du Chalet (translated from German).

172. JOHN, Sr. Helen James. "Rahner on Roles in the Church." *Review for Religious* 24, 526-533.

173. LAJE, E. "Karl Rahner ye el sentido teológico de la muerte." *Stromata* 21, 515-523.

174. LAKEBRINK, Bernhard. "Der Thomistische Platonismus und die moderne Theologie." In Ludwig Landgrebe, editor: *Beispiele. Festschrift für Eugen Fink.* The Hague: Martinus Nijhoff, pp. 254-269.

175. LATOUR, J. J. "Imago Dei invisibilis. Esquisses sur les relations de l'anthropologie chrétienne et de la psychologie du Christ." In H. Bouëssé and J. J. Latour, editors: *Problèmes actuels de christologie*. Travaux du symposium de l'Arbresle 1961. Paris. See esp. pp. 227-264, and also 401-409.

176. LEVI, A. "The Religious Teaching of Karl Rahner." *The Month* 34, 234-245.

177. LINDBECK, George A. "The *A Priori* in St. Thomas' Theory of Knowledge." In *The Heritage of Christian Thought*: Essays in Honor of Robert Lowry Calhoun, edited by Robert Cushman and Egil Crislis. New York: Harper & Row, pp. 41-63.

178. LINDBECK, George A. "The Thought of Karl Rahner, S.J." *Christianity and Crisis* 25, 211-215.

179. LOHFINK, Norbert, S.J. "Genesis 2-3 as 'Historical Etiology.'" *Theology Digest* 13, 11-17. (Condensation of No. 78.)

180. McGOLDRICK, P. "Sin and the Holy Church." *The Irish Theological Quarterly* 32, 3-27.

181. METZ, Johann Baptist; Walter Kern; Adolf Darlap; and Herbert Vorgrimler, editors. *God en wereld*. Hilversum: Five Volumes (Durch translation of No. 124.)

182. METZ, Johann Baptist; Walter Kern, Adolf Darlap; and Herbert Vorgrimler, editors. *Dios en el mundo*. Homenaje a Karl Rahner. Barcelona: Herder. (Partial translation of No. 124 by Manuel García Doncel.)

183. MEYER, B. "An Apostle of *aggiornamento*." *The Priest* 21, 852-855.

184. MORGENROTH, A. "Devotion to the Sacred Heart and Modern Man." *Review for Religious* 24, 418-428.

185. MOTHERWAY, Thomas J., S.J. "Supernatural Existential." *Chicago Studies* 4, 79-103 (especially on Rahner, 83-88).

186. MUNERA, A. and R. Boada. "La sacramentalidad de la iglesia según los teólogos actuales (Rahner, Semmelroth, Schillebeeckx)." *Ecclesiastica Xaveriana* 15, 69-90.

187. NIEL, Henri. "Honouring Karl Rahner." *The Heythrop Journal* 6, 259-269.

188. PÉREZ, T. "Karl Rahner, et mejor teólogo especulativo de hoy." In Propulsores del Concilio, Vol. 18, 9-30 (Bilbao).

189. PETER, Carl J. "The Position of Karl Rahner Regarding the Supernatural: A Comparative Study of Nature and Grace." *Proceedings of the Catholic Theological Society of America* 20, 81-94.

190. RIESENHUBER, Klaus, S.J. "Rahner's Anonymous Christian." *Theology Digest* 13, 163-171. (Condensation of No. 141.)

191. ROBLES, L. "Vida, muerte y eternidad del alma." *Teología espiritual* 9, 533-540.

192. SCHERER, Georg. *Anthropologische Aspekte der Erwachsesenbildung*. Osnabrück: Verlag A. Fromm.

193. SILOS, Leonardo R. "A Note on the Notion of 'Selbstvollzug' in Karl Rahner." *Philippine Studies* 13, 461-470.

194. TeSELLE, Eugene A., Jr. "The Problem of Nature and Grace." *The Journal of Religion* 45, 238-249.

195. TOMASZEWSKI, E. "La succession apostolique dans l'épiscopat à la lumière des récentes recherches bibliques et historiques" (Polish with French summary). *Roczniki teologiczno-kanoniczne* 12, 5-18.

196. VORGRIMLER, Herbert. *Karl Rahner. His Life, Thought, and Work.* London: Burns and Oates. (Translation of No. 89 by Edward Quinn.)

197. VORGRIMLER, Herbert. *Karl Rahner.* Paris: Fleurus. (Translation and adaptation of No. 89 by Charles Miller.) (Italian and Spanish translations also published, Rome and Madrid, respectively.)

198. WALDENFELS, H. "Genzai ni ikiru shingaku. K. Rahner no shingaku o megutte" (Living Theology in its Historical Setting. The Theology of Karl Rahner). *Katorikku Shingaku* (Tokyo) 7, 152-174.

199. "Karl Rahner in America." *Jubilee* 12, 22-23.

200. "Rahner on Change in the Church." *Tablet* 219, 108.

1966

201. VON BALTHASAR, Hans Urs. *Cordula oder der Ernstfall.* Einsiedeln. (See also No. 310.)

202. BOERACKER, H. Heilserfahrung und Heilsverwortung. Eine theologische Untersuchung über die Schriften Karl Rahners. Dissertation, Rome.

203. BORNHORST, G. Das Weltverständnis bei Karl Rahner. Dissertation, Magister theologiae, Würzburg.

204. GELPI, Donald L., S.J. *Life and Light.* A Guide to the Theology of Karl Rahner. New York: Sheed & Ward.

205. GELPI, Donald L., S.J. "Rahner's Theology of the Sacred Heart Devotion." *The Way* 22, 405-417.

206. GERBER, U. *Katholischer Glaubensbegriff.* Die Frage nach dem Glaubensbegriff in der katholischen Theologie vom I. Vatikanum bis zur Gegenwart. Gütersloh. See esp. 241-268.

207. HEINZ, R. *Französische Kantinterpretation in 20. Jahrhundert.* Bonn.

208. HILLMANN, E. "Anonymous Christianity and the Missions." *The Downside Review* 85, 361-379.

209. HIRSCHAUER, G. "Das Konzil und die 'grosse Hoffnung' der Theologen." *Werkhefte* 20, 237-246. Appears also as Chaper 11 in his *Der Katholizismus vor dem Risiko der Freiheit.* Nachruf auf ein Konzil. München. Published in paperback by Reinbek in 1969.

210. HOLZ, Harald. *Transzendentalphilosophie und Metaphysik.* Studie über Tendenzen in der heutigen philosophischen Grundlagenproblematik. Mainz: Matthias-Grünewald Verlag.

211. JOHN, Sr. Helen James, R.S.C.J. *The Thomist Spectrum.* New York: Fordham University Press. See 167-179: "Karl Rahner: Man as the Being Who Must Question Being."

212. KOEHNLEIN, M. Katholische Worttheologie. Eine kritische Analyse neuerer katholischer Theologie. Theology dissertation, Erlangen-Nürnberg.

213. LAFONT, G. *Peut-on connaître Dieu en Jésus-Christ?* Paris (Cogitatio Fidei 40). See 171-228.

214. De LAVELETTE, Henri, S.J. "Bulletin de théologie dogmatique." *Recherches de Sciences Religieuses* 54, 140-144, 159.

215. LENICQUE, P. "Manniska och kosmos. Karl Rahners teologiska vision." *Vår lösen* 57, 11-15.

216. LEVI, A. "The Religious Teaching of Karl Rahner." *Catholic Mind* 64, 4-13. (Reprint of No. 176.)

217. LINDBECK, George A. "Karl Rahner and a Protestant View of the Sacramentality of the Ministry." *Proceedings of the Catholic Theological Society of America* 21, 267-288.

218. McCRIMMON, M. "Karl Rahner's Approach to Secularization. A Review Article." *Japan Christian Quarterly* 32, 146-150.

219. McCUE, J. F. "Roman Catholic Perspective." *Dialog* (Minneapolis) 5, 176-181.

220. McDEVITT, P. "Pastoral Care." *The Irish Theological Quarterly* 33, 151-154.

221. MALINSKI, M. Das Leben der Kirche nach Karl Rahner. Dissertation, Rome.

222. MAXEY, M. N., R.S.C.J. "Original Sin Revisited in the Light of Karl Rahner's Supernatural Existential." *Barat Faculty Review* 1, 57-73.

223. MESA, B. "Sentido teológico de la muerte." *Franciscanum* 8, 99-101.

224. METZ, Johann Baptist. "Karl Rahner." In H. J. Schultz, editor, *Tendenzen der Theologie im 20. Jahrhundert. Eine Geschichte in Porträts.* Stuttgart: Olten. See 513-518.

225. METZ, Johann Baptist. "Freedom as a Threshold Problem between Philosophy and Theology." *Philosophy Today* 10, 264-279. (Translation of No. 126 by William J. Kramer.)

226. NIEL, Henri. "The Old and the New in Theology: Rahner and Lonergan." *Cross Currents* 16, 463-480. (See also No. 132.)

227. O'CALLAGHAN, D. "Indulgences." *The Irish Theological Quarterly* 33, 291-308.

228. O'MEARA, Thomas Franklin, O.P. "Karl Rahner on Priest, Deacon, Parish." *Worship* 40, 103-110.

229. RIEDLINGER, H. *Geschichtlichkeit und Vollendung des Wissens Christi* (Quaestiones Disputatae 32). Freiburg: Herder. See esp. 148-154.

230. RIESENHUBER, Klaus, S.J. "The Anonymous Christian According to Karl Rahner." Translation of No. 141 by Joseph Donceel, S.J., as "Afterword," 145-179, in No. 231.

231. RÖPER, Anita. *The Anonymous Christian.* New York: Sheed & Ward. (Translation of No. 83 by Joseph Donceel, S.J.)

232. SCHILLING, Sylvester Paul. "Karl Rahner." In *Contemporary Continental Theologians.* Nashville: Abingdon Press/London: S.C.M. Press. See 206-226.

233. SCHNEIDER, Richard. "A Transcendental Philosophy of the Question." *Continuum* 4, 150-153.

234. SIMONS, Eberhard. *Philosophie der Offenbarung.* In Auseinandersetzung mit *Hörer des Wortes* von Karl Rahner. Stuttgart: Kohlhammer.

235. TERÁN DUTARI, J. "Zum theologischen Verständnis der Gnade als Kreuz der Natur. *Zeitschrift für Katholische Theologie* 88, 283-314.

236. TRETHOWAN, Illtyd. "A Changing God." *The Downside Review* 84, 247-261.

237. VORGRIMLER, Herbert. *Karl Rahner: His Life, Thought, and Work.* Glen Rock: Paulist-Newman Press, Deus Books. (Translation of No. 89 by Edward Quinn.)

238. WALDENFELS, H. "Theologische Akkomodation. Erläutert an einem Modell." *Hochland* 58, 189-204.

239. WILSON, Barrie A. "The Possibility of Theology after Kant: An Examination of Karl Rahner's *Geist in Welt.*" *Canadian Journal of Theology* 12, 245-258.

240. "From Munich to Münster." *Tablet* 220, 1400-1401.

1967

241. BUCHRUCKER, A.-E. "Die Repräsentation des Opfers Christi im Abendmahl in der gegenwärtigen katholischen Theologie." *Kerygma und Dogma* 13, 273-296, especially 280ff.

242. CASALI, G. C. "E valida la tesi di K. Rahner che nega all'anima di Christo 'viatore' la visione beatifica? *Rivista di ascetica e mistica* 12, 264-279.

243. COWBURN, John, S.J. *Love and the Person.* London: Geoffrey Chapman. Published in the U.S. by Alba House (Staten Island, N.Y.) under the title *The Person and Love.* Philosophy and Theology of Love.

244. DAECKE, S. M. *Teilhard de Chardin und die evangelische Theologie.* Göttingen. See 408-410.

245. DEDEK, J. "The Theology of Devotional Confessions." *Proceedings of the Catholic Theological Society of America* 22, 215-222.

246. DONCEEL, Joseph, S.J. *Philosophical Anthropology.* New York: Sheed & Ward. Third edition of *Philosophical Psychology;* see Nos. 23 and 50.

247. FALK, Heinrich. "Can Spirit Come from Matter? *International Philosophical Quarterly* 7, 541-555.

248. GABORIAU, Florent, O.P. *Interview sur la mort avec Karl Rahner.* Paris: Lethielleux.

249. GRANFIELD, P. *Theologians at Work* (Personal Interviews). New York. See 35-50.

250. HARTMANN, Klaus. "On Taking the Transcendental Turn." *The Review of Metaphysics* 20, 223-249.

251. HOLZ, Harald. "Thomisticher Transzendentalismus: Möglichkeiten und Grenzen." *Kantstudien* 58, 376-386.

252. KRUSE, H. "Die 'Anonymen Christen' exegetisch gesehen." *Münchener theologische Zeitschrift* 18, 2-29.

253. LAKEBRINK, Bernhard. *Klassische Metaphysik*. Eine Auseinandersetzung mit der existentialen Anthropozentrik. Freiburg: Rombach.

254. de LUBAC, Henri, S.J. *Paradoxe et mystère de l'église*. Paris: Aubier Montaigne. See 153-156.

255. MASCALL, E. L. "Behind the Tortuous Style of Rahner." *Times* (18 November) 10.

256. METZ, Johann Baptist; Walter Kern; Adolph Darlap; and Herbert Vorgrimler, editors. *Orizzonti attuali della Teologia*. Rome. Volumes 1 and 2. (Italian edition of No. 124.)

257. O'MEARA, Thomas Franklin, O.P. "Karl Rahner, Theologian." *Doctrine and Life* 17, 21-37.

258. PAPAPETROU, K. *Prosopa kai Themata* (R. Bultmann, P. Tillich, D. Bonhoeffer, K. Rahner). Athens.

259. PRELLER, Victor. *Divine Science and the Science of God*. A Reformulation of Thomas Aquinas. Princeton: Princeton University Press.

260. ROBERTS, Louis. *The Achievement of Karl Rahner*. New York: Herder & Herder.

261. SCHROEDER, E. "Christian Humanism." *Journal of Ecumenical Studies* 4, 369-384.

262. SHEPHERD, William Charles. Karl Rahner and the Problem of Nature and Grace. Dissertation, Yale University.

263. SPECK, Josef. *Karl Rahners theologische Anthropologie*. Eine Einführung. München: Kösel Verlag.

264. SQUIRE, A. "Karl Rahner. A Spiritual Portent." *New Blackfriars* (1967/68) 49, 410-416.

265. Stranzinger, E. "Trinitätskonzeptionen in der neueren deutschen Theologie." *Wissenschaft und Weisheit* 30, 30-44, especially 39f.

266. WESS, P. Die Inkomprehensibilität Gottes und ihre Konsequenzen für die Gotteserkenntnis bei Thomas von Aquin und Karl Rahner. Ein krit. Vergleich mit dem Versuch einer Weiterführung im Hinblick auf eine Synthese mit der neueren protestant. Theol. und ein Gespräch mit dem moderenen Atheismus. Theology dissertation, Innsbruck University.

1968

267. De BECKER, G. "La théologie actuelle du Sacre Coeur." *Divinitas* 12, 173-190.

268. BOERACKER, H. "De gelovige en het evangeliewoord. Een onderzoek naar achtergronden van de theologie van Karl Rahner." *Tijdschrift voor Theologie* 8, 1-21.

269. BOOBYER, G. H. "Jesus as 'Theos' in the New Testament." *Bulletin of the John Rylands Library* 50, 247-261.

270. CHIRAT, H. "Quelques contributions catholiques à l'histoire des origines de la Réformation." *Revue des sciences religieuses* 42, 193-230.

271. COCHRANE, A. C. "The Theological Basis of Liturgical Devotion to Mary Re-examined." *Marian Studies* 19, 49-69.

272. CORETH, Emerich, S.J. *Metaphysics.* New York: Herder and Herder. (Partial translation—omits the Zusätze—of No. 49 by Joseph Donceel, S.J.)

273. CORRELL, D. K. "A Protestant Response to 'The Theological Basis of Liturgical Devotion to Mary Re-examined.'" *Marian Studies* 19, 70-75.

274. COUTAGUE, Paul, O.P. "Chronique teilhardienne. Teilhard et les recherches actuelles sur la philosophie de la nature." *Revue des Sciences philosophiques et théologiques* 52, 303-343; on Rahner 339-343.

275. DOHERTY, J. "The Celibacy of the Secular Priest: An Open Letter to Karl Rahner." *Catholic World* 208, 103-106.

276. EICHER, Peter. "Immanenz oder Transzendenz? Gespräch mit Karl Rahner." *Freiburger Zeitschrift für Philosophie und Theologie* 15, 29-62.

277. FILIPETTI, B. "Elementi del pensiero contemporaneo sull'ascetismo cristiano e monastico." *Vita Monastica* 22, 167-188.

278. FIORENZA, Francis P. "Introduction. Karl Rahner and the Kantian Problematic." In Karl Rahner, S.J. *Spirit in the World* (New York: Herder and Herder), xix-xlv.

279. GABORIAU, Florent, O.P. *Le tournant théologique aujourd'hui selon K. Rahner.* Tournai: Desclée.

280. GARCÍA-MURGA VÁSQUEZ, J. R. *Intimidad con Dios y servicio al prójimo.* Estudio y solución de esta antinomía a la luz de la teología de K. Rahner. Dissertation, Gregorian University, Rome. Published, Madrid.

281. GEISSER, H. "Die Interpretation der kirchlichen Lehre vom Gottmenschen bei Karl Rahner, S.J." *Kerygma und Dogma* 14, 307-330.

282. GUERARD DES LAURIERS, M. L. "La doctrine théologique du R. P. Rahner." *La pensée catholique* 117, 78-93.

283. GUTWENGER, E. "Zur Trinitätslehre von 'Mysterium Salutis' II." *Zeitschrift für katholische Theologie* 90, 325-328.

284. HODGSON, P. C. "Karl Rahner." In Wm. Jerry Booney and Lawrence E. Molumby, editors. *The New Day: Catholic Theologians of the Renewal.* Richmond: John Knox Press. See pp. 46-61.

285. KAISER, Ph. *Die gott-menschliche Einigung in Christus als Problem der spekulativen Theologie seit der Scholastik.* München: Max Hueber Verlag. See 264-290.

286. KELLER, A. *Sein oder Existenz?* Die Auslegung des Seins bei Thomas von Aquin in der heutigen Scholastik. München. See 142-153.

287. LEFEVRE, L. J. "Quelques remarques à propos d'une allocution radiophonique du R. P. Karl Rahner, S.J." *La pensée catholique* 112, 20-26.

288. LOHFINK, Norbert, S.J. "Text und Thema. Anmerkungen zum Absolutheitsanspruch der Systematik bei der Reform der theologischen Studien." *Stimmen der Zeit* 181, 120-126.

289. McKINNON, E. "The Transcendental Turn: Necessary but Not Sufficient." *Continuum* 6, 225-231.

290. MALEVEZ, Léopold, S.J. "Présence de la théologie à Dieu et à l'homme." *Nouvelle revue théologique* 90, 785-800.

291. MANN, P. "The Transcendental of the Political Kingdom." *New Blackfriars* 50, 805-812.

292. MANNERMAA, T. "Oleminenja ilmiö. Eräs Rahner-tutkimuksen perustehtävä." *Teologinen Aikakauskirja* 73, 128-134.

293. MAWSHINNEY, J. J. "The Concept of Mystery in Karl Rahner's Philosophical Anthropology." *Union Seminary Quarterly Review* 24, 17-30.

294. METZ, Johann Baptist. "Foreword: An Essay on Karl Rahner." In *Spirit in the World* (see No. 278), xiii-xviii.

295. METZ, Johann Baptist. *L'homme. L'anthropocentrique chrétienne.* Pour une interprétation ouverte de la philosophie de saint Thomas. Paris: Mame. (Translation of No. 63 by Michel Louis.)

296. MUCK, Otto, S.J. *The Transcendental Method.* New York: Herder & Herder. (Translation of No. 128 by William Seidensticker.)

297. MULLER, Charles. "Un teólogo para el hombre de hoy: Karl Rahner." *Teología y vida* 9, 296-309.

298. PANNENBERG, Wolfhart. *Was ist der Mensch?* Die Anthropologie der Gegenwart im Lichte der Theologie. Göttingen: Vandenhoeck und Ruprecht. (See also No. 408.)

299. PUNTEL, L. B., S.J. "Philosophie der Offenbarung. Kritische Überlegungen zum gleichnamigen Buch von E. Simons." *Philosophisches Jahrbuch* 76, 203-211. (See No. 234.)

300. REICHMANN, James B., S.J. "The Transcendental Method and the Psychogenesis of Being." *The Thomist* 32, 449-508.

301. ROBERTS, Louis. "The Collision of Rahner and Balthasar." *Continuum* 5, 753-757.

302. SCHOOF, M. *Aggiornamento. De doorbraak van een nieuwe katholieke theologie.* Baarn: Het Wereldvenster. (See also No. 417.)

303. STOHRER, Walter J., S.J. The Role of Martin Heidegger's Doctrine of Dasein in Karl Rahner's Metaphysics of Man. Dissertation, Georgetown University.

304. STASSEN, P. "The Anonymous Christians." *Christ to the World* 13, 246-247.

305. TAKAYANAGI, S. "Gendaishingaku ni okeru kyōkairontekikiso to kyūsaishi-tekiapurochi." *Katorikku shingaku* 14, 403-436.

306. TeSELLE, Eugene. "Identity of Indiscernibles?" *Continuum* 6, 424-428.

1969

307. AMSTUTZ, J. "Die Mission als kirchliche Wirklichkeit." *Nouvelle revue de science missionaire* 25, 241-249.

308. ARNALL, M. "Dear Father Rahner." *The Furrow* 20, 340-345.

309. BALIC, C. "Note on the Assumption." In *Mélanges de J.A. de Aldama, Diakonia Pisteos.* Granada: Biblioteca teologica Granadina. See 185-215.

310. VON BALTHASAR, Hans Urs. *The Moment of Christian Witness.*

Glen Rock, S.J.: Newman Press. (Translation of No. 201 by Richard Beckley.)

311. BEIERWALTES, W. "Kritisches über einige neuere Bestimmungen des Verhältnisses von Philosophie und Theologie." 81, 178-188, esp. 184ff.

312. BENT, Charles, N. *Interpreting the Doctrine of God.* Glen Rock, N.J.: Paulist Press.

313. BLEISTEIN, Roman and Elmar Klinger. *Bibliographie Karl Rahner 1924-1969.* Freiburg: Herder Verlag.

314. BOBLIOLO, L. "Nota all'articula del Padre Galli." *Divinitas* 13, 455ff. (See No. 330.)

315. BOLLMAN, Richard W., S.J. "Rahner's Trinity and the Contemporary Student." *The Priest* 25, 460-462.

316. BROZ, Ludek. "Entretien à Prague avec Karl Rahner." *Terre Entière* 36, 57-66.

317. CARMODY, John T. "Karl Rahner: Theology of the Spiritual Life." *Chicago Studies* 8, 71-86.

318. CHIRAT, H. "Questions disputées II. Un médiateur et des co-médiateurs." *Revue des sciences religieuses* 42, 45-57.

319. CITRINI, T. "Gesù Cristo rivelazione di Dio. Il tema negli ultimi decenni della teologia cattolica." *Venegono Inferiore:* La scuola cattolica. (Hildephonsiana 10). See 145-171.

320. DEWART, Leslie. *The Foundations of Belief.* New York: Herder and Herder.

321. DONCEEL, Joseph, S.J. *The Philosophy of Karl Rahner.* Albany: Magi Books, Overview Series (29pp.).

322. DORCY, M. and J. Jurich. "A Conversation with Karl Rahner. Interview by M. Dorcy and J. Jurich." *America* 120, 733-735.

323. DORR, D. J. "Karl Rahner's 'Formal Existential Ethics.'" *The Irish Theological Quarterly* 36, 211-229.

324. DYCH, William V., S.J. "Father Rahner and the Curia: Stalemate or Hope?" *Ave Maria* 109, Nr. 5, 6f.

325. DULLES, Avery, S.J. *Revelation Theology.* New York: Herder and Herder.

326. EICHER, Peter. "Der geschichtliche Mensch. Karl Rahners philosophische Reflexion zur Geschichtlichkeit." *Freiburger Zeitschrift für Philosophie und Theologie* 16, 197-221.

327. FAHLBUSCH, E. "Theologie der Religionen. Überblick zu einem Thema römisch-katholischer Theologie." *Kerygma und Dogma* 15, 73-86.

328. FLAMAND, J. "M. Blondel et K. Rahner. Une interprétation convergente des rapports de la nature et de la grace." In his *L'idée de médiation chez Maurice Blondel.* Louvain/Paris: Béatrice Nauwelaerts (Philosophes contemporains. Textes et études 15). See 509-517.

329. FOLKEMER, L. D. "Theological Excellence." *Jewish Quarterly Review* 59, 335-336.

330. GALLI, A. "Perché Karl Rahner nega la visione beatifica in Cristo.

Premesse filosofiche della cristologia Rahneriana." *Divinitas* 13, 417-456. (See No. 314.)

331. GEISSER, H. "Kontroverse um einen Reformplan des katholischen Theologiestudiums." *Theologia Practica* 4, 65-72.

332. GERKEN, Alexander, O.F.M. *Offenbarung und Transzendenzerfahrung.* Kritische Theses zu einer künftigen dialogischen Theologie. Düsseldorf: Patmos Verlag.

333. GLOWIENKA, Sr. Emerine. "Notes on Consciousness in Matter." *The New Scholasticism* 43, 602-613.

334. HOERES, Walter. *Kritik der transzendentalphilosophischen Erkenntnistheorie.* Stuttgart: W. Kohlhammer Verlag.

335. KLAUS, B. "Von der 'Pastoral-' zur Praktischen Theologie." *Zeitschrift für Religions und Geistesgeschichte* 21, 357-361.

336. KLINGER, Elmar. "Grosse Theologie auf engstem Raum. Zum 65. Geburtstag am Professor Karl Rahner." *Münstersche Zeitung* (5 March 1969).

337. KUNZ, E. *Glaube, Gnade, Geschichte.* Die Glaubenstheologie des Pierre Rousselot, S.J. Frankfurt. See 47-49.

338. LEHMANN, Karl. "Aufbruch und unermüdlicher Dienst. Karl Rahner zum 65. Geburtstag am 5 Marz 1969." *Publik* 2, Nr. 9 (28 February 1969), 26.

339. LEHMANN, Karl. "Das dogmatische Problem des theologischen Anzatzes zum Verständnis des Amtspriestertums." In F. Henrich, editor: *Existenzprobleme des Priesters.* München (Münchener Akademie-Schriften 50), 123-175, especially 169-171.

340. LEHMANN, Karl. "Den Glauben erschliessen. Karl Rahner zum 65. Geburtstag am 5 Marz 1969." In KNA Nr. 11 (21 February 1969), 3.

341. LEHMANN, Karl. "Bemühungen um eine 'Kurzformel' des Glaubens." *Herder Korrespondenz* 23, 32-38.

342. McCOOL, Gerald A., S.J. "Philosophy and Christian Wisdom." *Thought* 44, 485-512.

343. McCOOL, Gerald A., S.J. *The Theology of Karl Rahner.* Albany: Magi Books, Overview Series. (40 pp.; slightly revised version of No. 53.)

344. MALONEY, G. D. Le chrétien anonyme dans la théologie de Karl Rahner. Theology dissertation, University of Strasbourg.

345. MANN, P. "Masters in Israel IV." The Later Theology of Karl Rahner. *Clergy Review* 54, 936-948.

346. MANNERMAA, T. "Onko Karl Rahnerin uskonnonfilosofinen pääteos tulkittu virheellisesti?" *Teologinen Aikakauskirja* 74, 450-456.

347. MARINELLI, F. "Dimensione trinitatia dell'incarnazione." *Divinitas* 13, 271-343.

348. METZ, Johann Baptist. "Karl Rahner." *Enciclopedia filosofica* V, 526f.

349. METZ, Johann Baptist. "Offener Brief an Karl Rahner." *Publik* 2, Nr. 10 (7 March 1969), 25.

350. METZ. Johann Baptist. *Antropocentrismo cristiano.* Studio sulla

mentalità di Tommaso d'Aquino. Torino: Borla (Italian translation of No. 63 by Aldo Audisio.)

351. METZ, Johann Baptist; Walter Kern; Adolf Darlap; and Herbert Vorgrimler, editors. Rodolf Schnackenburg, French editor: *Le message de Jésus et l'interprétation moderne*. Mélanges Karl Rahner. Paris: Cerf. (Partial translation of No. 124.)

352. MULKERN, S. "Karl Rahner: An Analysis." *Catholic Library World* 40, 374-377.

353. NEAL, D. L. The Soteriology of Karl Rahner, S.J. Dissertation (M.A.), Exeter University.

354. OCHS, Robert, S.J. *The Death in Every Now*. New York: Sheed & Ward.

355. OTT, Heinrich. *Wirklichkeit und Glaube* II. Der persönliche Gott. Göttingen/Zürich. See 340-348.

356. PUNTEL, L. B., S.J. *Analogie und Geschichtlichkeit* I. Philosophie-geschichtlich-kritischer Versuch über das Grundproblem der Metaphysik. Freiburg (Philosophie in Einzeldarstellungen 4), esp. 81-93, 108-110.

357. ROBERTS, Louis. *Karl Rahner, sa pensée, son oeuvre, sa méthode*. Tours: Mame. (French translation of No. 260 by Michel Marton.)

358. RUBICEK, O. "Karl Rahner. 5 Anmerkungen zu seiner Theologie (Wie progressiv sind unsere Progressiven. II). *Kritischer Katholizismus* 2, Nr. 6, pp. 8f.

359. RYAN, Sr. R. "The Meaning of Death: Paul and Modern Theologians." *The Bible Today* 41, 2856-2861.

360. SCHUPP, F. "Die Geschichtsauffassung am Beginn der Tübinger Schule und in der gegenwärtigen Theologie." *Zeitschrift für katholische Theologie* 91, 150-171, esp. 163-165.

361. SHEPHERD, William Charles. *Man's Condition*. God and the World Process. New York: Herder and Herder.

362. SIMONS, Eberhard, and K. Hecker. *Theologisches Verstehen*. Philosophische Prologemena zu einer theologischen Hermeneutik. Düsseldorf (passim, esp. 218-226.)

363. TAKAYANAGI, S. "Incarnation, the Central Idea in K. Rahner's Theology" (in Japanese). *Katorikku Shingaku* 15, 217-261. *Louvain Studies* 11, 277-281.

364. TALLON, Andrew. "Getting to the Heart of the Matter: Spirit." *Louvain Studies* 11, 277-281.

365. TALLON, Andrew. Personization. Person as personization in Karl Rahner's philosophical anthropology. Dissertation, Louvain University.

366. TORELL, Jean-Pierre. "Chronique de théologie fondamentale." *Revue Thomiste* 69, 61-92 (passim).

367. VERHAAK, C., S.J. "De invloedssfeer van Joseph Maréchal. Een sector van de katholieke wijsbegeerte in de twintigste eeuw." *Bijdragen* 30, 436-448.

368. VERWEYEN, H. *Ontologische Voraussetzungen des Glaubensaktes*. Zur transzendentalen Frage nach der Möglichkeit von Offenbarung. Düsseldorf (passim).

369. VIDRÁNY, K. "Az ember helye Karl Rahner világképében" (Man's Place in Karl Rahner's Image of the World). *Vilagossag*, Nr. 2, 83-88.

370. WALDENFELS, H. *Offenbarung.* Das Zweite Vatikan. Konzil auf dem Hintergrund der neueren Theologie. München.

371. WALDENFELS, H. "Zur Heilsbedeutung der nichtchristlichen Religionen in katholischer Sicht." *Zeitschrift für Missionswissenschsft und Religionswissenschaft* 53, 257-278.

1970

372. BAKKER, L. *Freiheit und Erfahrung.* Redaktionsgeschichtliche Untersuchungen über die Unterscheidung der Geister bei Ignatius von Loyola. Würzburg. Passim.

373. BAGET BOZZO, G. "Teologia come antropologia?" *Rinovatio* 5, 17-39.

374. BOYER, Charles, S.J. "Sur le pluralisme théologique." *Doctor Communis* 23, 185-191.

375. BRESNAHAN, James F., S.J. "Rahner's Christian Ethics." *America* 123, 351-354.

376. BROWARZIK, Ulrich. *Glauben und Denken.* Dogmatische Forschung zwischen der Transzendentaltheologie Karl Rahners und der Offenbarungstheologie Karl Barths. Berlin: Walter De Gruyter. (Foreword by Rahner.)

377. CARMODY, John T. "Rahner's Spiritual Theology." *America* 123, 345-347.

378. CLARKE, Thomas E., S.J. "On Americanizing Karl Rahner." *America* 123, 337-339.

379. DONCEEL, Joseph, S.J. "Rahner's Argument for God." *America* 123, 340-342.

380. DYCH, William V., S.J. "Karl Rahner—An Interview." *America* 123, 356-359.

381. EBERHARD, K. D. Karl Rahner's Doctrine of the Supernatural Existential. Theology dissertation, Graduate Theological Union. (See also No. 437.)

382. EICHER, Peter. *Die anthropologische Wende.* Karl Rahners philosophischer Weg vom Wesen des Menschen zur personalen Existenz. Freiburg (Switzerland: Universitätsverlag. (Foreword by Rahner.)

383. GEFFRÉ, Claude, O.P. and Yves Congar, O.P. "Bulletin de théologie. Problèmes généraux." *Revue des Sciences philosophiques et théologiques* 54, 636-653; Rahner: 331-332, 335-337, 344-350, 357, 359, 362-364, 368-371.

384. GONZÁLEZ De MENDOZA, R. *Stimmung und Transzendenz.* Die Antizipation der existenzialanalytischen Stimmungsproblematik bei Ignatius von Loyola. Berlin. See esp. 229-237.

385. HAUGHEY, John C., S.J. "Karl Rahner." *America* 123, 335-337.

386. HEINRICHS, Johannes, S.J. "Sinn und Intersubjektivität: Zur Vermittlung von Transzendentalphilosophie und dialogischem Denken in einer 'transzendentalen Dialogik.'" *Theologie und Philosophie* 45, 161-191.

387. HENNING, J. "Hier wird's Ereignis. Geistesgeschichtliche Grundlagen einer theologischen Denkform." *Zeitschrift für Religions und Geistesgeschichte* 22, 193-211.

388. HIRSCHAUER, G. "Neue Inquisition oder: Karl Rahner hat immer recht!" *Werkhefte* 24, 310-314.

389. KELLY, Anthony J. "God: How Near a Relation?" *The Thomist* 34, 191-229.

390. KELLY, Anthony J. "Trinity and Process. Relevance of the Basic Christian Confession of God." *Theological Studies* 31, 393-414.

391. KOCH, T. *"Natur und Gnade. Zur neuernen Diskussion." Kerygma und Dogma* 16, 171-187.

392. KÜNG, Hans. *Menschwerdung Gottes.* Eine Einführung in Hegels theologisches Denken als Prologomena zu einer künftigen Christologie. Freiburg. See esp. 648-652.

393. LAPOINTE, Roger. "L'ontologie de Karl Rahner." *Dialogue* 8, 592-611.

394. DE LAVALETTE, Henri, S.J. "La 'théologie politique' de Jean-Baptiste Metz." *Recherche de science religieuse* 58, 321-350.

395. LEGRAND, F. "Le Père Rahner et la crise doctrinale actuelle." *Le Christ au Monde* 15, 154-156. In English: "Father Karl Rahner and the Present Doctrinal Crisis." *Christ to the World* 15, 146-148.

396. LEHMANN, Karl. "Karl Rahner." *Bilanz der Theologie im 20. Jahrhundert IV: Bahnbrechende Theologen,* edited by Herbert Vorgrimler and R. Vander Gucht. Freiburg. See 143-181. (See also No. 000.)

397. LEHMANN, Karl. "Kurzformeln des christlichen Glaubens." HVK 1, 274-295, esp. 281-283. (See also No. 454.)

398. McCOOL, Gerald A., S.J. "Rahner's Anthropology." *America* 123, 342-344.

399. MALONEY, Donald, S.J. "Rahner and the Anonymous Christian." *America* 123, 348-350.

400. MALDONADO, L. *Secularización de la Liturgia.* Madrid (Bibliotheca Oecumenica). See esp. 104-119.

401. MANNERMAA, T. "Eine falsche Interpretationstradition von Karl Rahners *Hörer des Wortes.*" *Zeitschrift für katholische Theologie* 92, 204-209.

402. MANNERMAA, T. *Lumen fidei et obiectum fidei adventicium.* Uskontiedon spontaanisuus ja reseptiivisyys Karl Rahnerin varhaisessa ajattelussa. (The Spontaneity and Receptivity of the Knowledge of Faith in Karl Rahner's Early Thought; with a summary in German). Helsinki.

403. MÜHLEN, H. "Gnadenlehre." *Bilanz der Theologie im 20. Jahrhundert III,* edited by Herbert Vorgrimler and R. Vander Gucht. Freiburg. See 148-192, esp. 169-174. (Published also in French.)

404. NAGY, F. "Sur un ouvrage récent consacré à l'encyclique *Humanae Vitae.*" *Science et esprit* 22, 99-109.

405. NOSSOL, A. "O Prof. Karl Rahner gósciem uczelni." *Zeszyty*

naukowe katolickiego uniwersytetu Lubelskiego. Kwartalnik 13 85-87.

406. OCHS, Robert, S.J. Time, Death, and the Sacred. As Essay on Karl Rahner's Theology of Death and the Unmanageable. Dissertation, Institut Catholique, Paris.

407. O'DONOGHUE, N.-D., O.C.D. "Rahner: Early Philosophy." *The Irish Theological Quarterly* 37, 322-325.

408. PANNENBERG, Wolfhart. *What Is Man?* Contemporary Anthropology in Theological Perspective. Philadelphia: Fortress Press. (Translation of No. 298 by Duane A. Priebe.)

409. PFAFFELHUBER, M. Die Kant-Rezeption bei Maréchal und ihr Fortwirken in der katholischen Religionsphilosophie. Philosophy dissertation, Freiburg.

410. RATZINGER, Josef. "Heil und Geschichte." *Wort und Wahrheit* 25, 3-14.

411. RENWART, L. "Efficacité des rites sacramentals?" *Nouvelle revue théologique* 92, 384-397.

412. REY, Bernard. "Théologie trinitaire et révélation biblique." *Revue des Sciences philosophiques et théologiques* 54, 636-653; Rahner, by way of Lafont (see No. 213) : 636-647.

413. ROBERTSON, J. C. "Rahner and Ogden: Man's Knowledge of God." *The Harvard Theological Review* 63, 377-407.

414. ROVIRA BELLOSO, J. M. "Models de relació Filosofia-Teologia en alguns teòlegs catòlicis del segle XX." *Analecta Sacra Tarrcon* 43, 239-286.

415. SANNA, I. *La cristologia antropologica di P. Karl Rahner.* Rome: Ed. Paoline (Biblioteca di cultura religiosa, seconda serie 152). (Dissertation, Lateran University.)

416. SCHÄFER, K. "Nochmals zum Thema Priestergruppen." *Stimmen der Zeit* 185, 361-378. Also in *SOG-Papiere* 3, 263-280.

417. SCHOOF, Mark. *A Survey of Catholic Theology* (title in England: *Breakthrough*). Glen Rock, N.J./Dublin: Paulist Newman Press/ Gill & Macmillan. (See No. 302.)

418. SIMONS, Eberhard. *Dove va la teologia?* Ebarhard Simons interroga Karl Rahner. Bologna.

419. SUDBRACK, J. "Fragestellung und Infragestellung der ignatianishcen Exerzitien." *Geist und Leben* 43, 206-226, esp. 216-219.

420. TALLON, Andrew. "Rahner and Personization." *Philosophy Today* 14, 44-56.

421. WENTSEL, B. *Natuur en genade.* Een introductie in en confrontatie met de jongste ontwikkelingen in de Rooms-katholieke theologie inzake dit thema. Kampen: Kok. See 102-168, 181-183, 239-244, 400-414.

422. WESS, Paul. *Wie von Gott sprechen?* Eine Auseinandersetzung mit Karl Rahner. Graz. Verlag Styria.

423. WOLF, U. A. *Ius divinum.* Erwägungen zur Rechtsgeschichte und Rechtsgestaltung. München (Jus ecclesiasticum 11), esp. 175-177.

424. YEARLY, L. H. "Karl Rahner on the Relation of Nature and Grace." *Canadian Journal of Theology* 16, 219-231.

425. "Karl Rahner." *Current Biography* 7, 38-40.

1971

426. BAUM, Gregory. "Truth in the Church. Kung, Rahner, and Beyond." *The Ecumenist* 9, 33-48. Appears also in J. J. Kirwan, editor; *The Infallibility Debate* (New York), 1-33.

427. BEGGIANI, S. "A Case for Logocentric Theology." *Theological Studies* 32, 371-406.

428. BERKOUWER, G. C. "Het conflict Kung-Rahner." *Gereformeerd Weekblad* 26, 249, 257f., 265f., 277. (See also No. 429.)

429. BERKOUWER, G. C. "The Küng-Rahner Debate." *Christianity Today* 15, 45-46. (English of No. 428.)

430. BOGDAHN, M. *Die Rechtfertigungslehre Luthers im Urteil der neueren katholischen Theologie.* Möglichkeiten und Tendenzen der katholischen Lutherdeutung in evangelischer Sicht. Göttingen, passim.

431. BRANICK, Vincent P., S.M. An Ontology of Understanding. Karl Rahner's Metaphysics of Knowledge in the Context of Modern German Hermeneutics. Dissertation, (See also No. 578.)

431a. BURI, F. "Zu Karl Rahners 'Kurzformel' des christlichen Glaubens," *Zur Theologie der Verantwortung*, pp. 85ff.

432. CONGAR, Yves, O.P. "Bulletin d'ecclésiologie." *Revue des Sciences philosophiques et théologiques* 55, 327-351; Rahner 340, 343-345.

433. CULLEN, F. P. The Christology of Karl Rahner. Dissertation, Nottingham University.

434. DEJAIFVE, G. "Un débat sur l'infallibilité. La discussion entre K. Rahner et H. Küng." *Nouvelle revue théologique* 103, 583-601.

435. DONCEEL, Joseph, S.J. "Rahner istenérve." *Merleg* 7, 149-154. (Translation of No. 379.)

436. DONCEEL, Joseph, S.J. "Second Thoughts on the Nature of God." *Thought* 46, 346-370.

437. EBERHARD, K. D. "Karl Rahner and the Supernatural Existential." *Thought* 46, 537-561. (See also No. 381.)

438. EICHHORST, C. J. "Demythologizing the Papacy. A Prophetic Inquiry." *Dialog* 10, 272-280.

439. FABRO, Cornelio, C.P. "Karl Rahner e l'ermeneutica Tomistica. La risoluzione-dissoluzione della metafisica nell'antropologia." *Divus Thomas* (Piacenza) 74, 287-338, 423-465. (See also No. 494.)

440. GALOT, Jean, S.J. *La conscience de Jésus.* Gembloux: Duculot; Paris: Lethielleux, esp. 169-172.

441. GARAUDY, Roger. *Del anatema al diálogo.* Con las ponencias de Karl Rahner y Johann Baptist Metz. Barcelona: Edics. Ariel.

442. GÓMEZ, F. "Justficación de la misión hoy, según J. Daniélou, K. Rahner, e Y. Congar." *Misceláneas Comillas* 55, 193-239.

443. GUGLIELMINETTI, P. Oh. M. L'estensione e l'approfondimento della nozione di sacramento in K. Rahner, E. Schillebeeckx, O. Semmelroth. Theology dissertation, Gregorian University, Rome.

444. HACKER, P. "The Christian Attitude toward Non-Christian Religions. Some Critical and Positive Reflections." *Zeitschrift für Missionswissenschaft und Religionswissenschaft* 55, 81-97.

445. HEBBLETHWAITE, Peter. "Karl Rahner's Commitment." *The Month* 3, 40-43.

446. HECK, Erich. *Der Begriff religio bei Thomas von Aquin.* Seine Bedeutung für unser heutiges Verständnis von Religion. München: Verlag Ferdinand Schöningh.

447. HILL, B. "Karl Rahner's Metaphysical Anthropology." *Carmelus* 18, 181-194.

448. HILL, E. "Karl Rahner's Remarks of the Dogmatic Treatise De Trinitate and St. Augustine." *Augustine Studies* 2, 67-80.

449. HUGHES, J. J. "Infallible? An Inquiry Considered." *Theological Studies* 32, 183-207.

450. KEEFE, Donald J., S.J. *Thomism and the Ontological Theology of Paul Tillich.* Leiden: Brill.

451. KNIGHT, D. B. The Implications for Spiritual Theology of Karl Rahner's Theology of Renunciation Studied in the Light of His Concept of Man. Theology dissertation, Catholic University, Washington, D.C.

452. KOEHNLEIN, M. *Was bringt das Sakrament?* Disputation mit Karl Rahner.

453. KÜNG, Hans. "Im Interesse der Sache. Antwort an K. Rahner." *Stimmen der Zeit* 96, 43-64 and 105-122. Also in *Fehlbar? Eine Bilanz*—Zürich (1973), 19-68, edited by Küng.

454. LEHMANN, Karl. "Karl Rahner." In *Bilan de la théologie du XX siècle II*, 836-874.

455. MACQUARRIE, John. *Twentieth-Century Religious Thought.* The Frontiers of Philosophy and Theology. London: SCM Press. Revised and expanded edition of No. 80; see pp. 293f.

456. MacSORLEY, H. J. "Response to Kung's Inquiry on Infallibility." *Worship* 45, 314-325.

457. MALEVEZ, Léopold, S.J. "Théologie et philosophie: leur inclusion réciproque." *Nouvelle revue théologique* 93, 113-144.

458. MANNERMAA, T. *Karl Rahnerin verhainen filosofinen antropologia.* Helsinki.

459. MARRANZINI, A. "La 'svolta antropologica' in teologia secondo Karl Rahner," in Marranzini, editor: *Associazione teologica italiana. Dimensione antropologica della teologia.* IV Congress nazionale, Arriccia 4-5 January 1971. Milano, 481-500.

460. MASSNER, N. "Christliche Erziehung als Ermächtigung und Bildung zur Freiheit. Zur pädagogischen Bedeutung der theologischen Anthropologie K. Rahners." *Vierteljahrsschrift für wissenschaftliche Pädagogik* 47, 105-115.

461. MEINVIELLE, Julio. "El problemo del conocimiento en Rahner." *Universitas* 20, 7-34.

462. MEYER, Charles R. *A Contemporary Theology of Grace.* Staten Island, N.Y.: Alba House.

463. DI NARDO, M. A. The Study of the Role of Symbol in the Writings of Karl Rahner, Mircea Eliade, and H. Richard Niebuhr. Some Implications for Contemporary Catechesis. Philosophy dissertation, Catholic University, Washington, D.C.

464. NICOLAS, J. M. "Vièrge jusque dans l'enfantement." *Ephemerides Mariologicae* 21, 377-382.

465. O'CONNELL, P. "A Reply to Karl Rahner." *The Priest* 27, 37-43.

466. PANNENBERG, Wolfhart. "Weltgeschichte und Heilsgeschichte," in H. W. Wolff, editor: *Probleme biblischer Theologie*. Gerhard von Rad zum 70. Geburtstag. München, 349-366, esp. 357f. and 361-363.

467. PESCH, O. H. "Unfehlbarkeit im Disput. Ein Streit zwischen Karl Rahner und Hans Küng." *Wort und Antwort* 12, 82-88.

468. PÜNDER, R. Kirche, Laie, Welt. Zu Sinn und Aufgabe des Christseins in der Welt bei K. Rahner. Theology dissertation, Gregorian University, Rome.

469. RATZINGER, Josef. "Offenbarung und Transzendenzerfahrung." *Theologische Revue* 67, 11-14.

470. RÖPER, Anita. *Objektive und subjektive Moral*. Ein Gespräch mit K. Rahner. Freiburg.

471. RUÍZ DE LA PEÑA, J. L. "La muerte en la antropologia de K. Rahner." *Revista Española de teología* 31, 189-212 and 335-360.

472. SÁNCHEZ DE MURILLO, J. "Dimensión escatológica de la vida cristiana según K. Rahner. Aportación a la teologia de la esperanza." *Ephemerides carmeliticae* 22, 38-94 (drawn from dissertation at the college of Sts. Teresa and John of the Cross, Rome).

473. SCHUPP, Franz. "Zwei Reflexionsstufen. Bemerkungen zu Pluralismus, Probabilität, Theorie und Kritik in der Theologie." *Zeitschrift fur katholische Theologie* 93, 61-73. (See also No. 633.)

474. SHEEHAN, Thomas J., S.J. Subjectivity and Transcendental Method as the Fundamental Groundwork of Karl Rahner's Theological Anthropology. Dissertation in philosophy, Fordham University.

475. STOCK, A. *Kurzformeln des Glaubens*. Zur Unterscheidung des Christlichen bei K. Rahner. Zürich.

476. SURLIS, P. "Rahner and Lonergan on Method in Theology." *The Irish Theological Quarterly* 38, 187-201. (See also No. 517.)

477. TALLON, Andrew. "Spirit, Matter, Becoming: Karl Rahner's *Spirit in the World (Geist in Welt)*." *The Modern Schoolman* 48, 151-165.

478. VANCOURT, R. "Faut-il changer de langage théologique? A propos du concept 'd'existential.'" *Esprit et vie* 81, 417-423.

479. VIRGOULAY, R. "Une justification théologique du rapport philosophie-théologie." *Revue des sciences religieuses* 45, 276-289.

480. VAN VOORST, B. "Küng and Rahner. Duelling over Infallibility." *Christian Century* 88, 617-622, 998-1000.

481. WIKMARK, Ö. "Auktoritetskris i den romers-katolska kyrkan?" *Svensk Teologisk Kvartalskrift* 47, 53-61.

1972

482. ANNESER, S. *Glaube im Ungläubigen, Unglaube im Gläubigen.*

Untersuchungen einer Tendenz im Glaubensverstandnis der letzten 2 Jahrzehnte. Kevelaer.

483. ARDUSSO, F., et al. *Introduzione alla teologia contemporanea.* Torino.

484. BLEI, K. *De onfeilbaarheid van de kerk.* Kamper: Kok. See 133-168 and 208-222.

485. BOFF, L. *Die Kirche als Sakrament im Horizont der Welterfahrung.* Versuch einer Legitimation und einer struktur-funktionalistischen Grundlegung der Kirche im Anschluss an das II. Vatikanische Konzil. Paderborn: Bonifacius-Druckerei. See 314-322 and passim.

486. BOYLE, J. Ph. Faith and Community in the Ethical Theory of Karl Rahner and Bernard Lonergan. Philosophy dissertation, Fordham University,

487. BRESNAHAN, James F., S.J. The Methodology of "Natural Law" Ethical Reasoning in the Theology of Karl Rahner and Its Supplementary Development Using the Legal Philosophy of Lon L. Fuller. Philosophy dissertation, Yale University.

488. CAMILLERI, N. "Il misterio della morte 'Anima separata' o 'cessata animazione?'" *Salesianum* 34, 97-115.

489. CARDONA, C. "Rilievi critici a due fondamentazioni metafisiche per una costruzione teologica." *Divus Thomas* (Piacenza) 75, 149-176 (with a summary in Latin).

490. CARR, Anne. The Theological Method of Karl Rahner. Philosophy dissertation, University of Chicago. (See also No. 528.)

491. CONGAR, Yves M.-J., O.P. "Bulletin de théologie. Ouvrages d'ensemble et de méthode." *Revue des Sciences philosophiques et théologiques* 56, 297-324; Rahner 298-299, 301-302, 208-312.

492. CONGAR, Yves M.-J., O.P. "Bulletin de théologie. Les normes de la foi et de théologie." *Revue des Sciences philosophiques et théologiques* 56, 640-660; Rahner 646-647, 649, 653.

493. FABRO, Cornelio, C.P. "Svolta Antropologica della Teologia?" *Studi Cattolici* 140, 665-675.

494. FABRO, Cornelio, C.P. *Karl Rahner e l'ermeneutica tomistica (La risoluzione-dissoluzione della metafisica nell'antropologia)* (Monographie del Collegio Alberoni 33). Piacenza: Ed. Divus Thomas. (See also No. 439.)

495. FRICK, E. G. The Meaning of Religion in the Religionswissenschaft of Joachim Wach, the Theology of Paul Tillich, and the Theology of Karl Rahner. An Inquiry into the Possibility of a Christian Theology of the History of Religions. Theology dissertation, Marquette University.

496. FRIEDMANN, E. H. *Christologie und Anthropologie.* Methode und Bedeutung der Lehre vom Menschen in der Theologie Karl Barths. Münsterschwarzach. (Münsterschwarzacher Studien 19), esp. 326-341 and passim.

497. GOTTSCHALCK, J. M. Review of *L'esprit dans le monde, Revista Portuguesa de Filosofia* 28, 99-102.

498. DE HAES, René. *Pour une théologie du prophétique.* Lecture thématique de la théologie de Karl Rahner. Louvain/Paris: Nauwel-

aerts (Recherches africains de théologie. Travaux de la faculté de théologie de Kinshasa 4).

499. HAUGHT, J. F. "What is Logocentric Theology?" *Theological Studies* 33, 120-132.

500. HOYE, William J. "Ist K. Rahner wirklich ein narzisstischer Solipsist, oder hat M. Sommer ihn noch nicht verstanden? *Trierer theologische Zeitschrift* 81, 183-185. (See No. 516.)

501. IMBELLI, R. P. "Karl Rahner's 'Itinerarium mentis in Deum.' " *Dunwoodie Review* 12, 76-91.

502. KEANE, Ph. S. Karl Rahner's Theology of the World. Theology dissertation, Catholic University, Washington, D.C. (Studies in Sacred Theology Series 231).

503. KENNY, John Peter, S.J. *The Supernatural.* Staten Island, N.Y.: Alba House.

504. KERSTIENS, F. "Zukunft und Hoffnung in der gegenwärtigen Theologie," in G. Scherer *et al*, editors: *Eschatalogie und geschichtliche Zukunft.* Essen (Thesen & Argumente 5), 66-88, esp. 73-77.

505. LAURENTIN, René, S.J. "Bulletin sur la vièrge Marie." *Revue des Sciences philosophiques et théologiques* 56, 433-491; Rahner 456-459.

506. LOTH, B. and A. Michel. "Karl Rahner," in *Dictionnaire de théologie catholique.* Tables générales, 3854-3856.

507. MARIOTTI, Piergiorgio. "Tomismo, realismo critico, ermeneutica." *Proteus* 3, 183-195. (Discussion of No. 494.)

508. OGDEN, S. M. "The Reformation That We Want." *Anglican Theological Review* 54, 260-273.

509. OZOROWSKI, Edward. " 'Konfrontacje' Karola Rahnera." *Studia Theologica Varsaviensia* 10, 171-178.

510. PETERS, A. "Der Tod in der neueren theologischen Anthropologie." *Neue Zeitschrift fur systematische Theologie und Religionsphilosophie* 14, 29-67.

511. REDFERN, Martin, editor. *Karl Rahner.* (Theologian Today Series). New York: Sheed & Ward.

512. RESWEBER, J. P. "La relation de l'homme à Dieu selon Karl Rahner et Maurice Blondel." *Revue des Sciences Religieuses* 46, 20-37.

513. RIHA, K. Immanenz und Transzendenz in der menschlichen Aktivität. Verglich der frühen Wissenschaftslehre J. G. Fichte mit der Erkenntnismetaphysik K. Rahners. Theology dissertation, Innsbruck University.

514. RUPP, E. Zur Kritik der transzendentalen und analytischen Wissenschaftstheorie. Philosophy dissertation, Free University of Berlin.

515. SCHAUF, H. "Zur Textgeschichte grundlegender Aussagen aus 'Lumen gentium' über das Bischofskollegium." *Archiv für katholisches Kirchenrecht* 141, 5-147, esp. 84-94.

516. SOMMER, Manfred. "Kommunikation und Narzissmuss. Zur Problematisierung des Wahrheitsbegriffs in der Kontroverse zwischen K. Rahner und H. Küng." *Trierer theologische Zeitschrift* 81, 40-49.

517. SURLIS, P. "Rahner and Lonergan on Method in Theology." *The Irish Theological Quarterly* 39, 23-42. (See also No. 476.)

518. THÜSING, W. "Neutestamentliche Zugangswege zu einer transzendental-dialogischen Christologie," in K. Rahner & W. Thüsing: *Christologie—systematisch und exegetisch.* Arbeitsgrundlagen für eine interdisziplinäre Vorlesung. Freiburg: Herder (Quaestiones Disputatae 55), 79-305.

519. TIEFENBACHER, H. and A. Schilson. "Die Frage nach Jesus Christus." *Herder Korrespondenz* 26, 563-570. esp. 564f.

520. TOINET, Paul. "Le probleme théologique du pluralisme." *Revue Thomiste* 72, 5-32.

521. TYRELL, Bernard. "The New Context of the Philosophy of God in Lonergan and Rahner," in Philip McShane, editor: *Language, Truth, and Meaning.* Dublin: Gill & Macmillan, 284-305.

522. WEISCHEDEL, Wilhelm. *Der Gott der Philosophen.* Grundlegung einer philosophischen Theologie im Zeitalter des Nihilismus II: Abgrenzung und Grundlegung. Darmstadt: Wiss. Buchgesellschaft in Zuz. arb. mit der Nymphenburger Verlagshandlung, München. See 60-75.

1973

523. ALLSOPP, M. E. "Karl Rahner's 'Existential Ethics.' A Study." *Australasian Catholic Record* 50, 118-129 and 331-340.

524. BECHTLE, R. "Karl Rahner's Supernatural Existential: A Personalist Approach." *Thought* 48, 61-77.

525. BLASER, K. "Vers une nouvelle Christologie. Quatre ouvrages récents" (among them: *Christologie—systematisch und exegetisch* by Rahner and Thusing). *Revue de théologie et philosophie* 23, 332-344.

526. BOUBLIK, V. *Teologia delle religioni.* Roma: Studium, passim.

527. CAPORALE, V. *Dimensione antropolagica della cristologia moderna.* Napoli: D'Auria, esp. 39-48, 91-101, 107-109.

528. CARR, Anne. "Theology and Experience in the Thought of Karl Rahner." *The Journal of Religion* 53, 359-376.

529. CLARKE, W. Norris, S.J. "A New Look at the Immutability of God," in Robert J. Roth, S.J., editor: *God Knowable and Unknowable.* New York: Fordham University Press, 43-72.

530. CONGAR, Yves M.-J., O.P. "Bulletin d'ecclésiologie." *Revue des Sciences philosophiques et théologiques* 57, 481-506; Rahner 483-486.

531. DEVREUX, A. R. "Der Vorgriff" (The Pre-Apprehension of Being) and the Religious Act in Karl Rahner. Philosophy dissertation, Georgetown University.

532. DUNNING, J. B. Human Creativity. A Symbol of Transcendence in Contemporary Psychology and the Theology of Karl Rahner. Implications for Religious Education. Philosophy dissertation, Catholic University. Abstract in *Religious Education* 70, 429f.

533. DUTARI, J. T. *Christentum und Metaphysik.* Das Verhältnis beider nach der Analogielehre E. Przywaras. München. See esp. 581-585, 590-593.

534. EBERHARD, K. D. "Rahner on Religious Education." *Thought* 48, 404-415.

535. EICHHORST, C. J. "From Outside the Church to Inside. Toward a Triumph of Grace in Catholicism." *Dialog* (St. Paul) 12, 190-196.

536. FABRO, Cornelio, C.P. "Il trasendentale esistenziale e la riduzione al fondamento: La fine della metafisica e l'equivoco della teologia transcendentale." *Giornale Critico de Filosofia Italiana* 52, 469-516.

537. FISCHER, Klaus P. Der Mensch als Geheimnis nach den Schriften Karl Rahners. Le mystère de l'homme d'après les écrits du P. Karl Rahner, S.J. Theology dissertation, Institut catholique, Paris. (See also No. 593.)

538. GRÜN, A. Erlösung durch das Kreuz. Karl Rahners Beitrag zu einem heutigen Erlösungsverständnis. Dissertation, Anselmianum Athenaeum, Rome.

539. VAN DER HEIJDEN, B. *Karl Rahner*. Darstellung und Kritik seiner Grundposition. Einsiedeln. (Sammlung Horizonte NR 6).

540. HOLZ, Harald. *Einführung in die transzendental Philosophie.* Darmstadt: Wissenschaftliche Buchgesellschaft.

541. KEANE, P. "Pluralism in the Works of Karl Rahner with Application to Religious Life." *Review for Religious* 32, 223-240.

542. KOTTUKAPALLY, J. "Infallible? Fallible?" *Indian Journal of Theology* 22, 92-111.

543. LAKELAND, P. "Rahner Critical of Küng." *National Catholic Reporter* 10, 3.

544. LANGEVIN, Gilles. "Le pluralisme en matière spirituelle et religieuse selon Karl Rahner." *Laval Théologique et Philosophique* 29, 3-17. (See also No. 609.)

545. LANTIN, Emmanuel M. L'homme et la foi dans la pensée de Karl Rahner. Dissertation, Institut catholique, Paris.

546. LAUTER, H.-J. "Die doppelte Aporetik der Trinitätslehre und ihre Überschreitung." *Wissenschaft und Weisheit* 36, 60-62.

547. LUKÁCS, L. "Az 'anonim keresztények' fölfedezése" (Discovery of the "Anonymous Christian"). *Vigilia* (Budapest) 37, 731-736.

548. McCOOL, Gerald A., S.J. "The Philosophical Theology of Rahner and Lonergan," in Robert J. Roth, S.J., editor: *God Knowable and Unknowable*. New York: Fordham University Press, 123-157.

549. MASSON, Robert. "Rahner and Heidegger: Being, Hearing, and God." *The Thomist* 37, 455-488.

550. MAY, G. " 'Normative Kraft des faktischen Glaubens' als Weg zur Einheitskirche der Zukunft? Bemerkungen zu einer Vision Karl Rahners." *Archiv für katholisches Kirchenrecht* 142, 3-16.

551. MEINVIELLE, Julio. "La ciencia humana de Cristo en Rahner." *Mikael* 1, 68-90.

552. NYIRI, T. "Karl Rahner emberképe" (Karl Rahner's Concept of Man). *Vigilia* (Budapest) 37, 723-730.

553. OCHS, Robert J., S.J. "Death as Act. An Interpretation of Karl Rahner," in M. J. Taylor, editor: *The Mystery of Suffering and Death*. Staten Island, N.Y.: Alba House, 119-138.

554. PAYGERT, A. "Wiara dzisiejszego chrzescijanina w oczach prof. Rahnera." *Novum* Nr. 7/8, 16-21.

556. PETERS, A. "Moderne evangelische Glaubensbekenntnisse und katholische Kurzfomeln des Glaubens." *Kerygma und Dogma*, 19, 232-253.

557. RATZINGER, Josef. "Noch einmal 'Kurzformeln des Glaubens.' Anmerkungen." *Internationale Katholische Zeitschrift* 2, 258-264. Also *Communio* 3, 258-264.

558. RIESENHUBER, Klaus, S.J. *Maria im theologischen Verständnis von K. Barth und K. Rahner*. Freiburg: Herder (Quaestiones Disputatae 60).

559. SCHLACHTENHAUFEN, H. D. A Comparison of the Theological Anthropology of Paul Tillich and Karl Rahner. Theology dissertation, Aquinas Institute of Theology, Dubuque, Iowa.

560. SCHMÖLDERS, W. Inkarnatorische Struktur. Funktion und Relevanz eines Denkmodells in der Theologie von Karl Rahner. Theology dissertation, Innsbruck University.

561. SCHROEDER, O. "Die Zukunft der Kirche nach Karl Rahner." *Werkhefte* 27, 133-135.

562. SLADECZEK, Franz-Maria, S.J. *Ist das Dasein Gottes beweisbar?* Wie steht die Existenzphilosophie Martin Heideggers zu dieser Frage? Würzburg: K. Triltsch (2nd edition).

563. SQUARISE, Cristoforo, O.F.M. Senso cristiano del corpo (Ricerca sull'antropología di K. Rahner). Dissertation, Lateran University, Academia Alfonsiana, Rome.

564. SZABÓ, F. "A halál teologiája Karl Rahnerél" (Karl Rahner's Theology of Death). *Vigilia* (Budapest) 37, 737-744.

564a. TALLON, Andrew. "Rahner Bibliography, Secondary Literature." *Theology Digest* 21, 185-192.

565. THOMPSON, W. M. The Enlightenment, Miracles, and Karl Rahner's Thought. A Study of the Miracle-Question in Current Theological Discussion in the Light of Karl Rahner's Thought. Philosophy dissertation, St. Michael's College, University of Toronto.

566. THOMPSON, W. M. "Rahner's Theology of Pluralism." *The Ecumenist* 11, 17-22.

567. THUNBERG, L. "Allt mänskosläktet av ett blod. Monogenismproblemet hos Karl Rahner." *Svensk teologisk kvartalskrift* 49, 49-62.

568. TOINET, Paul. "Le principe de développement dogmatique et les idées du temps." *Revue Thomiste* 73, 211-238.

569. UÑA JUAREZ, A. "La iglesia del futuro. Reflexiones de K. Rahner." *Ciudad de Dios* 186, 57-85.

570. WEISSMAHR, B. *Gottes Wirken in der Welt*. Ein Diskussionsbeitrag zur Frage der Evolution und des Wunders. Frankfurt. See 35-39 and passim.

571. WIEDERKEHR, D. "Konfrontationen und Integrationen der Christologie." *Theologische Berichte* (Zürich) 2, 11-119, esp. 76-81.

572. WINTERHOLLER, H. Schöpferische Freiheit in christlicher An-

thropozentrik. Zur Freiheitslehre Karl Rahners. Theology dissertation, Gregorian University, Rome.

1974

573. ALTMANN, Walther. *Der Begriff der Tradition bei Karl Rahner.* Bern: Lang.

574. BLEISTEIN, Roman, S.J., editor. *Bibliographie Karl Rahner 1969-1974.* Freiburg: Herder.

575. BLEISTEIN, Roman, S.J. "Einleitung: Entstehung und Entwicklung der *Schriften zur Theologie.*" In No. 620, pp. 13-23.

576. BOURKE, Vernon J. "*Esse*, Transcendence, and Law: Three Phases of Recent Thomism." *The Modern Schoolman* 52, 49-64.

577. BRACKEN, Joseph A., S.J. "The Holy Trinity as a Community of Divine Persons. II. Person and Nature in the Doctrine of God. *The Heythrop Journal* 15, 257-270.

578. BRANICK, Vincent P., S.M. *An Ontology of Understanding.* Karl Rahner's Metaphysics of Knowledge in Context of Modern German Hermeneutics. St. Louis: Marianist Communication Center.

579. BRECHTKEN, J. "Transzendenz der Zukunft. Zur temporalen Interpretation der Gottesfrage bei Metz und Rahner." *Theologie und Glaube* 64, 146-161.

580. BREUNING, W. "Christologie—systematisch und exegetisch." *Theologische Revue* 70, 177-186.

581. BÜMLEIN, Klaus. *Mündige und schuldige Welt.* Überlegungen zum christlichen Verständnis von Schuld und Mündigkeit im Gespräch mit Paul Tillich und Karl Rahner. Göttingen: Vandenhoeck & Ruprecht.

582. BURKE, Ronald Raymond. Rahner and Revelation. Doctoral dissertation, Yale University.

583. CARMODY, John T. "Karl Rahner's Brave New Church." *America* 130 (16 February), 109-111.

584. CLARKE, W. Norris, S.J. "What Is Most and Least Relevant in the Metaphysics of St. Thomas Today? *International Philosophical Quarterly* 14, 411-434.

585. COLEMAN, G. D. Religious Experience as Guide of Spiritual Living. A Study in Ignatius of Loyola and Karl Rahner, His Interpreter. Doctoral dissertation, St. Michael's College, University of Toronto.

586. CORETH, Emerich, S.J. Hommage to Karl Rahner on the occasion of the two numbers of the journal dedicated to him on his 70th birthday: *Zeitschrift fur katholische Theologie* 96, 3-5.

587. DONCEEL, Joseph, S.J. "Transcendental Thomism." *The Monist* 58, 67-85. Also in *Listening* 9, 157-164.

588. DULLAART, L. *Kirche und Ekklesiologie.* Die Institutionlehre Arnold Gehlens als Frage an den Kirchenbegriff in der gegenwärtigen systematischen Theologie. München/Mainz. See esp. pp. 134-165, 174-179.

589. FABRO, Cornelio, C.P. *La svolta antropologica di Karl Rahner.* Problemi attuali. Milano: Rusconi Editore.

590. FABRO, Cornelio, C.P. "La svolta antropologica in teologia." *Miscellanea francescana* 74, 433-463.

591. FAHLBUSCH, E. "Karl Rahner. Theologie in der Nachfolge des Thomas von Aquin." *Materialdienst des Konsfessionskunlichen Instituts* 25, 22-25.

592. FARRELLY, J. "Man's Transcendence and Thomistic Resources." *The Thomist* 38, 426-484.

593. FISCHER, Klaus P. *Der Mensch als Geheimnis.* Dis Anthropologie Karl Rahners. Mit einem Brief K. Rahners. Freiburg. Herder.

594. FITZPATRICK, P. J. "Infallibility—A Secular Assessment." *Irish Theological Quarterly* 41, 3-21.

595. DE FRANCA MIRANDA, Mario, S.J. O misterio de Deus em nossa vida. A doutrina trinitaria de Karl Rahner. Dissertation, Gregorian University. See also No. ....

596. FRIES, Heinrich. "Ökumenisches Amtsverständnis?" *Stimmen der Zeit* 192, 555-564.

597. GALST, J. "Valeur de la notion de personne dans l'expression du mystère du Christ." *Gregorianum* 54, 69-97.

598. GIRONÉS, G. "Respuesta a K. Rahner sobre la teologia trinitaria." *Anales del seminario de Valencia* 9-14, Nr. 17.

599. GRABSKA, Stanislawa. "La liberté chrétienne d'après les écrits de Karl Rahner." *Ephemerides theologicae Lovanienses* 50, 75-91.

600. HEBBLETHWAITE, Peter. "Relaxing with Karl Rahner. Herr Professor at Age 70." *Commonweal* 101, 111-112.

601. VAN DER HEIJDEN, B. "Zur Offenbarungstheologie Karl Rahners." *Liber annualis* (Rome: Gregorian University).

602. HEINRICHS, Johannes, S.J. "Ideologie oder Freiheitslehre? Zur Rezipierbarkeit der thomanischen Gnadenlehre von einem transzendental-dialogischen Standpunkt." *Theologie und Philosophie* 49, 395-436.

603. VAN HOOF, G. "Het geloof van een minderheid." *De Standaard* (Amsterdam) (8 November), 15.

604. HOYE, William J. "A Critical Remark on Karl Rahner's *Hearers of the Word.*" *Antonianum* 48, 508-532.

605. KASPER, Walter. *Jesus der Christus.* Mainz. See esp. pp. 56-62.

606. KATTUKAPALLY, Joseph. "Nature and Grace: A New Dimension." *Thought* 49, 117-133.

607. KEEFE, Donald, S.J. "Biblical Symbolism and the Morality of in vitro Fertilization." *Theology Digest* 22, 308-323.

608. KÖSTER, F. "Die Begründung der Mission am Beispiel der Theologie Karl Rahners." *Zeitschrift für Missionswissenschaft und Religionswissenschaft* 58, 241-257.

609. LANGEVIN, Gilles. "Le pluralisme en matière spirituelle et religieuse selon K. Rahner," in *Le Pluralisme. Pluralism. Its Meaning for Today.* Montreal: Fides. (See also No. 544.)

610. LEHMANN, Karl. "Karl Rahner und die Pastoral," in *Theologie und Religion aktuell.* Beihefter zum Anzeiger für die katholische

Geistlichkeit, 23. Folge (February) I-VI (with a Bibliography by Albert Raffelt).

611. LOTZ, Johannes Baptist, S.J. "Zur Thomas-Rezeption in der Maréchal-Schule." *Theologie und Philosophie* 49, 375-394, esp. 388-390.

612. McCOOL, Gerald A., S.J. "Is St. Thomas's 'Science of God' Still Relevant Today?" *International Philosophical Quarterly* 14, 435-454.

613. McCOOL, Gerald A., S.J. "Scientific Theology: Bonaventure and Thomas Revisited." *Thought* 49, 374-396.

614. MANZANO, Isidoro, O.F.M. "Reflexiones en torno a los fundamentos del conocer human según Rahner. Con ocasión de un libro de Fabro sobre Rahner." *Antonianum* 49, 320-344. (See No. 589.)

615. MASCALL, E. L. "Thomism, Traditional or Transcendental?" *Tijdschrift voor Filosofie* 36, 323-341.

616. MERTENS, Jos. "Functie en wezen van de intellectus agens volgens S. Thomas." *Tijdschrift voor Filosofie* 36, 267, 322.

617. MESSNER, M. "Die ewige Unruhe zum je grösseren Gott. Zur Theologie des Gebetes und ihrem ignatianischen Hintergrund nach Karl Rahner." *Geist und Leben* 47, 244-256.

618. METZ, Johann Baptist. "Karl Rahner—ein theologisches Leben. Theologie als mystische Biographie eines Christenmenschen heute." *Stimmen der Zeit* 192, 305-316. (Separately published in: *Die Sendung*, Vol. II, 3-13, and in *Nachrichten und Berichte*. Westfäl. Wilhelms-Univ. Münster (22 April), pp. 17f.

619. MUCK, Otto, S.J. "Phänomenologie, Metaphysik, Transzendentale Reflexion." *Zeitschrift für katholische Theologie* 96, 70-75.

620. NEUFELD, Karl H., S.J. and Bleistein, Roman, S.J. *Rahner-Register*. Eine Schlüssel zu Karl Rahners *Schriften zur Theologie* I-X und zu seinen Lexikonartikeln. Zürich: Benziger Verlag.

621. NEUFELD, Karl H., S.J. "Beobachtungen im Umgang mit Karl Rahners *Schriften zur Theologie*. In No. 620, pp. 177-200; survey of important reviews of the Schriften on pp. 193-200.

622. NEUFELD, Karl H., S.J. "Fortschritt durch Umkehr. Zu Karl Rahners bussgeschichtlichen Arbeiten." *Stimmen der Zeit*, 192, 274-281.

623. NEUMANN, K. "Suchen und suchend verstehen. Die Christologie Karl Rahners." *Christ in der Gegenwart* 26, 221f.

624. NICOLAS, J. H. "L'Acte pur de Saint Thomas et le Dieu vivant de l'Evangile." *Angelicum* 51, 511-532.

625. PANNENBERG, Wolfhart. "Tod und Auferstehung in der Sicht christlicher Dogmatik." *Kerygma und Dogma* 20, 167-180, esp. 172, 175ff.

626. PIEKARSKI, S. "Jubileusz Karla Rahnera." *Mysl Spoleczna*, n. 13.

627. PIET, J. H. "Where in the World is God?" (Christianity and Hinduism). *Reformed Review* 27, 131-147.

628. RESWEBER, Jean-Paul. Essai sur le discours théologique à la lumière de la critique heideggerienne de la métaphysique. Theology dissertation, University of Strasbourg, 1973. Available from Lille:

University of Lille II, Service de reproduction de thèses; see also No. 669.

629. ROTTER, Hans, S.J. "Kann das Naturrecht die Moraltheologie entbehren?" *Zeitschrift für katholische Theologie* 96, 76-96.

630. RUPP, G. E. *Christologies and Cultures.* Toward a Typology of Religious World Views. The Hague: Mouton. See esp. pp. 204-210 and 210-214.

631. SCHILSON, A. and Walter Kasper. *Christologie im Präsens.* Kritische Sichtung neuer Entwürfe. Freiburg. See esp. pp. 80-89, 142f. (Second edition 1977, expanded.)

632. SCHOONENBERG, Piet, S.J. "Continuiteit en herinterpretatie in de Drieeenheidsleer." *Tijdschrift voor Theologie* 14, 54-72.

633. SCHUPP, Franz. *Auf dem Weg zur einer kritischen Theologie.* Freiburg: Herder (Quaestiones Disputatae 64). See esp. pp. 27-42 and passim.

634. TALLON, Andrew. "Spirit, Freedom, History. Karl Rahner's *Hörer des Wortes (Hearers of the Word)." The Thomist* 38, 908-936.

635. TIERNEY, B. "Infallibility in Morals. A Response." *Theological Studies* 35, 507-517.

636. TRACY, G. E. On the Nature of Symbol as Set Out in the Theology of Karl Rahner, S.J. Philosophy dissertation, Boston College.

637. WALOSZCYK, K. "Assemblée liturgique et mystère de l'Eglise à la lumière de la théologie contemporaine" (in Polish, with French summary). *Studia theologica Varsaviensia* 12, 15-44.

638. WILHELMSEN, Frederick D. "The Priority of Judgment over Question: Reflections on Transcendental Thomism." *International Philosophical Quarterly* 14, 475-493.

1975

639. BAUER, Gerhard. *Christliche Hoffnung und menschlicher Fortschritt.* München/Mainz: Kaiser-Grünewald.

640. BOYLE, John P. "Faith and Christian Ethics in Rahner and Lonergan." *Thought* 50, 247-265.

641. BURNS, P. J. "Apologetic of Liberation and Fulfilment." *Communio* 2, 323-342.

642. DE CLERCK, P. "La fréquence des Messes. Réalités économiques et théologiques." *La Maison-Dieu* 121, 151-158.

643. FLURY, J. "Was ist Fundamentaltheologie?" *Theologische Zeitschrift* 31, 351-367.

644. FÜSSEL, K. Die sprachanalytische und wissenschaftstheoretische Diskussion um den Begriff der Wahrheit in ihrer Relevanz für eine systematische Theologie. Theology dissertation, Münster/Westf. See esp. pp. 440-459.

645. GERVAIS, Pierre. L'interprétation des énoncés dogmatiques dans la théologie de Karl Rahner. Dissertation, Institut Catholique, Paris.

646. GIBELLINI, R. "Visti in città." *Città e provincia* 3 (16 March), 7.

647. GIRONELLA, Juan Roig. "El pluralismo teólogico ante la filosofía del lenguaje." *Espíritu* 24, 47-86.

648. GONZÁLEZ DE CARDENAL, Olegario. *Jesús de Nazaret.* Approximación a la cristología. Madrid: B.A.C.

649. GRÜN, A. *Erlösung durch das Kreuz.* Karl Rahners Beitrag zu einem heutigen Erlösungsverstandnis. Münsterschwarzach (Münsterschwarzacher Studien 26).

650. JÄGER, N. Die Heilsmöglichkeit der Nichtchristen und die Notwendigkeit der Mission. Das II. Vatikanische Konzil auf dem Hintergrund der Theologiegeschichte. Theology dissertation, Münster/Westf. See esp. pp. 161-217.

651. JÜNGEL, Eberhard. "Extra Christum nulla salus—als Grundsatz natürlicher Theologie? Evangelische Erwägungen zur 'Anonymität' des Christenmenschen." *Zeitschrift für Theologie und Kirche* 72, 337-352.

652. JÜNGEL, Eberhard. "Das Verhältnis von 'ökonomischer' und 'immanenter' Trinität. Erwägungen über eine biblische Begründung der Trinitätslehre im Anschluss an und in Auseinandersetzung mit Karl Rahners Lehre vom dreifaltigen Gott als transzendentem Urgrund der Heilsgeschichte." *Zeitschrift für Theologie und Kirche* 72, 353-364. See also No. 697.

653. KELLY, Anthony J. "Is Lonergan's 'Method' Adequate to Christian Mystery?" *The Thomist* 39, 437-470.

654. KÜNG, Hans. "Anonyme Christen—wozu?" *Orientierung* 39, 214-216. (See also H. R. Schlette, *ibid.*, pp. 265f.)

655. LEGRAND, Hervé-Marie. "Bulletin d'ecclésiologie. Recherches sur le presbytérat et l'épiscopat." *Revue des Sciences philosophiques et théologiques* 59, 645-724; on Rahner see pp. 704-706.

656. LOERSCH, S. Die Theologie Dorothee Sölles. Darstellung und Kritik. Theology dissertation, Münster. See esp. pp. 374-389.

657. McCOOL, Gerald A., S.J. "Introduction: Rahner's Philosophical Theology," in his *A Rahner Reader.* New York/London: Seabury Press/Darton, Longman and Todd, xiii-xxviii.

658. McCOOL, Gerald A., S.J. "Social Authority in Transcendental Thomism," in George McLean, O.M., editor: *Philosophy and Civil Law.* pp. 13-23.

659. MILLER, Jeremy, O.P. "Rahner's Approach to Moral Decision-Making." *Louvain Studies* 16, 350-359.

660. De FRANCA MIRANDA, Mario, S.J. *O misterio de Deus em nossa vida.* A doutrina trinitária de Karl Rahner. São Paulo: Ed. Loyola (Coleção Fé e realidade 1). See also No. 595.

661. MITTERSTIELER, E. *Christlicher Glaube als Bestätigung des Menschen.* Zur "fides quaerens intellectum" in der Theologie Karl Rahners. Frankfurt.

662. MODA, A. "Una svolta nella recerca teologica: la cristologia di Rahner-Thüsing." *Humanitas* 30, 123-137.

663. MÜLLER, W. *Être-au-monde. Grundlinien einer philosophischen Anthropologie bei Maurice Merleau-Ponty.* Bonn (Studien zur franz, Philos. des 20. Jahrhunderts 6), esp. pp. 231-266.

664. MUSSNER, F. "Warum noch Konversionen?" *Internationale Katholische Zeitschrift: Communio* 4, 331, 338.

665. NEGRI, L. "Implcazioni apologetiche del discorso teologico rahneriano." *Ephemerides carmeliticae* 26, 104-175.

666. PEARL, Th. "Dialectical Panentheism: On the Hegelian Character of Karl Rahner's Key Christological Writings." *Irish Theological Quarterly* 42, 119-137.

667. PEDUN, C. "Rahner's Theological Investigations." *The Illif Review* 32, 47-55.

668. PORRO, C. *Cristologia in crisi?* Roma: Ed Paoline. See pp. 27-39.

669. RESWEBER, Jean-Paul. *La théologie face au défi herméneutique.* M. Heidegger, R. Bultmann, K. Rahner. Bruxelles/Paris/Louvain: Vander-Nauwelaerts. (See No. 628.)

670. ROACH, R. R. "An Excessive Claim: Rahner's Identification of Love of God with Love of Neighbor." *Studies in Religion* 5 (1975/1976) 247-257, 360-372.

671. SCHLETTE, H. R. "Rahner, Küng und die anonymen Christen." *Orientierung* 39, 174-176. (See No. 654.)

672. SCHMIDT, P. "Theologische Anthropologie und Religionspädagogik." *Theologie und Philosophie* 50, 404-415.

673. SCHOONENBERG, Piet, S.J. "Christologische Diskussion heute." *Theologisch-praktische Quartalschrift* 123, 105-117.

674. SHIM, J. S.-T. Glaube und Heil. Eine Untersuchung zur Theorie von den "anonymen Christen" Karl Rahners. Theology dissertation, Tübingen.

675. STEVENS, C. "Karl Rahner: People's Theologian." *Our Sunday Visitor Magazine* 63, N. 16, p. 1.

676. TAPPEINER, D. A. "Sacramental Causality in Aquinas and Rahner." *Scottish Journal of Theology* 28, 243-258.

677. THOMAS, Dean. *Post-Theistic Thinking: The Marxist-Christian Dialogue in Radical Perspective.* Philadelphia: Temple University Press.

678. THOMPSON, W. "Renewed Interest in the Discernment of Spirits." *Ecumenist* 13, 54-59.

679. TORRANCE, Th. F. "Toward an Ecumenical Consensus of the Trinity," *Theologische Zeitschrift* 31, 337-350.

680. VACEK, Edward, S.J. "Development within Rahner's Theology." *The Irish Theological Quarterly* 42, 36-49.

681. VANDERVELDE, G. *Original Sin.* Two Trends in Contemporary Roman Catholic Reinterpretation. Amsterdam: Rodopi.

682. VANSTEENKISTE, P. Clemente, O.P., ed. *Rassegna de Letteratura Tomistica* 7, 438-440. Notice on No. 494.

683. VARGAS-MACHUCA, A., ed. *Teología y mundo contemporáneo.* Homenaje a K. Rahner en su 70 cumpleaños. Madrid.

684. WOOD, Charles M. "Karl Rahner on Theological Discourse." *Journal of Ecumenical Studies* 12, 55-67.

1976

685. ANTES, P. "Christus und Christentum in der Sicht der grossen Weltreligionen." *Theologie und Philosophie* 51, 385-396.

686. BERCIANO, M. "Influjos de la filosofía de Heidegger en la teología reciente: R. Bultmann, P. Tillich, K. Rahner." *Burgense. Collectanea scientifica* 17, 445-473.

687. BRESNAHAN, James F., S.J. "Rahner's Ethics: Critical Natural Law in Relation to Contemporary Ethical Methodology." *The Journal of Religion* 56, 36-60.

688. BURKE, R. "Reviewing Rahner's Rules for Theology." *Encounter* 37, 315-325.

689. CAREY, W. H. The Concept of Salvation in the Writings of Karl Rahner, S.J. Doctoral Dissertation, New York University.

690. CARRERAS, J. M. *Significación teológica de Juan Martinez de Ripalda, en la pensamiento de K. Rahner con referencia a la teoria de los cristianos anónimos.* Resumen de la disertación para el doctorado en la faculdad de teología pontificia y civil Lima. Lima.

691. CATTAUI DE MENASCE, G. "Riflessioni critiche sulla cristologia di Rahner." *Divinitas* 20, 175-184.

692. DE H-ÍDÉ, S. "Rahner and Lonergan." *Studies* 65, 63-67.

693. DRACK, B. "Grundkurs des Glaubens." *Schweizerische Kirchenzeitung* 144, 778-780.

694. EICHER, Peter. "Wovon spricht die transzendentale Theologie? Zur gegenwärtigen Auseinandersetzung um das Denken von Karl Rahner." *Theologische Quartalschrift* 156, 284-295.

695. FISCHER, Klaus P. "Wo der Mensch an das Geheimnis grenzt. Die mystagogique Struktur der Theologie Karl Rahners." *Zeitschrift für katholische Theologie* 98, 159-170.

696. GEYER, C. F. "Philosophie und Theologie." *Neue Zeitschrift für systematische Theologie und Religionsphilosophie* 18, 1-21.

697. JÜNGEL, Eberhard. "The Relationship between 'Economic' and 'Immanent' Trinity." *Theology Digest* 24. (See No. 652.)

698. KEHL, Medard. *Kirche als Institution.* Zur theologischen Begründung des institutionellen Charakters der Kirche in der neueren deutschsprachigen katholischen Ekklesiologie. Frankfurt: Josef Knecht. See esp. pp. 171-238.

699. KLINGER, Elmar, editor. *Christentum innerhalb und asserhalb der Kirche* (dedicated to K. Rahner). Freiburg: Herder (Quaestiones Disputatae 73).

700. LANGEVIN, Gilles. "L'apport du P. Karl Rahner à la christologie. Présentation et traduction d'un texte-synthèse," in *Le Christ hier, aujourd'hui et demain.* Québec: Pr. Univ. Laval. See esp. pp. 259-276.

701. LEGRAND, Hervé-Marie. "Bulletin d'ecclésiologie." *Revue des Sciences philosophiques et théologiques* 60, 649-697; on Rahner: 674, 678-680, 686-687.

702. McCOOL, Gerald A., S.J. "Duty and Reason in Thomistic Social Ethics," in Robert O. Johann, editor. *Freedom and Value.* New York: Fordham University Press. See pp. 137-159.

703. MANCINI, Guy, O.S.B. The Understanding of the Experience of God According to Karl Rahner and Bernard Lonergan. Master's Thesis, Indiana University.

704. MAYRHOFER, F. "Gestorben wird irgendwann während des Lebens. . . . über ein Seminar zur Euthanasie." *Salzburger Nachrichten* (10 May).

705. MESOTTEN, B. "Het testament van teoloog Karl Rahner." KNACK (Brussels) (8 December), 179-180.

706. METZ, Johann Baptist. "Theologie als Biographie. Eine These und ein Paradigma." *Concilium* 12, 311-315.

707. MEYER, M. Universales Heil, Kirche und Mission. Studien über die ekklesial-missionarischen Strukturen in der Theologie K. Rahners und im Epheserbrief. Theology dissertation, Munster/Westf. Exegetical part published as *Kirche und Mission im Epheserbrief*. Stuttgart, 1977.

708. MOTZKO, Maria Elizabeth. Karl Rahner's Theology. A Theology of the Symbol. Doctoral Dissertation, Fordham University.

709. PEUKERT, Helmut. *Wissenschaftstheorie—Handlungstheorie—Fundamentale Theologie*. Analysen zu Ansatz und Status theologischer Theoriebildung. Düsseldorf: Pasmos Verlag. See pp. 43-49. Paperback edition (Frankfurt, 1978: Suhrkamp Taschenbuch Wiss. 231); see esp. pp. 47ff.

710. PUNTEL, L. B. "Hans Küng, die Logik und die theologische Redlichkeit. Bemerkungen zur Kritik des Tübinger Theologen am Begriff 'anonymes Christentum.'" *Orientierung* 40, 3-6.

711. RUIZ DE LA PEÑA, Juan Luiz. "Espiritu en el mundo. La antropología de Karl Rahner." *Antropologías de siglo XX*, edited by Juan de Saghagun Lucas. Salamanca: Sígueme Editore (Hermeneia 5), 180-201.

712. SACHOT, M. "*La théologie face au défi herméneutique* par Jean-Paul Resweber." *Revue des Sciences religieuses* 50, 169-173.

713. SECKLER, M. Einführung in den Begriff des Christentums. Zu K. Rahners neuestem Werk." *Herder Korrespondenz* 30, 516-521.

714. SCHEURICH, H. Karl Rahners These vom anonymen Christentum. Darstellung—Kritik—Würdigung. Theology dissertation, Halle University, Wittenberg.

715. SOBOSAN, J. B. "Anonymity and Christianity." *Homilectic and Pastoral Review* 76, 62-69.

716. SOLTERER, J. "Natural Law and Economics: Reflections on Desan, Rahner and Schumpeter." *Review of Social Economy* 34, 53-62.

717. TAYLOR, D. A. Unio hypostatica in the Christology of Karl Rahner. Philosophy dissertation, Oxford University.

718. VANSTEENKISTE, P. Clemente, O.P., editor. *Rassegna de Letteratura Tomistica* 8, 434-436.

719. WALDENFELS, H. "Anthropologia negativa." *Zeitschrift für Missionswissenschaft und Religionswissenschaft* 60, 55-60.

720. WALDENFELS, H. "Die neuere Diskussion um die 'anonymen Christen' als Beitrag zur Religionstheologie." *Zeitschrift für Missionswissenschaft und Religionswissenschaft* 60, 161-180.

721. WEGER, K. H. "Das 'anonyme' Christentum in der heutigen Theologie." *Stimmen der Zeit* 194, 319-332.

722. LES CHRÉTIENS. Paris: Hachette (Encyclopédie du monde actuel 4463), see Rahner entry.

1977

723. BRADLEY, Denis J.M. "Rahner's *Spirit in the World:* Aquinas or Hegel?" *The Thomist* 41, 167-199.

724. BORZAGA, Reynold. *In Pursuit of Religion: A Framework for Understanding Today's Theology.* Palm Springs: Sunday Publications.

725. BRANDENBURG, A. "Theologisches Dokument seiner Zeit. Zu Karl Rahners *Grundkurs des Glaubens.*" *Catholica* 31, 66-68.

726. BUCKLEY, James J. Karl Barth and Karl Rahner in the Christian Community. Analysis, Comparison, and Assessment. Doctoral dissertation, Yale University.

727. BÜRKLE, H. *Einführung in die Theologie der Religionen.* Darmstadt. See esp. pp. 28-33.

728. CARR, Anne. *The Theological Method of Karl Rahner.* Missoula, MT: Scholars Press for the American Academy of Religion.

729. CARROLL, D. "Hierarchia Veritatum: A Theoretical and Pastoral Insight of the Second Vatican Council." *The Irish Theological Quarterly* 44, 125-133.

730. CONLON, James J. "Karl Rahner's Theory of Sensation." *The Thomist* 41, 400-417.

731. CORDUAN, Winfried. Elements of the Philosophy of G.W.F. Hegel in the Transcendental Method of Karl Rahner. Doctoral dissertation, Rice University.

732. COUTO, F. "Katholische Theologie. Zu Karl Rahners *Grundkurs des Glaubens.*" *Theologie und Glaube* 67, 422-431.

733. DÖRING, H. *Abwesenheit Gottes.* Fragen und Antworten heutiger Theologie. Paderborn. See esp. pp. 384-386.

734. DOUD, Robert E. "Rahner's Christology: A Whiteheadian Critique." *The Journal of Religion* 18, 144-155. From his doctoral dissertation, under this title, Claremont Graduate School, 1977.

735. EICHER, Peter. "Erfahren und Denken. Ein nota bene zur Flucht in Meditative Unschuld." *Theologische Quartalschrift* 157, 142-143. (Response to No. 741.)

736. EICHER, Peter. *Offenbarung.* Prinzip neuzeitlicher Theologie. München. See esp. pp. 347-421.

737. FAHLBUSCH, E. "Zum 'Begriff des Christentums.' Resümierende und kritische Bemerkungen zum *Grundkurs des Glaubens* von Karl Rahner." *Materialdienst des Konfessionskundlichen Instituts* 28, 36-40.

738. FIGL, J. *Atheismus als theologisches Problem.* Modelle des Auseinandersetzung in der Theologie der Gegenwart. Mainz. See esp. pp. 146-176.

739. FISCHER, Klaus P. "Kritik der 'Grundpositionen'? Kritische Anmerkungen zu B. van der Heijdens Buch über Karl Rahner." *Zeitschrift für katholische Theologie* 99, 74-89. See

740. FISCHER, Klaus P. "Grundkurs des Glaubens. Karl Rahners 'Ein-

führung in den Begriff des Christentums.' " *Theologie und Philosophie* 52, 67-71.

741. FISCHER, Klaus P. "Wovon erzählt die transzendentale Theologie? Eine Entgegung an Peter Eicher." *Theologische Quartalschrift* 157, 140-142. See No. 735.

742. GEENSE, A. "Men is altijd Christen om het te worden." *De Bazuin* (Utrecht) (4 March).

743. HEBBLETHWAITE, Peter. "The Status of 'Anonymous Christian.' " *The Heythrop Journal* 18, 52-53.

744. HEINEMANN, H. "Gottliches Recht? Versuch einer Differenzierung." *Theologische Quartalschrift* 157, 279-291.

745. VAN HOUT, H. "Gekruisigde theologie. De kritische funktie van het kruis in de dogmatiek van Karl Rahner," in *Proef en toets*. Theologie als experiment. Bijdragen bij gelegenheid van het tienjarig bestaan van de Katholieke Theologische Hogeschool te Amsterdam. Amersfoort. See pp. 103-116.

746. LAMMARONE, L. "Il 'divenire di Dio' e Giovanni Duns Scoto." *Miscellanea francescana* 77, 45-94.

747. KERN, Walter, S.J. "Karl Rahners *Grundkurs des Glaubens*. Kleine Einführung in eine grosse Einführung." *Stimmen der Zeit* 195, 326-336.

748. KRÖGER, A. "Totale Pluriformität? Zu Karl Rahners Aufsatz: 'Dogmen- und Theologiegeschichte—gestern und morgen." *Der Fels* 8, 246-248.

749. LAURET, Bernard. "Bulletin de Christologie, II. Christologie proprement dite." *Revue des Sciences philosophiques et théologiques* 61, 567-604; on Rahner see pp. 567-574, 595.

750. LOTZ, Johannes Baptist, S.J. "Die transzendentale Verwiesenheit des Menschen auf die geschichtlich ergangene christliche Offenbarung" *Geist und Leben* 50, 74-77.

751. McHUGH, J. "Faith and Prayer in Secular Culture. Report on Karl Rahner's Vision of Faith and Prayer in the Church." *Cross and Crown* 29, 44-50.

752. MANSER, J. *Der Tod des Menschen*. Zur Deutung des Todes in der gegenwärtigen Philosophie und Theologie. Bern. See esp. pp. 70-80.

753. MARRANZINI, A. " 'Corso base della fede' de Karl Rahner." *La civiltá cattolica* 128, 462-468.

754. MARRION, M. "Theological Formation: The Two Approaches to Christ." *Contemplative Review* 10, 10-14.

755. METZ, Johann Baptist. *Glaube in Geschichte und Gesellschaft*. Studien zu einer praktischen Fundamentaltheologie. Mainz. Passim.

756. MOLONEY, Robert. "Seeing and Knowing. Some Reflections on Karl Rahner's Theory of Knowledge." The Heythrop Journal 18, 399-419.

757. O'DONOVAN, Leo Jeremiah, S.J.; J. Peter Schineller, S.J.; John P Galvin; Michael A. Fahey, S.J. "A Changing Ecclesiology in a Changing Church: A Symposium on Development in the Ecclesiology of Karl Rahner." *Theological Studies* 38, 736-752.

758. OZOROWSKI, E. "K. Rahnera podstawowy kurs wiary (Grundkurs des Glaubens)." *Studia theologica Varsavienia* 15, 236-243.

759. PATER, G. H. Karl Rahner's Historico-theological Studies on Penance. The Retrieval of Forgotten Truths. Doctoral dissertation, Notre Dame University.

760. POWER, D. N. "Confessing as Ongoing Conversion." *The Heythrop Journal* 18, 180-190.

761. RAFFELT, Albert. "Aspekte gegenwärtiger Christologie." *Lebendige Seelsorge* 28, 34-40, esp. 35, 39-40.

762. RENWART, L. "Jésus-Christ aujourd'hui." *Nouvelle revue théologique* 109, 208-249, esp. 234f, 238f, and passim.

763. SCHEFFCZYK, Leo. "Erwagungen zu Karl Rahners *Grundkurs des Glaubens.*" *Internationale katholische Zeitschrift* 5, 67-71.

764. SCHEFFCZYK, Leo. "Christentum als Unmittelbarkeit zu Gott. *Internationale katholische Zeitschrift* 6, 442-450.

765. SCHILLEBEECKX, Edouard. "Rahner verteld ons over de afgronden van het menselijk bestaan," in K. Rahner: *Was is een Christen?* Tielt: Lanoo, pp. 5-9.

766. SCHWEIZER, E. "Aspekte der Theologie heute: Karl Rahners *Grundkurs des Glaubens.*" *Universitas* 32, 389-396 (abridged version of No. 767).

767. SCHWEIZER, E. "Moderne katholische Dogmatik. Karl Rahners *Grundkurs des Glaubens* (on Bultmann/Rahner)." *Neue Züricher Zeitung* (25 February).

768. SESBOÜÉ, B. "Le procès contemporain de Chalcédoine." *Recherche de science religieuse* 65, 45-79 (on Rahner, Tillich, Moltmann, Pannenberg, and others).

769. STICH, Helmut. *Kernstrukturen menschlicher Begegnung.* Ethische Implikationen der Kommunikationspsychologie. München: Johannes Berchmans Verlag.

770. THOLEN, N. "Schwieriger Grundkurs." *Frankfurter Hefte* 32, 59-61.

770a. THOMAS, O. C. "Being and Some Theologians." *Harvard Theological Review* 70, 137-160, especially 141-142.

771. TRETHOWAN, Illtyd, O.S.B. "Christology Again." *The Downside Review* 95, 1-10.

772. WALDENFELS, H. *Die Offenbarung.* Von der Reformation bis zur Gegenwart (in collaboration with Leo Scheffczyk). Freiburg. See esp. pp. 175-178 and passim.

773. WALSH, Michael J. *The Heart of Christ in the Writings of Karl Rahner.* An Investigation of Its Christological Foundation as an Example of the Relationship between Theology and Spirituality. Rome: Gregorian University Press (Analecta Gregoriana 209).

774. WENICH, B. "Zur Theologie Karl Rahners." *Münchener theologische Zeitschrift* 28, 383-398.

775. WIEDERKEHR, D. "Chancen und Grenzen anthropologischer Theologie. Zu Karl Rahners *Grundkurs des Glaubens.*" *Wissen und Weisheit* 40, 197-204.

776. WOHLGSCHAFT, H. *Hoffnung angesichts des Todes.* Das Todesproblem bei Karl Barth und in der zeitgenössischen Theologie des deutschen Sprachraums. München.

777. WOLFINGER, F. "Zu Karl Rahners *Grundkurs des Glaubens.*" *Orientierung* 41, 45-48.

778. *Dizionario teologico interdisciplinare.* Torino: Mariette, 3 vols. See the following: B. Seveso. "Il progetto di K. Rahner e l'Handbuch der Pastoraltheologie," I, 94-97; G. Ferretti. "L'analisi trascendentale (K. Rahner)," I, 167-168; F. Ardusso. "Rinnovamento della teologia fondamentale in Germania, I, 190-191; L. Serentha. (Zum Aufriss der Dogmatik), I, 274-275; L. Sartori. "Teologia delle religioni non cristiane. La cosidetta 'linea Rahner,'" III, 407-409; G. Angelini. "Rahner," III, 604-609; and passim in the alphabetical part.

1978

779. BERNING, V. *Gott, Geist und Welt.* Paderborn. See esp. pp. 52-55.

780. BEUTTER, Friedrich. "Christliche Ethik in der pluralen Gesellschaft." *Theologische Zeitschrift* 34, 212-220 (on Rahner pp. 212-213).

781. BLANDINO, G. "La dottrina trinitaria di K. Rahner," in G. Blandino: *Questioni dibattute di teologia* II. Rome: Città nuova editore, pp. 187-237.

782. CORDUAN, Winfried. "Hegel in Rahner. A Study in Philosophical Hermeneutics." *Harvard Theological Review* 71, 285-298.

783. CULLITON, Joseph T. "Rahner on the Origin of the Soul. Some Implications Regarding Abortion." *Thought* 53, 203-214.

784. GARADJA, V. I. "Transcendentalism and History—A Dialogue between the Christian Philosophy and the Present Time." *Dialectics and Humanism* 5, 137-144.

785. GIRONELLA, Juan Roig. "El cuerpo, puerta de entrada al ser y puerta de salida hacia el ser." *Espiritu* 27, 155-161.

786. GREINER, F. "Die Menschlichkeit der Offenbarung. Die transzendentale Grundlegung der Theologie bei K. Rahner in lichte seiner Christologie." *Zeitschrift für katholische Theologie* 100, 596-619.

787. GREINER, F. *Die Menschlichkeit der Offenbarung.* Die transzendentale Grundlegung der Theologie bei Karl Rahner. München (Münchener Monographen zur histor. und systemat. Theologie 2).

788. GRUBER, Lambert. *Transzendentalphilosophie und Theologie bei Johann Gottlieb Fichte und Karl Rahner.* Frankfurt (Disputationes Theologicae 6).

789. GUSTAFSON, J. *Protestant and Roman Catholic Ethics.* Chicago.

790. HAIGHT, Roger. "Grace and Liberation: An Interpretation of History." *The Thomist* 42, 539-581.

791. HENTZ, Otto, S.J. "Foundations of Christian Faith: An Introduction in the Idea of Christianity." *Thought* 53, 433-441.

792. HERBERG, J. *Kirchliche Heilsvermittlung.* Ein Gespräch zwischen Karl Barth und Karl Rahner. Frankfurt. (Disputationes Theologicae 5).

793. KERN, Walter, S.J. "Hundert Jahre Theologie. Zum Jubiläum der

Innsbrucker Zeitschrift für katholische Theologie." Stimmen der Zeit 196, 651-664.

794. KING, J. Norman. "The Experience of God in the Theology of Karl Rahner." *Thought* 53, 174-202.

795. KNAUER, P. *Der Glaube kommt vom Hören.* Ökumenische Fundamentaltheologie. Graz. Passim.

796. KOCH, H. G. "Ignatius für Zeitgenossen." *Anzeiger f. d. kath. Geistlichkeit* 87, 286-288.

797. B. JU. KUZMICKAS. "Transcendental'naja antropologija Karla Rahnera," *Voprosy filosofii* 32, 150-156.

798. McCOOL, Gerald A., S.J. "Karl Rahner on Christian Faith.'" *America* 138, 138-139.

799. McCOOL, Gerald A., S.J. "Twentieth-Century Scholasticism." *The Journal of Religion* 58 (Supplement), S198-S221 (Supplement edited by David Tracy entitled *A Colloquy on the Thought of Aquinas and Bonaventure*).

800. MASSON, Robert. Language, Thinking and God in Karl Rahner's Theology of the Word: A Critical Evaluation of Rahner's Perspective on the Problem of Religious Language. Theology dissertation, Fordham University.

801. METTE, Norbert. *Theorie der Praxis.* Wissenschaftsgeschichtliche und methodologische Untersuchung zur Theorie-Praxis-Problematik innerhalb d. prakt. Theologie. Düsseldorf. See esp. 126ff.

802. METTE, Norbert. "Zwischen Reflexion und Entscheidung I. and II. Der Beitrag Karl Rahners zur Grundlegung der praktischen Theologie." *Trierer theologische Zeitschrift* 87, 26-43, and 136-151.

803. MEYNELL, H. "On Objections to Lonergan's 'Method.' " *The Heythrop Journal* 19, 405-410.

804. MICHIELS, R. "De theologie van Karl Rahner." *Collationes* 8, 264-292.

805. MICHIELS, R. "Rahners *Grundkurs des Glaubens* of zijn theologisch testament." *Collationes* 8, 342-358.

806. MOLNAR, Thomas Steven. *Christian Humanism:* A Critique of the Secular City and its Ideology. Chicago: Franciscan Herald Press.

807. NEUMANN, K. Der Praxisbezug der Theologie bei Karl Rahner. Theology dissertation, München.

808. NIGRO, C. "Osservazioni," in G. Blandino. *Questioni dibattute di teologia* II. Rome: Citta nuova editore. See pp. 237-241.

809. OEDINGEN, K. "Eine kritische Studie zu Rahners *Grundkurs des Glaubens.*" *Tijdschrift voor filosofie* 40, 502-509.

810. OTTE, Klaus. *Lernen als reflexiv vollzogene Existenz.* Die Analyse eines Lernprozesses in der Theologie dargestellt an Karl Rahner: Das Leben der Toten. Bern/Frankfurt/Las Vegas: Peter Lang. Preface ("Begleitwort") by Rahner.

811. RATZINGER, Josef Cardinal. "Vom Verstehen des Glaubens. Anmerkungen zu Rahners *Grundkurs des Glaubens.*" *Theologische Revue* 74, 177-186.

812. RICOEUR, Paul. " 'Response' to Karl Rahner's Lecture: On the

Incomprehensibility of God." *The Journal of Religion* 58 (Supplement—see No. 793), S126-S131.

813. ROWLING, Richard J. *A Philosophy of Revelation according to Karl Rahner.* Washington, D.C.: University Press of America.

814. SALA, R. "Les cristologies actuals" (in Catalan). *Questions de Vida Cristiana* 91, 64-76.

815. SCHEFFCZYK, Leo. "Thought Structures of Contemporary Theology" (in Polish, with German summary). *Zeszyty Naukowe Katolickiego Uniwersytetu Lubelskiego* (Lublin) 21, 17-23.

816. SCHELLEVIS, L. De betekenis van Jezus mensheid. Een onderzoek narr de christologie van Karl Rahner. Doctoral dissertation, Utrecht (with a summary in German).

817. TALLON, Andrew. "In Dialogue with Karl Rahner: Bibliography of Books, Articles, and Selected Reviews, 1939-1978." *Theology Digest* 26, 365-385.

818. TRIPOLE, Martin R. "Philosophy and Theology—Are They Compatible? A Comparison of Barth, Moltmann, and Pannenberg with Rahner." *Thought* 53, 27-54.

819. VANSTEENKISTE, P. Clemente, O.P., editor. *Rassegna de Letteratura Tomistica* 10, 191-195 (notice on No. 589).

820. VOGELS, H.-J. "Personen oder Weisen? Zur Trinitatslehre Karl Rahners." *Rheinischer Merkur* 33 (18 August), 20.

821. VORGRIMLER, Herbert. *Der Tod im Denken und Leben des Christen.* Düsseldorf. See esp. pp. 76-79.

822. WEGER, Karl-Heinz, S.J. *Karl Rahner.* Eine Einfuhrung in sein theologisches Denken. Freiburg: Verlag Herder (Herderbücherei 680).

823. WIEDERKEHR, D. "Christologie im Kontext." *Theologische Berichte* 7, 11-62, esp. pp. 48-56.

824. WIKMARK, Ö. Ofelbarket och evangelium. En studie i Karl Rahners, Hans Küngs och Walter Kaspers uppfattning av kyrkans och läroämbetets infalibititet. Berlings, Lund: Ohlsonns (with a summary in German).

825. "Sowjetische Philosophiezeitschrift befasst sich mit Rahner," in *KNA—Ökumenische Information* Nr. 26 (28 June), 11.

1979

826. ALCALÁ, M. "La tensión teologia-magisterio en la vida y obra de Karl Rahner." *Estudios Eclesiásticos* 54, 3-17.

827. AMATO, A. "Dall'uomo al Cristo, Salvatore assoluto, nella teologia di K. Rahner. La 'cristologia trascendentale' al suo primo livello di reflessione." *Salesianum* 41, 3-35.

828. COOKE, Bernard. "Horizons on Christology in the Seventies." *Horizons* 6, 193-217 (on Rahner see esp. 206-207).

829. FRIES, Heinrich. "Theologische Methode bei John Henry Newman und Karl Rahner. Karl Rahner zum 75. Geburtstag." *Catholica* 33, 109-133.

830. GIROTTO, Bruno. "Il problema dell'essere nel pensiero di K. Rahner." *Filosofia* 30, 555-584.

831. HEBBLETHWAITE, Brian. "Time and Eternity and Life 'After' Death." *The Heythrop Journal* 20, 57-62.

832. HOYE, William J. *Die Verfinsterung des absoluten Geheimnisses.* Eine Kritik der Gotteslehre Karl Rahners. Düsseldorf: Patmos Verlag (series 'Theologische Perspektiven').

833. KASPER, Walter. "Karl Rahner—Theologe in einer Zeit des Umbruchs. Forschungsberichte und Kritik." *Theologische Quartalschrift* 159, 263-271.

834. KENNEDY, Eugene. "The Quiet Mover of the Catholic Church. Theologian Karl Rahner." *The New York Times Magazine* (23 September), pp. 22, 23, 64, 66-70, 72, 74-75.

835. LASH, Nicholas. "Time and Eternity and Life 'After' Death: A Comment." *The Heythrop Journal* 20, 67-71.

836. MASSON, Robert. "Can Rahner Bridge the Linguistic Divide?" *Horizons* 6, 219-239.

837. MENGUS, R. "Karl Rahner en pratique." *Nouvelle revue théologique* 104, 378-380.

837a. NEUMANN, K. *Der Praxisbezug der Theologie bei Karl Rahner* (freiburger theol. Studien, 118). Freiburg.

838. O'DONOVAN, Leo J., S.J. "On Karl Rahner: *Foundations of Christian Faith:* An Introduction to the Idea of Christianity." *Religious Studies Review* 5, 194-199.

839. PERINI, G. "Pluralismo teologico e unità della fede. A proposito della teoria di K. Rahner." *Doctor Communis* 22, 135-188.

840. PETER, Carl J. "A Shift to the human subject in Roman Catholic theology." *Communio* 6, 56-72 (Rahner and Lonergan).

841. RAFFELT, Albert. "Karl Rahner. Bibliographie der Sekundärliteratur 1948-1978," in Herbert Vorgrimler, editor: *Wagnis Theologie* (See No. 845), pp. 598-622.

842. ROBERTSON, John C., Jr. "On Karl Rahner: *Foundations of Christian Faith:* An Introduction to the Idea of Christianity." *Religious Studies Review* 5, 190-194.

843. RODRÍGUEZ MOLINERO, José Luis. *La antropología filosófica de Karl Rahner.* (Col. Acta Salamanticensia. Filosifia y Letras). Salamanca: Univ. Salamanca.

843a. RÖPER, Anita. *Ist Gott ein Mann?* ein Gespräch mit Karl Rahner.

844. TALLON, Andrew. *Personal Becoming.* Karl Rahner's Metaphysical Anthropology. *The Thomist* 43, 1-177. (With a Foreword by Karl Rahner.)

845. VORGRIMLER, Herbert, editor. *Wagnis Theologie.* Erfahrungen mit der Theologie Karl Rahners. Freiburg/Basel/Wien: Herder. Includes 37 articles and updated bibliography of secondary literature.

846. ZÜRICH, A. "Carlo Rahner nega di essere filosofo e si autoqualifica dilettante in teologia." *Divus Thomas* (Piacenza) 82, 19-28.